IDENTITIES: NATIONS, PROVINCES AND REGIONS, 1550-1900

Proceedings of the III Anglo-Spanish
Historical Studies Seminar
held at the University of East Anglia,
25-26 October 1996

W0006565

Editors

Isabel Burdiel
Universitat de València
James Casey
University of East Anglia

1999

COVER ILLUSTRATION

The front cover shows the royal arms of the Spanish and British monarchies in the seventeenth century.

ACKNOWLEDGEMENTS

The editors acknowledge the financial sponsorship of the Cañada Blanch Foundation and the British Council. They are also grateful for the support of Sr Dámaso de Lario and the Cultural Office of the Embassy of Spain in the United Kingdom. The original colloquium, of which the proceedings are collected in the present volume, was organised by the University of East Anglia in collaboration with the University of Valencia. The editors would also like to acknowledge the hard work of Jenni Tanimoto and Helena Spurrell in the preparation of the final type script.

ISBN 0 9536068 0 5

Published by: **School of History**
                  University of East Anglia,
                  Norwich NR4 7TJ,
                  England

CONTENTS

PREFACE

The birth of history as a professional discipline in the West was closely associated with new universities, new state archives and a sense that the nation state was the culminating point of a protracted process known as 'state building'. A century later renewed regional resources for historical research and the juxtaposition of demands for regional autonomy with the emergence of supranational institutions leaves us less sure.

The contingencies of dynasticism and the exigencies of war, in the early modern period, may have buttressed some kind of unity in both the Iberian peninsula and the Atlantic archipelago. But our uneasiness about the simple application of what are now contested appellations - Spain or Britain - reveals important changes taking place in our political cultures and the interface between those cultures and the writing of history.

This third seminar in the Anglo-Spanish Historical Studies series took as its theme a vitally important, and indeed urgent, topic. We believe it is another example of the ways in which comparison of the two countries' historical experience can prove valuable and instructive. Nationalism, or proto-nationalism, and the creation of national identity are here set alongside the histories of regions struggling with issues of autonomy and subordination; composite monarchies, newly formed states and states in crisis are compared, as are perspectives from the 'centre' and the 'periphery'. To remind us that exclusive focus on an Anglo-Spanish axis will not tell us everything we have the very striking contribution of Peter Aronsson on the same range of problems in a Scandinavian context.

At a moment when, from the Balkans to Ireland, regional, national and international forces, cultural demands and political realities seem to be pulling one against another, how we construct and reconstruct perceptions of past experience is vitally important. These papers and the discussions attendant upon them remind us of the value of the wider, comparative focus and of the necessity to maintain such dialogue.

Colin Davis
Professor of English History
15 June 1998

1

IDENTIDADES: NACIONES, PROVINCIAS Y REGIONES (1550-1900)

INTRODUCCION

ISABEL BURDIEL
(Universidad de Valencia)

Durante los últimos veinte años, el problema de la identidad se ha convertido en un tema central de discusión de las ciencias sociales. El debate académico aparece así asociado a la emergencia de reivindicaciones o conflictos de orden político, social y cultural que afectan a una nueva articulación de las identidades nacionales, raciales, religiosas, de género, etc. Todas ellas, con sus particularidades, se presentan como formas de experiencia y de acción que resisten el universalismo y la uniformización que parecía ser su destino a finales del siglo XIX.

Sin embargo, una de las paradojas características de este fin del siglo es que las visibles tendencias hacia la globalización de la economía y de los estilos de vida, se ven contrarrestadas (al menos aparentemente) por las también evidentes tendencias hacia el particularismo identitario y la aspiración (más o menos violentamente expresada) de forzar su reconocimiento social y político.

En los albores de la modernidad, el Estado–nación fue el horizonte acomodo, organización y/o anulación de la singularidad, la diferencia y la pluralidad social y cultural. Al acabar el siglo XIX, su éxito como forma de organización política de las sociedades modernas parecía incontestable. A fines del siglo XX, los científicos sociales se preguntan hasta qué punto aquel tipo de organización política está preparado por su propia historia – y por el entramado de valores que la sustentaron– para acomodar la diversidad lingüística, cultural, étnica y religiosa que es patente en la gran mayoría de las sociedades modernas. Una diversidad que se resiste a ser anulada en nombre de la vieja idea del Estado-nación y que, sin embargo, parece incapaz de prescindir de ella en el momento de articular sus aspiraciones.

En efecto, el Estado-nación es algo más que la forma política por excelencia de organización de las sociedades modernas. Es también y, sobre todo, el marco cultural y discursivo profundo que determina todo lo que podemos decir, u oponer a él. Su configuración como tal se realizó mediante un proceso histórico (las más de las veces violento) de anulación o uniformización de las diversidades antes señaladas (y de otras muchas) incluyendo aquellas que hoy se representan a sí mismas como expresión de identidades nacionales previas y alternativas a las que fueron capaces de imponerse a través de su proyección estatal.

El éxito a medio y largo plazo de cada uno de los Estados-nación modernos ha estado, hasta ahora, estrechamente relacionado con su capacidad para construir un alto grado de consenso – en el sustrato profundo del 'sentido común' - sobre ese tipo particular de uniformización excluyente. Aquella que busca identificar Estado y nación convirtiendo toda diferencia (articulada como tal) en una alteridad esencialmente disruptora y antagonista de su propia esencia. La amplitud y profundidad cultural de ese consenso es innegable, incluso hoy a finales del siglo XX. En la práctica, es el origen último de las evidentes dificultades que encontramos para escapar al círculo lingüístico (y por lo tanto analítico) del discurso estatal-nacional en el momento mismo en que pretendemos abordar su estudio en tanto que producto histórico.

Con esta reflexión comienza el excelente trabajo del profesor Enrique Ucelay-Da Cal que inagura este volumen, resultado de las discusiones que al respecto tuvieron lugar durante el III Seminario de Estudios Históricos Hispano-Británicos, celebrado en la Universidad de East Anglia durante el último fin de semana de octubre de 1996. El objetivo de aquel Seminario era proporcionar un marco de reflexión comparada acerca de las condiciones, comunes y particulares, que dieron lugar a la configuración del Estado-nación en Europa desde finales del siglo XVI. El volumen está organizado –como lo estuvo en su momento el Seminario- en torno a la discusión de dos textos centrales – a cargo de los profesores Enrique Ucelay-Da Cal y John Morrill- sobre la formación del Estado y de la idea de nación en España y Gran Bretaña, respectivamente. Cada uno de esos textos es objeto de una serie de reflexiones y críticas cruzadas por parte de destacados especialistas británicos y españoles, incluyendo como contrapunto la perspectiva escandinava ofrecida por el profesor Peter Aronsson.

Siguiendo aquella propuesta, los trabajos de los profesores Joan-Lluis Marfany sobre el nacionalismo catalán, James Casey sobre Valencia y Steven Ellis sobre Irlanda, desarrollan críticamente algunos de los supuestos más globalizadores de las ponencias-marco de Ucelay-Da Cal y John Morrill. Por su parte, los trabajos de los profesores Salvador Albiñana e Isabel Burdiel discuten el papel desempeñado, en los siglos XVII y XIX respectivamente, por la nociones de decadencia y fracaso como elementos profundamente anclados (paradójicamente) en la gestación de una identidad potencialmente española, y en su cuestionamiento. Mención especial merece la espléndida colaboración del profesor Pablo Fernández Albaladejo al poner de manifiesto las poco valoradas concordancias entre los casos británico y español por lo que se refiere a la idea, y por lo tanto a la posibilidad misma, de una Historia de España y de una Historia Británica que pueda legítimamente utilizar las mayúsculas.

Como apunta esta última colaboración (y todas ellas en conjunto), la Historia, en su doble y profundamente contaminado sentido de aquello que pasó y aquello que escribimos sobre lo que pasó, fue entonces (y lo es ahora) la gran constructora de aquella forma de identidad excluyente y abstractamente totalizadora que denominamos Estado-nación. De hecho, toda configuración identitaria moderna se ha legitimado a través de la (su) historia produciéndola al mismo tiempo a su servicio. De la misma manera, todo cuestionamiento de formas de identidad totalizadoras (por ejemplo, el que oponen las naciones sin Estado a los Estados-nación que pretenden abarcarlas), está esencialmente articulado en torno a la Historia, en el doble y contaminado sentido a que acabo de referirme.

Las implicaciones analíticas de esa situación, producto ella misma de la historia que la ha creado y la relata, constituyen el horizonte de pensamiento de esta colección de ensayos y el origen último de las tensiones teóricas que, más o menos explícitamente, aparecen en todos ellos. Dichas tensiones particulares hacen referencia a aquella más general que existe entre experiencia y lenguaje, o entre lo que algunos llamarían 'realidad' y 'discurso', en lo que se refiere a la noción misma de nación, y a las aspiraciones políticas y retóricas envueltas en la misma.

En términos más concretos, todos los ensayos de este volumen, al referirse a la problemáticas de identidad nacional en Gran Bretaña, España y Escandinavia, han debido plantearse el reto que implica reconocer la existencia de experiencias de identidad alternativas a las que acabaron siendo hegemónicas y, al mismo tiempo, la existencia paralela de discursos que, al mismo tiempo que dan cuenta de ellas, las crean y legitiman como tales experiencias previas a la retórica que las envuelve. Un universo de representaciones y de prácticas que se retroalimentan hasta un punto en que resulta difícil encontrar (en sus concreciones históricas analizables) algún tipo de dicotomía válido entre las dos grandes concepciones del problema-nación que se disputan su campo de estudios. Es decir, entre una concepción esencialista e historicista de la experiencia-nación, por una parte, y una concepción modernista, funcionalista e invencionista de la idea-nación, por otra.

De forma generalmente implícita, y en ocasiones à contre-coeur, todos los ensayos publicados demuestran (más que ninguna otra cosa) que "esencialismo" e "invencionismo" estuvieron estrecha e inevitablemente unidos en los diversos procesos históricos de construcción (y cuestionamiento) de los Estados-nación modernos en Gran Bretaña, España y Escandinavia. Por ello, su lectura conjunta ofrece un panorama muy útil acerca de las posibilidades de la historia comparada del proceso de construcción de los Estado-nación europeos que ilumina, a su vez, algunas de las aporías insalvables a las que parece abocado su cuestionamiento, tal y como aparece hoy planteado en las formas de legitimación que adoptan las naciones sin Estado y que quieren serlo.

Tras su lectura, es quizás más fácil, y también más complejo, entender el sentido último de la afirmación de John Pocock con que cierra John Morrill su colaboración: la historia británica (como la española) es la historia del problemático e incompleto experimento de creación e interacción de diferentes naciones. De la nación española y de la británica, por supuesto, pero también de la escocesa y la vasca, la catalana o la irlandesa. Todas ellas se requirieron y se requieren mútuamente para ser, o ser 'a la contra' en tanto que todas participan de un mismo sentido común nacional y estatal construido como tal históricamente y que, por lo tanto, a la historia como disciplina compete analizar, convirtiéndose así, de paso y una vez más, en la protagonista última de un proceso que la afecta por partida doble.

NACIONALISMOS EN ESPAÑA

ENRIC UCELAY-DA CAL

(Universitat Autònoma de Barcelona)

La percepción de la sociedad española como 'excepcional' dentro de Europa representa el principal inconveniente para la plena maduración de la historiografía española. Al contrario, tal plenitud se hubiera demostrado por la incorporación sin trabas de las problemáticas hispánicas al ámbito de los estudios europeos. Qué duda cabe que tradiciones culturales externas - especialmente la francesa y la inglesa - que datan del siglo XVI han tendido a reforzar la idea de la 'diferencia' española ante sus propios desarrollos históricos. Así lo 'español' ha servido como una temática ajena, contraria, 'el otro', para la formación de identidades en el arco de países vecinos. Al mismo tiempo, como reflejo, el 'excepcionalismo' ha sido un recurso cultural e ideológico para la elaboración de una identidad española.

Dada la dependencia que tiene la narración histórica respecto a la política que de múltiples maneras pretende explicar, la historiografía general europea ha tendido a excluir temas hispánicos, hasta el punto que, en los manuales, las cuestiones españolas no figuran en la agenda interpretativa a partir de los capítulos pertinentes a la segunda mitad del siglo XVII. La respuesta hispánica ha sido paralela: en la medida de lo posible, dejar fuera interacciones con la dinámica más global, para insistir en la erudición sobre matices propios. Mientras que poco o nada en la tradición historiográfica española ha favorecido la corrección del supuesto foráneo del 'excepcionalismo', y que los estudios extranjeros sobre temas hispánicos han quedado igualmente segregados, como 'hispanistas', en un campo propio pero aislado. A su vez, el desarrollo de estudios sobre las particularidades ibéricas, empezando por Cataluña y siguiendo por un largo reguero en las últimas décadas, ha tendido a agudizar el abuso del 'excepcionalismo', ya que cada campo naciente se ha afirmado como único y naturalmente 'excepcional', desvinculado del antiguo marco hispánico.

A mi parecer, sólo será posible superar el lastre del 'excepcionalismo' hispánico, en cualquiera de sus acepciones, mediante un esfuerzo por integrar toda la problemática ibérica (cuestiones lusas incluídas) en un contexto analítico genuinamente europeo. Para empezar, tal impulso serviría para redefinir la misma noción de qué es Europa y superar la comprensión limitada - pero hasta ahora operativa - que reemplaza el complejo mosaico continental por el conjunto reduccionista de lnglaterra (sin Escocia ni Irlanda), Francia, Alemania y el norte de Italia. Por el contrario, una perspectiva capaz de incluir al mismo tiempo el espacio báltico y el meridional con el extremo oriental del continente, lejos de reducir el protagonismo histórico hispánico, lo recogería en toda su amplitud y sería capaz de hacer los distingos necesarios para que problemáticas españolas generales existieran interpretativamente junto a matices catalanes o vascos (etc.), tal como éstos han existido en la realidad.

Tal paso requiere que las explicaciones hispánicas se abran hacia afuera, en vez de cerrarse, reforzadas por posicionamientos políticos interiores que resultan incomprensibles para el observador lejano. Como sabe quién haya hecho el intento, transformar cuestiones propias en inteligibles a un lector foráneo no se resuelve mediante una sencilla traducción, ya que el mismo lenguaje político cambia según las circunstancias geográficas y culturales. Hay, pues, que 'traducir', más que palabras, conceptos, para situar el discurso interpretativo propio a un nivel de abstracción que le permita acceder al meollo de la cuestión a un lector culturalmente ajeno, pero no por ello menos capacitado para entender el asunto. Dar este paso significa operar sin la carga de detalle y erudición que, con frecuencia, hace fascinante el trabajo histórico al especialista o al lector interesado del país. De rebote, el beneficio es que, al buscar elementos generales o comunes, así como enfoques comparativos, se gana distancia ante las temáticas domésticas que, de tan añejas y manidas, pueden parecer muertas interpretativamente, cuando en realidad casi están a punto de nacer para el análisis.

El ensayo en inglés que aquí se presenta y que acompaña este pequeño sumario en castellano ha procurado dar un paso en esta dirección, para plantear un esquema global sobre el desarrollo histórico de los nacionalismos en España - tanto centrípetos como centrífugos- capaz de ser situado en cuzllquier discusión equivalente en las Islas Británicas. Una confrontación erudita hubiera sido más bien poco provechosa, situarse en un paradigma compartido, muy monográfico, de relaciones bilaterales. Aun así, la discusión resultante sería más bien estrecha, para el deleite de superespecialistas. Es mucho mejor, desde mi punto de vista, la reflexión que puede llegar a ser compartida en su intención y, por lo tanto, entendida por ambas partes, aunque la interpretación concreta que aporte sea discutida o hasta rechazada.

Las ideas que se presentan en el ensayo forman una secuencia. En primer lugar, se argumenta que los diversos nacionalismos visibles a finales del siglo XX en España son de hecho una sola dinámica. Por ello, cualquier análisis debería incorporar tanto continuidades centrípetas como centrífugas, como interrupciones históricas generales o particulares. Se debería mirar el desarrollo de actitudes nacionalistas como parte del proceso de construcción del Estado, que por lo tanto incorpora imágenes y argumentos tanto en la dirección que deriva del afianzamiento del poder real como en otras que sacan su persistencia de la afirmación de intereses particularistas, poderes locales que son, a la vez, parte del desarrollo estatal y rivales de su crecimiento. De esta forma, se puede superar la disyuntiva - todavía dominante en la sociología pertinente entre los partidarios de entender los nacionalismos como 'vínculos primordiales' y aquéllos que los entienden como meras manipulaciones ideológicas, debate éste que se refleja, con mucho primitivismo, en las controversias hispánicas sostenidas por la historiografía española y sus competidores 'nacionales', así como en la disputa sobre la validez de la 'Historia local'.

En segundo lugar, se habría que dar mayor importancia a la dinámica del conflicto civil en la sociedad española y/o sociedades hispánicas. Las guerras civiles son una realidad endémica en la historia española, inseparable de la construcción del Estado. En vez de contemplar este hecho como una especie de desgracia o tara histórica, habría que recoger el hecho, no como algo accidental, y sí como un aspecto central de la construcción de las formas políticas hispánicas. En términos generales, las guerras civiles por doquier son un mecanismo social clave para la refundición y reelaboración de los símbolos políticos a lo largo del tiempo, ya que sirven como experiencias que a la vez fijan modelos ideológicos y los comunican a sectores sociales: en última instancia, la implicación es que la vida parlamentaria, con su función clave en el desarrollo ideológico moderno y contemporáneo, es esencialmente la guerra civil por otros medios, fuertemente ritualizados y capaces de mantener la sociedad civil en pie, sin ruptura. Si la España contemporánea, en especial, ha sido una 'sociedad de guerra civil', ésto lo reflejarán tanto la forma y manera de actuar del

Estado unitario como los impulsos surgidos de las sub-sociedades que han compuesto el todo social. Por lo tanto, el nacionalismo español y los nacionalismos rivales hispánicos son productos de la dinámica histórica de guerra civil, sobrepuesta a la tradición a la vez centrípeta y centrífuga del poder, que viene desde el Medioevo.

En tercer lugar, el desarrollo del Estado en España se produce como imperio; luego una visión estrictamente peninsular, preocupada por la definición del supuesto 'Estado-Nación', resultará por fuerza insuficiente. En realidad, España sufrió una prolongada crisis de descolonización, tan pionera como lo fue la fundación de su poder interoceánico. Asi, las guerras de independencia de las colonias, en especial la experiencia cubana, fueron tambien contiendas civiles, con poderosos efectos sobre la vida política metropolitana. Los discursos coloniales - de forma más indirecta en la primera mitad del siglo XIX, de manera directa en la segunda - condicionaron la formulación de los discursos nacionalistas en España, transformando la noción de identidad y, por ello, confrontando una nueva 'españolidad' con otras 'formas de ser' hasta entonces ambiguas.

Tales identidades actuaron en un medio peninsular determinado por el definitivo desarrollo capitalista, visible sobre todo en la urbanización, cada vez más intensa con la entrada del siglo XX. El crecimiento económico español configuró un gran arco urbano desde Sevilla hasta Bilbao, pasando alternativamente por Madrid o Barcelona, devenidas las únicas ciudades verdaderamente grandes de España. La tensión de fondo, entre un interior agrario y el sistema de ciudades, convirtió la presión urbanizadora en la fuente de un complejo de discursos de rivalidad entre ciudades como centros de servicios que ha condicionado toda la evolución de la meritocracia y del 'Estado asistencial' en España hasta el presente. Finalmente, para terminar, se argumenta en el ensayo que - aunque pueda parecer paradójico - los nacionalismos competitivos peninsulares han fracasado en la España contemporánea, vista ésta desde el final del siglo XX. El españolismo - llevado al paroxismo por la dictadura franquista - no ha logrado imponerse de manera efectiva, más bien el contrario. Pero tampoco los nacionalismos rivales han podido derrotar al españolismo, ni se han mostrado capaces, de suplantarlo.

NATIONALISMS IN SPAIN.
Some Interpretative Proposals

ENRIC UCELAY-DA CAL
(Universitat Autònoma de Barcelona)

I. Problems of Perspective and Historiography

Studies of nationalism in Spain have dealt almost exclusively with individual cases. Either they talk of Spanish selfhood and ignore the development of other nationalisms within Spain, or the interest is centered on a specific area and the construction of its peculiar discourse of personality, while disregarding the role of the state in fostering opposition to itself. While the first approach still tends to be true of foreign studies of nationalism in Spain, the second has intensely characterized the abundance of local studies that have been produced within the country in the last twenty years. Equally, there is a long-standing habit of treating Spain as an exceptional case. On the one hand, Spanish historians, often far too self-absorbed, tend not to compare their findings with broader questions, while Europeanists generally omit Spain from their reflections, considering 'Iberian Studies' as a marginal area to more general continental trends, at least after the seventeenth century.

Thus, it is no easy matter to discuss the development of nationalisms in Spain. The moment the observer chooses a non-reductionist approach in the spirit of *Histoire totale*, it becomes difficult even to know exactly about whom he is speaking, given the natural dispersion of the subject or subjects: Spaniards but also Catalans, Basques, Galicians, and so forth. Further, there is a problem of perception: identity is not just how any group perceives itself but also how other groups perceive it. In the abstract, this might seem an easy idea to handle; in practice it is not.

Let me suggest some reasons why. In the first place, we are all trained to think in terms of states, even though specialized legal historians such as Lalinde, may reasonably fret over the careless, "indiscriminate" use of the term. But the state is a discourse, a kind of language with a mesmerizing effect. It convinces us that what is only ritual, interpersonal relations, a variety of services both pleasant and unpleasant, some considerable real estate and a sizable patrimony is also a tangible, organic 'thing' with a 'life' of its own. The great political philosophies of the eighteenth and early-nineteenth centuries all consolidated such reification. By the Congress of Vienna in 1815, the criterion was firmly established that states speak only to other states, hence the modern codification of diplomacy. This dependency on the short-hand of statism means that, from abroad, the first tendency is to think of all of Spain as 'Spanish', in the way continental Europeans confuse the ideas of 'English' and 'British'. Since Spain is alleged to be one of the first historic 'nation-states', having roughly today's shape on the Iberian Peninsula since 1516, such an approach would seem clear enough. Accordingly, foreigners will see any other existing identities beyond the 'Spanish' as folkloric, 'regional', 'dialectal', in the same way that, in the British case, Scots or Welsh are seen from abroad as always less than the 'whole'.

Taken as a single explanation, such a perspective is clearly wrong. However, it might be an acceptable starting point, but only if we begin to accept scientific relativism. Thus, we could do something apparently strange, which runs counter to any linear training, and accept simultaneous contradictory explanations. In sum, since we are speaking of a social, human reality, based on conflicts of identity, different perspectives (both of observers and the observed) literally mean different social realities which exist at the same time in the same place. This leads to a peculiar aspect of the ways outsiders tend to see Spain and peripheral nationalists. We are all trained to think in terms of single rather than plural realities and by extension in terms of states. If foreigners for some reason discover that Basques or Catalans are not simple, generic Spaniards, it is very easy for them to turn completely around, and simply become converts to the alternative nationalist position, swallowing such a stance whole. So, in the same way that there are outsiders (a vast majority), as well as a multitude of Spaniards, who only can see Spain through determined historical lenses (this is very clear in British anti-Spanish tradition), one can find foreigners (a small minority), and evidently many Catalans or Basques, who pretend that Spain is a fiction, and that in reality only Catalonia or Euskadi exist. Again, either avowal is false if taken as a single explanation, but each is as real as the affirmation of the existence of the other (at least from perspectives grounded in social psychology or anthropology). If relativism is applied, it is possible to see the direct relation between one perspective and the other. Such questions of simultaneous perspective, as well as the terminological difficulties that are their direct consequence, point directly to the limits of traditional historiography of nationalism. The problem of simultaneously perceived identities, and the degree to which they can function as some sort of reality, have not been clarified by historiography, as least as practiced in a Hispanic context. Basically there are three historiographic positions, which can be summarized critically here as: (1) the errors of statist (nationalist) historiography; (2) the errors of nationalist (anti-statist) historiography; (3) the errors of antinationalist (often antistatist) historiography.

Statist history identifies state boundaries with a long-term moral unity, as in the Spanish usage *la Península* (where the Iberian Peninsula stands for Spain, without Portugal, Gibraltar or Andorra), akin to the English concept of the British Isles or the French *hexagone*. In fact, every state is only a permanent project to unify the space it formally controls, a utopian aspiration. We ought not to confuse a project with a result, especially when the idea is an a historical continuity designed to justify the origin of the state. Statist historiography reflects a cumulative state agenda, mystically identified with an imaginary collective agenda of 'everybody'. This, on the right, is explained by reference to *Raison d'État*, and, on the left, to popular will. Either way, arguments are almost always sanctimonious, revealing debts to a determined morality of collective will, democratic or otherwise.

As a reaction to the first mass-education schoolbooks in the late nineteenth century, anti-statist nationalists inveighed against the obvious manipulation of statist nationalist history. But anti-statist nationalism and its historiography reply with their own trick of special pleading. Anti-statist nationalists proceed from a paradox: they denounce the falsities of official state history (from the premise 'it cannot be a real nation, because we are!'), but, at the same time, they reproduce their own version of statist history, because this is accepted as the 'real' level of historically exercised power. Since anti-statist nationalists crave legitimacy in the most traditional sense, they grant the standard state model (with the recognition it implies) a central role in their scheme of things: their problem is only that they do not have such a state.

To contradict the spiritual continuity of state which is so central to statists and their historical agenda, anti-statist nationalists have tended to present a specific reading of *Volksgemeinschaft*, the equivalence between man and land, where time or history only add on to both sides of the equation. The continuity of the state model, derived from the supposed interrelation of institutions and territory, is here inverted to an equally idealized situation where continuity is based on the fixed relation between population and geography. This Montesquieu-ish vision of climate, location, and the like, fixing the parameters of a 'submerged' people, naturally distant from power and close to the land, can have many expressions convenient to particularist historians, without visibly dabbling in *Blut und Boden* excesses. Such a perspective often purports to be much superior to the statist claim that the collective spirit is embodied over time in the central, symbolic development of the state (from tribes to kings to the King to, finally, the sway of parliament, progressively ever more representative, in the Whiggish way). In this view, with the mix of territory and society, only local institutions acquire validity, and can be considered as 'real', capable of transferring identity. However, the anti-state model is equally manipulative, insofar as continuity is confused with inalterability.

In the face of both statist nationalist and anti-statist nationalist historiographies, there appeared anti-nationalist history, primarily (but not exclusively) linked to the Marxist tradition and the alleged superiority of class-consciousness among proletarians of all countries: only the working-class movement can aspire to monopolize the apparatus of the state. The key premise of anti-nationalist historiography is the importance of breaks or interruptions (such as revolutions) in the flow of historical time. In this view, the so-called 'turning points' in history occur here, with the intervals in between as clearly secondary pauses leading up to the periods of movement or historical evolution. Logically, this perspective offers a complete contradiction to the other two interpretations, since both nationalist historiographies stress continuity, while the anti-nationalist position stresses the opposite. Nationalism anywhere is an always messy subject to deal with, half fiction and half fact, obsessively historicist, aggressively in the present but persistently harking back to the past. In contrast, modern social movements pretend to do away with history at a pen stroke.

The problem with anti-nationalist history is the fact that the interruption is justified by what can be called a replacement teleology. Some global moral argument serves as an axiom on which to base historical interruptions, and simultaneously points to a new goal of all development. The introductory premise and the assumed conclusion of history are essentially the same, simply the realisation of the goal of either socialism (as with Marxists), sexual equality (as with feminists), or even exponential economic expansion (the capitalist 'new goal' in liberal historiography). But replacement teleology gives itself the appearance of science in the face of nationalist emotionalism. It sanctifies its own critical stance, avoiding the obligation to apply an equally fastidious analysis to its own historical trajectory. If, as Hobsbawm has insisted, both statist and anti-statist nationalisms are centered around the question of jobs and the control of the state apparatus, the same can be said of all other social movements.

This paper, to approach the problem of nationalisms in Spain and place it in a long-term European perspective, will develop an explanation which joins the Spanish centralist tradition to its 'peripheral' or centrifugal equivalents. Symbols, derived from structures of power and authority, can serve as tracers for such an enquiry insofar as they are repeatedly used as forms of communication over time, even if their formal meanings or interpretations keep varying in accordance with social change and political fashion. A corpus of repeated arguments may be called 'paleonationalism' if they are understood as a historical process by which a given justification of power congeals and becomes a stepping stone for a new, more aggressive affirmation. Such theses became the basis of both Spanish and anti-Spanish nationalisms as the Crown turned into a state over a period of centuries: Spanish nationalism and its competitors (as well as the more minor regionalisms) all have a common origin and therefore a common heritage. Politically this may have had little effect since independence is not the necessary product of original ideas; but to be aware of this point can have important implications for historical reassessment.

Starting from dynastic union and composite monarchy, Spanish politics has been marked by stressful and simultaneous centripetal and centrifugal tendencies. There is no scientific consensus over the historical existence of either nation or state. Both are ongoing projects, open-ended ways of understanding power. So we can speak of 'paleonationalism' (or 'proto-') as readily as of a corresponding 'paleo-' or 'proto-statism', without them meaning terribly different things. This paper prefers to stress the theme of nation-building rather than the simultaneous state-building because the former permits, perhaps, a broader reference to political imagery beyond constitutional formulae and juridical documents. If, as Pocock admonishes, metaphors and legal formulations must be read in appropriate historical context, literary and visual representation serve as a vivid reminder of the vitality of reference and of the inventiveness of succeeding generations seeking to better legitimate tactical situations or strategic goals in their jockeying for power. This means that, while, at any given time, historians, jurists, poets, iconographers and other laureates of power are always alluding to alleged facts - either centripetal or centrifugal - nevertheless nothing is objective beyond the fact of their affirmation. Such decorative or erudite special pleading is merely a defensive argument for a better position in 'turf wars' or long-term political squabbles. But this ongoing process of cumulative political definition - which we are calling 'paleonationalism' - is conditioned by outside perspective. Outsiders saw 'Spaniards', whatever these might be in their own minds. Spaniards saw Catalans or Basques or Castilians, but could interpret that variety as an expression of unity (i.e. as 'Spaniards') or as deep division, depending on their interest. Similarly, whether or not the Spanish monarchy was really an articulated state, foreigners saw it as a fearsome and coherent instrument and a threat: it was thus a 'virtual reality', perceived rather than existing. The variability of the notion of kingship - power as 'empire', but empire as any of a number of institutions - meant that part and whole never needed to be clearly defined until confronted with the new reality of citizenship, in the second half of the nineteenth century.

The explanation offered here will therefore start from the basis that (1) all the antagonistic nationalisms are in fact a single process, at least in Spain; any adequate analysis should assume both centripetal and centrifugal continuities and the impact of historical interruptions, in order to produce a coherent interpretative model, not dependent on linkage with one or other nationalist cause or with the presumptions of replacement teleologies (i.e., those arguments which suppose that some other factor, such as class identity, is 'more real' than willful national ascription). (2) Civil wars are a key social mechanism for fusing and re-elaborating political symbols over time. Ultimately, the implication is that parliamentary life, with its role in developing modern ideological debate and argument, is essentially civil war by other means. (3) Focusing on the concept of empire offers advantages over the quite contradictory notion of 'nation-state'. In many ways, Spain suffered the first crisis of de-colonization in Europe, long before the need for redefining ambiguous institutions overwhelmed other powers. The theme of Spanish 'degeneration', popular with British and French cultural critics in the nineteenth century, was no more than a mirror to the fears of loss of territory or prestige. (4) If ferocious centralist nationalism of identity arose out of colonial civil wars in the second half of the nineteenth century, and anti-Spanish territorial nationalisms sprang up in reply, this tension was fed by urban rivalries, above all the bitter race between the capital Madrid and the eternal 'second city' Barcelona. The prime index of industrialization and altered social patterns, of the regression of traditional society, has been urbanization. In Spain, urbanization fed controversy over how urban hinterlands are to be redefined, in order to create a framework for careers open to talent, around which modern national movements have taken shape. Finally, (5) Spanish nationalism seems to have climaxed and failed, but rival nationalisms are not capable of replacing it: this is the central paradox of the current Spanish political system since Franco's death. The upshot is a stalemate, doubtless pregnant with future difficulties.

II. The Quarry of Legitimization: Inherited Vocabularies of Power

A central unsolved debate looms persistently over Spanish historiography: What is Spain? A question not just of identity but of definition, the "Problem of Spain" as it is usually referred to for over a century, signifies an object of study that is most elusive. The Spanish nationalist tradition turned Seneca and Trajan into 'Spaniards' and referred to 'Moslem Spain'. In reply, recent critical trends have been careful to speak of Hispania or al-Andalus. So to ask 'What is Spain?' begs other questions: 'When was Spain?' or the even more complex 'Where is Spain?' A hackneyed debate, which merely turns round in circles, usually means that both sides are talking about different things at the same time. The vast upsurge of 'local' history - part of the autonomist process that accompanied the democratic transition out of dictatorship after 1976-77 - has fueled active Catalan, Basque and other replies to the effect that Spain is, as it were, 'Not In My Back Yard'. In sum, Spanish historiography tends to be at loggerheads with such studies for pride of place. All ultimately clamor for the authenticity of being there first. In the search for foreign approval, hispanists are often brought in to lend their authority to the claims of one side or the other. By training, hispanists are reared on a 'Spanish' viewpoint, but, once in tune with a 'regionalist' perspective, can convert with vehemence. A political battle of words is, scientifically speaking, a semantic argument. Perhaps the best way to re-situate the ongoing discussion is precisely to analyze the vocabularies of confrontation and their etymologies, so as to separate, in historical terms, substance from rhetoric. The development of parallel discourses of 'paleonationalism' and of much later, mature nationalisms can be traced by reference to historical periods (or to 'layers', as in a mental archaeology). All rival Hispanic historiographies have 'dug' backwards through such 'layers' because they have all been deeply politicized. As has happened in many other societies (like Morocco, a neighboring example), Spain's history can be understood as a permanent tension between the pull towards centralization and the push towards fragmentation. The medieval Christian kingdoms expressed their political identity in two parallel ways that conditioned the development of both dynastic rule and local sovereignties. The crown (especially that of Castile) was legitimated with allusions to a Hispanic 'imperial ideal', which mixed the memory of Roman and Gothic peninsular unity with dreams of religious unification, expansion and chiliasm. In reply, a strong local patriotism, expressing the interests of nobles or urban patricians, affirmed local institutions, common particularism against outside interference.

This contradiction became a key factor between the twelfth and the fourteenth centuries, with the definition of specific cultural traditions and the redefinition of the past established through troubadour culture, as well as late-medieval rationalization of law. It incorporated a series of elements into an ideal of authority common to all Iberian Christian states, especially as a crusader logic became more important as a means of legitimization. Chiliasm (the millenial myth of the 'once and future king' who would return to set his country right or the Final Judgment as the ultimate object of worldly rule) and local law (medieval parliaments and municipalities setting the limits of royal power) together helped to create a patriotic religious identity, justified in retrospect, with reference to a myth of origins and goals derived from a sense of mission. Thus defined, simultaneously legitimating and limiting, kingship came to embody the 'Roman'–'Frankish' contradiction. This also meant that ideas of past and future were confused and jumbled together in the growing justification of a more integrated state system. The effects of this duality continued visible in what could be termed the growing 'paleonationalism' of high and low state service to the unified Spanish Crown of the late Trastámaras and of the Habsburgs in the passage from the fifteenth to the sixteenth centuries. Such a 'paleonationalism' should be understood as the cumulative development of attitudes surrounding the exercise of power over time, rather than as the coherent sentiment of a fully-conscious citizenry, (which would be an evident anachronism). Forged out of feudal civil wars, the identity of the united Crown was imperial (with a vast American empire as a sudden windfall), insistent on the need for religious unity (hence the importance of the Inquisition). Needless to say, this imperial identity was contradictory, and nurtured sentiments that looked to the past (the hidden apocalyptic strains), as well as to the future (Castilian as the language of the state in the making, reflecting the high noon of empire). On the one hand, such identity also led to a common Spanish experience of service to the Crown, a normative administrative procedure and a corporate identity on the part of the state's servants. On the other, however, this same institutional growth, nourished by the sense of imperial mission, encouraged a peculiar style of decision-making, with an exalted notion of bureaucratice due process above any pratical sense and a rampant taste for legalisms, that together had the peverse effect of nurturing a generalised faith in lat-minute improvisation. Such patterns of behaviour, became characteristic, went beyond the élite and worked their way into the customs of a diversified society.

Accordingly, any sense of imperial destiny and administrative cohesion as a historical need of the united Crown was permanently confronted with the appeal of localism, focused on the component crowns with their particular laws and customs. The greater whole never quite convinced all those sectors that did not derive immediate benefit from its momentary greatness. From the uprisings in Castile, Valencia and Mallorca (1519-23) against the foreign 'Flemish rule' of Charles I to the revolt of the Catalans against Philip IV (1640-53), particularism kept resisting the expansion of absolutist power. Even without violence, local patriotism was kept alive by the insistent respect for local law against bureaucratic fiat, summarized in the terms *fueros* and *foralismo* (needless to say, such privileges or 'liberties' were not only territorial but also social). By the seventeenth century, the discourse of Spanish politics was already patterned into a permanent, very legalistic debate between the relative superiority of royal prerogative and local rights, each accusing the other of being a form of abuse that misunderstood the basic contractual nature of power. 'Habsburg paleo-nationalism' incorporated medieval 'Frankish' patriotic identity and the cult of local law (frontiers of kingdoms, *fueros*, *Cortes*, municipal charters and rights, as well as strictly feudal sovereignties, all as opposed to integrative, generic Roman law and central administration) into a greater symbolic whole. But it did so only as a permanent tension with the ideal of kinghood-statehood conceived as apocalyptically justified, as a parallel medieval inheritance (i.e., the Crown has higher authority than local authority, even higher than the Church, because when it realized its final goal the millennium would arrive). The power discourse of Ferdinand of Aragon (admired by Macchiavelli) became the messianic justification of empire, with Charles V as the 'perfect Christian knight' of the Western *Oekumene* struggling against unbelievers.

Thus, the macro-, 'Roman', tradition of internal 'Hispanic' Imperium (the Iberian Peninsula as a recreation of Roman symbolic legitimacy) was vastly expanded in the sixteenth century to an external 'two world' empire. But this affected the symbolic trappings of authority. A greater Crown required the creation of a new central mythology, which naturally grew out of those of the Christian kingdoms, especially out of the later crusader logic. So the new power of the Renaissance Crown, heading towards absolutism, became inseparably tied to not only the chiliasm of the past, but the realization of a new imperial dream, as aspiration to messianic leadership apparently come true. But the local micro-vision of the diverse kingdoms within an imperial realm was actively retained, not merely in the distinction between administration and power/authority, but also in the way the world-empire was understood and identified with: the Castilian crownlands tended to look to the Americas, to the Low Countries and Germany, while the Aragonese crownlands were more oriented to the Mediterranean and Italy.

After the bitter conflict over the succession to the Spanish Crown (1701-15), the 'paleonationalism' of the Bourbons further perfected the pressure towards centralization through the imposition of French-derived administrative reform, which included a far stricter insistence on the efficiency to be gained by the imposition of a single state language. Paradoxically, pro-Habsburg nostalgia mixed freely with the reams of *foralista* enhanced literature as an interclass vehicle for counteracting Bourbon (i.e. constitutionalist) centralization, enhanced, as the latter was, with the triumphs of the late civil war. Nevertheless, by the time the reformist drive wound down at the end of the eighteenth century, with the reign of Charles IV, official Bourbon 'paleonationalism' or 'proto-statism' had itself assumed all the appeal to things popular and local, usually referred to as *tipismo* or *casticismo*, absorbing the Habsburg inheritance of symbols and organizational habits.

In sum, from the fifteenth to the nineteenth centuries, identity was suppressed in aggressive images, derived from expansionist imperial or missionary experience, which took the form of a series of injunctions of the 'other', whether at the institutional level of state or church, or at the sentimental core of the locality. This world view had much to do with the distribution of opportunities for social mobility within the various Spanish communities: those who could profit from service to state or church (or from the economic proximity to the needs of either or both) tended naturally to adapt to the discourse of dynastic 'paleonationalism'; those left out, or left behind, tended to grumble in a thousand petty disputes over local privileges ignored or trampled upon by centralizers. In the measure that Castilian was the language of Bourbon bureaucracy, the remaining spoken idioms became a vehicle almost exclusively of lower class expression, of interest mostly to churchmen dedicated to assuring catechism and correct dogmatic devotion among the peasantry. This meant that, in an 'enlightened' age, Catalan (a working cultural vehicle through to the victory of Philip V, and never effectively stamped out as the language of local administration), Galician (a rich literary language in the late Middle Ages), the multiple Basque tongues (the major written form of which was the "Biscay" variant, in which, however, precious little was expressed beyond some religious texts), or the local Romance variants like Asturian Bable or Old Aragonese, all tended to be increasingly regarded as vestiges, not actively defended by cultivated spokesmen for particularism and *fueros* (even in the Catalan case).

However, it is not so much a question of the existence of a specific ideology of state identity or, conversely, of particularistic exaltation. Nationalist historiography has persisted in pretending that patriotic sentiments are a sustained emotion, a feeling for place that has existed from the origin of a community up to the present. So clearly historical, the pretence has generated criticism for more than a century. Anti-nationalist historiography, however, denies too much: the idea that no statist or local feelings existed or that these were purely private and socially inchoate until the French Revolution arrived and gave them clear ideological expression seems equally ingenuous. Doubtless, nationalism as a formed or mature ideology, with expressions ranging from the institutional French style to the ethnic German version, is a product of late-eighteenth and early-nineteenth centuries. But it had to come out of somewhere, and, all too often, contemporary historians fail to pay much heed to what early modernists are talking about. In the case of Spain, that continuity was provided by the abundance of juridical and socio-political writing that accompanied the rise of absolutism, much of this production being *arbitrismo* or proposals for administrative improvement of society and the bureaucracy, often with the implicit hope of landing the author a job. In addition, many Spanish societies, like the Catalan or the Basque, were abundantly litigious, leading to an extremely 'lawyerly' outlook, which conditioned the development of both social and economic theory and of history. The essence of a jurist's attitude is the citing of precedents, and it is precisely in this way that statist or particularistic 'paleonationalism' was sustained.

The corpus of literature formed a repertoire of ideas, arguments, justifications, proofs and examples which could be mined over and over again, in a cultural context that has not traditionally welcomed an imaginative approach to serious matters. The Inquisition survived until 1834, and other forms of censorship far longer, leaving fantasy to grow unhindered in the arts (provided, of course, holy matters were ignored). Nevertheless as a major power in the sixteenth, seventeenth, and eighteenth centuries, Spain had to call on foreign know-how, and works not deemed dangerous or subversive to throne and altar were often promptly translated in a 'Spanish version' that usually omitted such details as were deemed questionable. As more was added to the socio-political canon, more possibilities existed for reproducing and reworking previous formulations, especially once the French Revolution and invasion opened the doors to much wider speculation, insofar as Napoleon reconciled the 'dynastic principle' with the revolutionary ideal of the representative, 'national principle'. 'Paleonationalism' in one or other guise was a quarry of legitimization, whereby any new political idea could be justified historically, giving proof of deep, Hispanic roots in a society trained by long thought-control and rigorous border searching to have little admiration for foreign sources. In the same way that the liberals in Cadiz insisted that the constitutional convention was no more than the resurgence of the medieval *Cortes* or that mid-nineteenth century republicans insisted that they were no more than the re-embodiment of sixteenth-century protesters, so the later regionalist movements refurbished *foral* (i.e. medieval constitutionalist) arguments, and Franco's propagandists found material for justifying his dictatorship.

The mid-nineteenth century is the usual starting point for analysis of Hispanic nationalisms, when bourgeois extremists began to explore the romantic vein in new ways through the cult of the non-Castilian languages. This was basically an occasional literary pastime for the some of the better educated. Quite naturally, such romantic effusions tended to emphasize a backward-looking, Catholic ideal of idyllic peasant society, hence facilitating the elite rediscovery of popular idiom alive beneath the official language of the state. One thing led to another: the Romantic awakening in Spain, as elsewhere, actually was no more than the recovery and manipulation, in a new context of representative, liberal government, of far older political arguments.

III.   Civil War Culture and Civic Culture

It is increasingly evident that internal definition of identity within states is forged in great measure by civil wars: the major case study has probably been the United States, but Britain or France serve just as well. In fact, the role of civil wars is just beginning to be studied. There has always been a strong tendency to think of violent internal conflict as the opposite of the normal situation of society, which would be civil peace. However, far from considering civil wars as exceptions, historians are now beginning to look at them as crucibles of identity, special moments of élite-popular interaction which permit the creation of a new identities to be sustained in more stable periods. Such an approach to the subject of intra-societal hostilities would be linked to the idea, two centuries old in physics but rather new in historiography, that through change nothing is lost, but just transformed. The concept of civil war would revise the classic Almond-Verba formulation of "civic culture", since this, and the parliamentary institutions that it fosters, would be the outcome of internal conflict based on the acceptance of ambiguity, on coming to terms with former enemies, rather than persisting in the will to destroy them. In a legislative environment, both sides accept the continuation of an unending symbolic war, expressed verbally by ritually chosen proxies, to avoid enduring an indecisive physical combat.

The contradictory images of religious and remote historical sanction that were shared and disputed by partisans of crown and particularistic sovereignties were incorporated into the composite Monarchy of the Renaissance. Both the 'Roman' and 'Frankish' implications of authority were moulded by the intense conflict of the second half of the fifteenth century. In an Iberian context, one could point to a succession of civil wars experienced in common, which gave rise to a complex historical memory regarding dynastic legitimacy, much as the War of the Roses did in England. To all this, was added the Castilian conquest of Granada, the Portuguese and Castilian assault on the Maghrib, the conflicts of both Castile and Aragon with France in Italy, the discovery of America and the conquest of an intercontinental empire beyond all medieval imagination. 'Civil war logic' would fuse older medieval ideas with new elements to create what can be termed 'Habsburg paleonationalism'. This series of parallel conflicts would be followed in the sixteenth century by the conflicts generated by the progressive unification of the different crowns in a single Hispanic imperial monarchy: the growth of central power under Charles V was met by multiple expressions of armed resistance in both Castile and the Aragonese crown lands, at the time of the conquest of the Americas and the religious conflicts in Germany; the attempt to integrate the imperial monarchy under Philip II and the challenges - Flanders, Granada, Portugal, Aragon - to that more limited but more intense process, have given rise to the thesis of a 'general crisis' in the 1590s. The imperial monarchy floundered in a similar 'general crisis' of the seventeenth century, with civil wars in Portugal and in Catalonia, as well as elsewhere in the Iberian Peninsula and Italy. Under the nostalgic neo-medievalism of Charles V, the contradiction between the recognition of the pre-eminent imperial drive and the jealous defense of particularistic 'freedoms' was not crucial, at least beyond Central Germany. But in the measure that Philip II, self-conceived top bureaucrat, set in motion greater rationalisation, latent conflicts arose (most spectacularly in the Low

Countries). By pretending to resolve the problem of the gap between power, authority and administration, Philipine reform posed the contradiction bluntly. The reform would gradually acquire overtures of absolutism - i.e., everything was justified by 'efficiency', especially in the seventeenth-century reform spearheaded by Olivares; but conflict was visible long before. The insistence on an ideologically homogeneous society assuring imperial coordination was the ideal background to a 'seventeenth-century crisis' as experienced by the Spanish Crown in the 1640s and to the failure of Olivares' projected union. Spain was too evidently an extended empire, and 'paleonationalism' never gelled into any more substantial feeling, as happened elsewhere with the consolidation of dynastic power in the seventeenth century. On the contrary, the enemies of Spanish hegemony, like the Dutch or the English, clearly forged a sense of common destiny in the face of the Spanish threat. Within the Iberian Peninsula, Portugal succeeded in 1640 in establishing its independence, creating a selfhood openly based on the *"perigo espanhol"*. The revolt of the Catalans, also in 1640, though it momentarily fused high and low 'paleonationalist' discourse, ultimately failed, leaving behind a running ambiguity.

The War of Spanish Succession can be considered as a peninsular civil war, again involving Portugal and the Aragonese Crown as well as Castile. Once the Spanish Crown achieved unity through war, it engaged in administrative and, eventually, social reorganisation, which provoked a traditionalist defence of local customs (*tipismo*). At the same time, the combined experience of harsh civil war and invasion by foreign armies reinforced the patriotic reaffirmation of *castizo* (i.e., nativist) attitudes against outlandish fashion and ideas. This meant the qualitative change to dynastic nationalism with the Bourbons, after the victory of Philip of Anjou in the Succession struggle, gathered strength as the power of Crown officials grew. Slowly, over the eighteenth century, the Bourbon fusion of power with authority and administration created a sense of unity and a common symbolic identity. But, at same time, it was not either powerful or successful enough to begin to overcome older identities as in France, or in Britain after 1707 (with the Jacobite failure in 1745). Rather, the new Bourbon 'paleonationalism' would be like a varnish, a new layer superimposed on older ones, covering without obliterating.

The relative successes and failures of the new symbolic logic can be seen in different ways. Above all, Bourbon 'paleonationalism' was the product of a civil war logic, re-shuffling older images and upper class/lower class arguments in an innovative and lasting way. The new nationalism was therefore the discourse of the winning side in the internal conflict, and of the new state with its disorientating methods and reforms. In the measure that social habits also adjusted to the changes, however, the new discourse of identity, with its additional symbols, became slowly accepted. But the new identity was also - at least in the first half of the century - only that of partisans of state construction, either by class, place or region. Accordingly, the legitimization of the refashioned relation between power, authority and administration was centered even more on the ideal and the practice of efficiency, in a much more complete way than in the previous century. Efficiency justified changing customs and laws, centralizing, all in the name of relative (hierarchical) equality under the Crown. This signified an identity based on 'modernization' (i.e. 'Enlightenment') in the face of the past. But, at the same time, the new Bourbon discourse was superimposed, as is natural and logical, on Habsburg symbolic baggage (plus, of course, on Renaissance and even older medieval imagery solidly in place everywhere). Bourbon 'paleonationalism' implied a certain revolutionary change born out of civil war, aiming ultimately at a compromise in support of absolutism that would permit the increase of economic productivity under a power still very traditionally conceived. Therefore the most intrinsic symbols of authority were only slightly readjusted. Everything in the tradition of defining power/authority or administration that did not contradict the basic principles of Bourbon reform (i.e., the combination of civil war logic with the cult of efficiency) was assimilated as much as possible, because in the short term this reinforced Bourbon strength. Logically, this meant that all opposition to Bourbon reformism was expressed in the rhetoric of 'good old' Habsburg 'paleonationalism' or even 'medieval patriotism' against the innovative, 'foreign', 'French' nature of 'false' Bourbon reform. This could go from the harsh defense of local administration against central reform (as in the vicious debate over *fueros* in the eighteenth century) to direct pressures in the capital and elsewhere, with noble-urban mob alliances in the name of traditional customs (as in 1766).

In the measure that Bourbon reformism exhausted itself, or that the problem of colonial reform burned out the possibilities for renovation of the administration from within, early state or dynastic nationalism became not only a more attractive option for those in power, eager to utilize any means of support, but also a welcome concession to those formerly in opposition. With Charles IV (1788-1808), the official statist discourse finally lost its civil war logic (after three generations), and a new *tipista* 'Spanish' nationalism was adopted by the Monarchy, especially potent as the progress of the French Revolution scandalized all classes of opinion. The more that institutional aspects of reform were blocked by the very despotic nature of Bourbon power, the more all political factions had recourse to *tipismo* as an easy way to garner support in the country. The 1793-95 war against France permitted the full assumption of *tipismo* discourse, including old anti-French prejudices in the name of a state-building cause.

Both Spain and Portugal were involved in the fight against the French Revolution, in the 1793 coalition. When Godoy withdrew Spain from the anti-revolutionary cause, Portugal was left isolated, dependent on British goodwill for retaining Brazil against Spain's progressively closer ties to the Thermidorians and then to Bonaparte. The upshot came with the "War of the Oranges" between Spain and Portugal in 1801. This was followed, in 1807, by Spanish acquiescence in the French invasion of Portugal, and then, in 1808, the full-scale French takeover of Spain. Contrary international alignments bred peninsular conflict, which in turn became an explicit internal war, simultaneously reflecting international contradictions. Thus, the "Spanish Revolution" was at the same time the "War of Independence". After the Fernandine restoration, the implicit civil war model (*patriotas* vs. *afrancesados*) became an explicit struggle between secularising liberals and ardent clericalist defenders of traditional religious norms, with renewed French and British intervention in both countries through the 1830s. The shared process of civil war, begun around 1820, did not end until the 1870s, first in Portugal (Saldanha's last coup in 1870) and then Spain (Martínez Campos' coup in 1874). This sustained dynamic of internal warfare as the expression of the confrontation of the main warring parties led to successive post-war settlements based on the principle that parliamentary life is symbolic civil war. By 1874, the practice of peaceful alternation of parties in government mimicked the violent successions in power of the previous fifty years. In both countries, this situation has lasted through the twentieth century (see Figueiredo's concept of closely parallel Iberian histories). In both cases, with differing chronologies, there would be an experiment in intra-monarchical dictatorship, leading to a republican regime, overthrown by the military, who established a dictatorship, which, again in both cases, lasted into the mid-1970s, giving way to democratic parliamentary regimes, and joint European integration. In Spain, however, the move to symbolic civil war in parliamentary terms led to the rise of anti-Spanish nationalisms, while in Portugal this did not occur outside of Africa, or, less vehemently, Madeira and the Azores.

The process described was not just defined internally. External references were also permanent, right up to the present. One can begin by pointing to Portugal: Galicia (for linguistic reasons), Andalusia with the Algarve, and even to some extent Asturias, León, Extremadura, all have local identities forged, from the fifteenth century onwards, at least partially as a reflection of the existence of the border with Portugal. This outside presence would help define a local image of self-identity as an alternative to an agenda of Spanish state building. This would be comparable to the role of the kingdoms of Upper and Lower Navarre in conditioning Basque 'foralism' from the mid-sixteenth century onwards. Similarly, the old Aragonese crownlands retained a permanent, tangible relation with the varied societies of the Italian peninsula until the mid-nineteenth century, when the Garibaldian *Risorgimento* (1861) and the opening of the Suez Canal (1867) radically transformed the traditional trade routes of the western Mediterranean. Spain was enough of an imperial construct to see Portugal and Italy as areas of expansion: In any case these were far more likely to fear Spanish intervention than to serve as possible threats. But France, recovered as a power, repeatedly invaded Spain, from the seventeenth to the nineteenth centuries, with consequent territorial loss and successive struggles to impose French dynasts on the Spanish throne. After the early nineteenth century, however, Spain's neutrality in continental wars proved to be a disadvantage to continued nation-building, since the feeling of unity derived from attack was increasingly dissipated, without being replaced by any other sense of common purpose, as happened in other neutral States like Switzerland or Sweden.

Mass-élite communication is a permanent cultural interaction, determining the ongoing development of both high and low culture. Be it musical forms, elements of dress, slang or political norms, upper-class habits and popular custom have continuously borrowed from each other, marked always by a rhythm of delays and distortions. Such social interaction is naturally conditioned by sectional traits, usually quite visible to those living within a given polity, but subsumed into a generic by foreigners. Inter-state wars reinforce such generic stereotypes insofar as outsiders' perceptions, often heightened and typified by propaganda, are brought aggressively into political consciousness by invasion or sustained conflict. Enemy perceptions affect political communities generally by reinforcing precisely the elements of unity that alien vision incorporates, all the while increasing inter-class communication. Civil wars, on the contrary, accentuate internal cleavages, religious, class or territorial, all at once. Differences previously ignored now become terrible wrongs - both real or imagined - and sustain a new notion of community forged out of the struggle. After the fighting stops, no matter who has won, such stereotypes of internal differentiation become partisan symbolic groupings that condition political attitudes and focus solidarity for very long periods of time. Starting with André Siegfried, French political science has stressed the surprising vitality of spaces of political affinity - for or against the memory of 1791-94 - for almost two hundred years. In the measure that most ideological bonds are at least in part inherited, civil wars - the religious conflicts of the sixteenth and seventeen centuries and the revolutionary wars of the late eighteenth and early- nineteenth centuries in western and central Europe - have served to define partisan loyalty, even party solidarity, supposedly freely chosen, within a wider framework.

In other words, civil wars lay down the markers, the "places of memory" described by Nora and others, that mark off ideological borders. At the same time, the birth of what has been called 'civic culture' is clearly related to the groupings established by civil wars, especially in the British and Anglo-American contexts. Westminster is the 'mother of Parliaments' not because of Whiggish harking back to Runnymede but rather because the stability of a party system grew directly out of the English Civil War of the mid-seventeenth century. The Stuart Restoration of 1660 and its parliamentary expression preserved an agreement to disagree, and, by extension, from an acceptance of ambiguity there derived multiple potential interpretations of contractual formulae, that gave scope for later analogous stabilizations of the contending sides in civil strife in other countries. Such lessons in the channeling of open warfare into mostly verbal party violence are as important (if not more so) as the abstruse points of constitutional theory, much discussed in the Enlightenment and which served to establish the foundations of liberal and democratic thought. For parliamentary contest to become stabilized as civil war by other means, however, one has to have arrived at a sort of consensus born of stalemate regarding more naked forms of confrontation. Basically, the majority opinion has to hold that violence beyond certain limits is simply too expensive; within those limits anything can go.

In Spanish political experience, such consensus has not been reached successfully except in the last twenty years. By 1875-85 élites had agreed to limit the cost of peninsular civil war, but no such consensus emerged regarding colonial civil strife in Cuba. Violent de-colonization, repatriation of colonials, paying for the loss, and general readjustment opened a broad political discussion about the democratization of liberal institutional practice. Putting liberal theory into social practice, seemed merely the straightforward task of opening politics to the masses and to merit. But, in fact, the talk of "regeneration" in the wake of the de-colonisation "disaster" meant that, during the first four decased of twentieth-century Spain, every ideological platform offered its own exclusive and aggressive model of a "nationalising" state, with its promise of public service and assitance, to social clienteles anxious for urbanisation, promotion and /or professional recognition. In a tightly networked society, with modernisation increasingly defined by the corporate associations of both left and right, the interplay between the sonorous language of political representation and the strains of effecctive participation in institutions eventually brought parliamentary life to an end, with new internal war and prolonged dictatorship.

IV. The Structures of Power Behind Words and Images

We have seen how the images and words being used in Spain to describe both nation-building and the development of nationalisms are similar between Spanish and anti-Spanish currents, and the degree to which their expression is not merely reiterative but inherited and accumulative. Terms, formulations, reasonings and rationalizations keep being re-utilised in markedly different historical contexts and so change their meaning over time. The vocabularies of power are therefore a kind of ideological quarry to which any political orientation can turn for ready-made answers and 'proofs'.

If such repetition, despite changed meanings, is sustained, then the usual History of Ideas approach becomes fruitless insofar as it is the search for an explanatory hypothesis. No matter how rich *Ideengeschichte* may be, the erudition involved will only clarify the how, not the why. This situation poses epistemological problems of the kind historians sedulously avoid. Most historians are accustomed to a relation of privilege with their objects of study: subjectivity resides in the object, while the observer strives for 'objectivity'. This means that there is a considerable trade in concepts that are taken for granted and not defined, much less explored. Even those interpretative schools that call for a greater awareness of material contradictions do not encourage extensive clarification of basic concepts. There is a kind of hidden corporate consensus that such questions are best left to sociologists, political scientists or even philosophers. So historians, however much they plead that their work entails fundamental search for facts, are endlessly caught up in semantic arguments, as formative ideas, being used with vagueness, bounce back and forth. Of all such conceptual loose cannon lurching below mental decks, one of the most egregious is the notion of the 'nation-state'.

Seemingly convenient, with something of a Teutonic ring thanks to the hyphen, 'nation-state' offers succour to the historian too busy to clutter his work with muddled antecedents. But scholars of nationalism tend to insist on the post-1789 nature of that phenomenon: alluding to the 'nation-state' becomes a convenient way not having to confront the conundrum between nation and nationalism, while subscribing implicitly to the functionalist argument (the state being the substantive part of the conjunction) and thus avoiding untrendy primordialism. 'Nation-state' is a virtually meaningless notion, comfortable because it points to a certain *je ne sais quoi* and serves as a signpost that political 'feudalism' - another wonderfully messy term - is coming to an end, but is not quite over yet. In historiographic practice, early modern historians rarely speak of 'nation-states' with any sense of confidence. Some Spanish juridical historians, like Clavero, go so far as to argue that the 'state' is a nineteenth-century legal structure. Nevertheless, in the sixteenth century, outside Spain the Spanish model of centralizing absolutism, however much over-rated, served to provide a focal image of abusive and oppressive power, much in the way that the 'Grand Turk' and his seraglio served as the icon for the same beyond European borders.

Today, the idea of empire has a singularly bad reputation. Such entities are held to be extinct and immoral. Although the name is avoided today, however, it remains to be seen whether empires have in fact disappeared at the present time (Russia, China, India, Indonesia, even the European Union, among other examples), much less that they will never rise again. Radicals like J.A. Hobson and extreme socialists like Lenin managed to transform it into a synonym for overseas colonialism, a most limited reductionism. The Soviets, in the measure that they held an empire papered over in red, were most interested in defining the concept restrictively, so that it would best apply to their capitalist enemies rather than to themselves. The term empire, as Koebner showed, became confused with capital export, as well as with the crowned ritual with which many major states - like Austria-Hungary, unified Germany or Great Britain - in the 1870s chose to adorn their naked power. As Republics began to proliferate after 1917-18, the obsolescence of the idea seemed self-evident. The flap provoked by A.J. Mayer's suggestion of the "survival of the Old Régime" up to World War I is an indication of historians' reluctance to use the concept. Nevertheless, the notion of empire was always ascribed to large territorial entities, too large, it was presumed, to be mere kingdoms. Great Britain is an explicitly imperial idea, as Elizabethan or Jacobean sources demonstrate; equally so France and Germany and, needless to say, Spain. We could define empires quite simply as very large aggregations of lesser territories (including traditionally recognized States), with a certain tendency to keep growing if at all possible; their characteristic feature is that they are always open-ended, implying the potential for expansion, at least as an aspiration that conditions identity. So familiar was the concept that in the nascent United States the term was a familiar way of alluding to the federal whole. In France, as Rémond indicated, it was the Bonapartist imperial tradition that, precisely for being synthetic, defined best the sense of state continuity and function. Before World War I, virtually every state in Europe - from Sweden to Turkey - was deemed in some sense an empire, unless it happened to be a "balkanized" piece that had fallen or been prised off, and even such fragments - Greece, Serbia, Rumania or Bulgaria - were built on the dream precisely of becoming one. Switzerland was the exception that proved the rule, hence its alleged peculiarity. The inter-war years were not so different: the central defining fact of Soviet rule, beyond ideology, was the fact of empire. Whatever the increasingly complicated taxonomy of fascism holds, it seems clear that the anti-communist régimes all hoped in some way to mix the retention of pre-war imperial forms with the pressures of some sort of social integration of the masses, a point made for Spanish fascism rather clumsily by H.R. Southworth years ago. Only the tacit Soviet-American agreement in favor of de-colonization that helped sustain the Cold War finally sank the concept of empire, rendering it momentarily unacceptable, at least until refurbished by Paul Kennedy.

Spain in the nineteenth century was the pioneer of de-colonization and its discontents. Because of this, Spain became a byword for 'decadence'. Historians such as Macaulay, Buckle or Motley, confident in the Protestant tradition, could not help stressing the rapid 'degeneration' of Spanish virility, a product of enervating cruelty, political and religious abuse and Catholic lack of enterprising spirit. Every time that Gallic institutions shuddered, French political discourse kept looking over its shoulder at Spanish decay as an object lesson in how far and fast a people could sink. The curious result has been that the historiography of de-colonization, written after Suez, is unanimously dated from the imposed fragmentation of the German overseas empire in 1919, assuming the Spanish example was due to some deeper or older cause. Nevertheless, the effects of a century of redefining state roles are clearly visible in Spain, from 1808 to 1898, in ways that, despite being smothered by the then contemporary analogy to political and economic liberalization, point to problems visible in France and the United Kingdom in the second half of the twentieth century.

The immense impact of liberalism on modern political thinking has led to massive insistence on the importance of the internal political institutions of states at the expense of other questions. Marxism redirected attention to the control of the economy, but only by excluding many other aspects. In sum, the territorial 'form' of a state is as important a factor as its institutional 'content' in conditioning both the formulation of policy by élites and the manipulation of popular enthusiasms. Perhaps parallel to the Ottoman Empire or the Habsburg monarchy, modern Spain was characterised by an ongoing need to redefine both its territorial 'form' and institutional 'content'. Certainly, the liberal struggles of the nineteenth century were provoked in large part by the loss of Latin America and the need to find a substitute for maritime empire, so that French imperial overreach had much to do with the breakdown of the French monarchy in the 1780s or even that the loss of British North America helped to facilitate the reorganization of English politics, in time to meet the threat of French Revolution.

French invasion in 1808, with its ideological trappings, changed the nature of Spanish identity, although it did so in a cumulative way, reincorporating the inheritance of the past into a radically changing political framework. The Bourbon administration was fragmented into local juntas, which only came together in an effort to create a political framework that could maintain the struggle against the outsiders who had kidnapped the dynasty. This meant the introduction of representative liberalism (embodied in the Constitution of 1812), even though it had to be presented as the recovery of an indigenous feudal parliament suppressed by absolutist centralism. The impact of harsh foreign occupation and bitter internal strife forged for the first time a real sense of Spanish nationhood, expressed as a real nationalism, which combined historical imagery with concepts of citizenship and representative government. Though liberals and neo-absolutists battled for decades over the significance of the changes wrought by Napoleon's invasion, both sides had essentially assumed a new national identification, with the debate (beyond its capitalist overtones) being about the nature of political representation. Still, successive civil wars underlined the old centripetal-centrifugal tension.

In sum, modern Spanish 'institutional nationalism' appeared out of Napoleonic invasion. Medieval forms, Habsburg 'paleonationalism' and Bourbon proto-statism had a cumulative effect, one upon the other. The depth of social alteration, the very destruction of the traditional social tissue represented by the 1808-14 conflict, permitted an intense shuffling of symbols, both upper and lower class, at a moment when, for the first time in more than three centuries there was no central authority. Furthermore, French invasion provoked a bitter civil war. This burned out a good part of the statist contents of the Bourbon inheritance, which rode out the conflict in the glorification of *tipismo* (i.e. 'Spanishness'). Older civil war logic, incorporated into Bourbon patriotic discourse was brought to the fore (the popular legitimization of eighteenth-century changes, now perceived as the good old ways threatened by external change). Even older neo-Habsburg baggage was resurrected (anti-French and other xenophobic sentiment, or counter-Reformation religiosity such as the cult of the Immaculate Conception), together with medieval images (the sense of continuity of the hidden, awaited king, identified with the absent Ferdinand VII). But these themes were now mixed in with a new civil war logic based on the immediate situation. The Regency implied a high degree of popular approval or participation necessary for legitimization, so the war against the French became accordingly "Our Revolution". The collapse of royal administration gave the army a new role, the incorporation of guerrillas into the military hierarchy gave the impression of a spiritualized social mobility, the appearance of Juntas which reproduced the old kingdoms recalled historical localism and common law. At the same time, the conflict unleashed all the unitary emotions provoked by foreign attack and occupation: the traditional Spanish dislike of France became as important for the sense of collective self as the Portuguese fear of Spain. The result was a complex reaffirmation of both localism and broad Spanishness without any feeling of contradiction. While similar to the past, such ambiguity was also very different, given the new ideological values attached to older symbols.

The "War of Independence" (i.e. 'War of Nation-Building') forged a new symbolic identity, with all manner of illustrative myths. Since the war was a revolution in the liberal sense, which created new participatory institutions "with the People", this new nationalism was above all institutionally defined. This was the importance of the Constitution of 1812, beyond all the other proclamations, Juntas and mechanisms by which the State was reinvented during the conflict. Thus, after

1808-14, the basic components of Spanish nationalism were fixed in a more or less modern form, although with more than one pattern of expression. In the first place, this nationalism incorporated a sequence of accretions from the past: the idea of authority as linked to chiliasm but compensated by the stability of religious unity (an ideal looked for in whatever form, so that, e.g., by the end of the nineteenth century atheists will dream of atheistic religious unity); localism (exemplified by Juntas), but also the conviction that Spain as a whole had an over-riding, unified mission; efficiency as an ideal for the state but, tempered by the multiple exceptions expressed as *fueros*, both local (regional law, municipal exemptions), and corporate (Church, army, university, press). These elements, accumulated from the medieval, Habsburg or Bourbon past redefined by the civil war experience of 1808-14, were welded to the eighteenth century revolutionary idea of the 'institutional nation' (the nation understood as the whole of the citizens expressing themselves through their properly elected representatives, with kinghood serving to incarnate the historical continuity of the state, something that radicals could modify by stressing the transformation of the latter). Thus the Old Régime idea of a 'nation' as civil society within the state (which would include institutions of the Crown plus the Crown itself) would become a new concept of 'nation', in which state and civil society were to be forever one.

Nevertheless, the new Spanish nationalism carried the implicit contrast of its 'paleonationalist' origins: while the 'high' tradition fed into a 'Greater Spain' discourse, at home with the imperial state however liberal, the 'low' encouraged an exclusively peninsular 'little Spanish' ideal. Such a polarity shaped right and left. It is easy to see that there was an extensive emotional and intellectual vocabulary by the time Romantic writers gave shape to such a hoard of images and metaphors. Mid-nineteenth century authors who started to dust off local curiosities were, therefore, merely picking up themes that particularist writers had been defending a few decades before. Juaristi offers a good example of this sort of borrowing: intrigued by the obsessive anti-Semitism of nineteenth century defenders of Basque *foral* rights, he shows how the themes of Basque racial purity date back to the angry quarrel between *vizcaínos* and ex-Jewish 'converts' for the leading role in the burgeoning Spanish administration of the sixteenth century, a bureaucratic battle that stirred much writing on Basque 'pure blood'. But Romanticism brought a systematic rationalization of accumulated ideas and images in what until then had been a process of discussion between central and local power contained within a religious framework. Inspired by Romantic fashion, the mid-nineteenth century spokesmen for both statist and local identities refurbished alleged popular memory in ballads of crusader kingdoms, and pretended to merge this directly with the model of institutional nationalism as an expression of the state imposed by liberal revolution. With of foreign attack still fresh in people's minds and civil wars omnipresent to keep the question of identity on the boil, the new mix of Spanish nationalism served all options, dominating literature, rhetoric and even street names and urban design. By 1868, the so-called "Glorious Revolution" (with echoes of Whig triumphalism) fixed both the institutional sense of Spanish nationalism and its imagery.

But the search for nationalist authenticity passed from literature to politics because of the failure of the Spanish liberal revolution, as it limped along through the nineteenth century, to provide effective state services. Liberalism was advocated by lawyers and journalists but effected by military officers. All were anxious for social promotion through a new kind of state service, but their rivalry also had its drawbacks, not the least of which was the continued divergence between legal principles and effective action. The more inefficient the state was, the more it contradicted the promise of liberal modernization, and the more it failed its stated ideals, the more it tended to get defensive and nasty, especially as regards the dissatisfied. At first, popular protest was channeled as usual to manifestations of local patriotism: Carlist *foralism* and republican federalism shared the conviction that general elections, even with universal manhood suffrage, were not as genuine as local politics. This was the sense of both the republican experiment of 1873-74 and the Carlist insurrection of 1872-76. But the civil war that really marked the future was the so-called "Long War" in Cuba, 1868-78. The Caribbean conflict had no easy solutions: pacification did not hold, and the "Long War" was followed by the "Short War" (1879-81) and by sustained guerrilla activity, banditry and more 'Yankee meddling' until the Cuban "War of Independence" broke out in 1895.

After the conservatives had re-established restrictive policies in 1876, a long period of liberal reform government, notably in 1885-1890, definitely made institutional nationalism the basis of the political system, since it incorporated the democratic functions upon which liberal institutions could flourish and expand, such as universal suffrage, trial by jury, freeing of slaves. But the culmination of liberalism brought discontent. A half-century of peninsular civil wars regarding the political definition of nationhood, between 1820 and 1876, created weariness with the revolutionary institutional message. Increasingly, the contradiction between stated goals and what was in fact delivered politically or administratively generated scepticism about the model of institutional nationalism as an expression of the state. Paradoxically, the ultimate triumph of liberalism was its failure, which set off a process of mutual antagonism between the official discourse of Spanish nationalism and the reply of alternative nationalist projects, both in the mainland and the colonies, clearly visible in the 1890s. Hereafter, Spanish and peripheral nationalisms continued to feed off each other emotionally.

After the failure of federalism and the defeat of Carlism, the 1880s were a period of renewed thinking about the state's territorial organization. The great unresolved subject was the reform of local administration (municipal, provincial, regional): although everyone was in agreement that the provincial system copied from France in 1833 did not work, there was no agreement as to how to replace it, and the unresolved colonial question (a part of local reform) made it impossible to discuss calmly. But any form of devolution was bound up with military administration of overseas territories. By the time the liberal government offered autonomy to the Caribbean islands in 1897, Cuba was in open revolt, which ultimately involved the United States and brought the loss of all Spanish overseas territories outside Africa. Thus it was that the colonial mess introduced an overseas civil war momentum, born of the Cuban internecine conflict, to metropolitan politics. The rise of Cuban nationalist identity since the 1830s, with its 'lone star' imitation of Texan independence and its permanent attraction to the United States, presented the first real alternative to Spanish institutional nationalism. After all, Cuba was the most advanced capitalist regional economy within the imperial state, the first to have a railway (even before Catalonia) and easily the most attuned to trends in the world market. The result was independent revolt, Spanish repression, and the appearance of new hysterical nationalisms of identity, 'us or them', on both sides. Such a Spanish nationalist discourse ('unionism' or 'Spanish unconditionalism', summarised as *españolismo*) was unknown in peninsular politics until the impact of renewed colonial war in the 1890s, when it was introduced by the militarist press, representing discontented middle-level officers. By obvious routes, Cuban independence quickly sprouted imitations in the Canary Islands, while Catalan, Galician and Basque immigrant associations in the Americas copied the prevailing discourse of national self-determination in the Western Hemisphere and applied it to nostalgic memories of the 'old country', in turn influencing metropolitan movements. The new colonial wars polarized what heretofore had been a juridical debate between politicians, turning it into a potentially violent conflict between the army officer corps, clinging doggedly to unity after being defeated by separatists, and the new alternative nationalist movements in industrialized Catalonia and the Basque Country. This hysterical nationalism of identity was perfectly adaptable to new *fin-de- siécle* European ideologies, linked to imperialism and visible in the 1890s crises of Portugal, Italy and France. But European influences played only a secondary role, though such copycat readings helped to dignify and polish ideas.

Obviously the rise of communications – as much for the rapid relaying of information as for physical transport of goods or persons, implied in the mid-nineteenth century rise of telegraph, undersea cable, steam engine, railroad and screw propeller - deeply altered the nature of power. The key to all power is in the efficacy of delegation. Before the 'communications revolution' a governor of a province was effectively free to decide in proportion to the distance that separated him from the capital. By the 1870s, outlying provinces virtually anywhere were under direct tutelage of central authorities, or would soon be so. Practical autonomy, with little theoretical justification, thus gave way to theoretical autonomy, often with difficult practical implementation. After the mid-nineteenth century, with faster communications, increased information led to a certain 'demonstration effect' based not so much on proximity, as on the fact of similar events in other places at the same time. As the twentieth century advanced and the amount of detail daily received in the media grew incommensurably, such comparisons became models for political organization and strategy. For nationalisms in a Spanish metropolitan context, far removed from American examples, this sort of analogy had its impact: the *Risorgimento* in Italy, Austro-Hungarian dualism, German unification, Balkan events, the Boer War, the outcome of the Great War, and so on, all provided as much inspiration for a new 'Spanish' awakening as for the arousal of regional nationalisms.

This external momentum, expressed formally in the changing tone of Spanish nationalism (with an increasingly hysterical emphasis on identity by the Right, on institutions by the Left), generated the rise of regionalist movements, committed to securing administrative reforms made necessary by colonial defeat. The 1898 'disaster' led to a re-examination of the myths of Spanish statehood and served to openly question the values forged out of the French invasion/civil war of 1808-14. From this point on, reform of local administration (that is, the basic guarantees for any deepening of the democratic process within liberal institutions) came to be indissolubly linked to the intimate psychological identity embodied in the mythology of the state. This explosive combination rendered parliamentary reform within the monarchy impossible up to 1923, made military-led reform impractical in 1923-30, and turned renewed parliamentary reform under a Republic into a source of extremely violent symbolic conflict, leading up to a new civil war in 1936-39. As a result, army intervention has dominated Spanish politics for most of the twentieth century down to the shift to democracy in the mid-1970s. Much of that militarism, not surprisingly, was focused on Barcelona.

V. Social Pressures for Structural Change Using Old Vocabularies

Recent interpretations of the so-called 'Industrial Revolution' are insisting more and more on the importance of what might be termed 'social software', specifically attitudes or forms of behavior, as a key to understanding the rise of mature liberal-capitalist societies, rather than putting the interpretative weight on the chain reaction of productive hardware, the development of technology, as was popular among historians such as Landes only a few decades ago. Certainly such an approach is scarcely new: the debate over the relation between Protestantism and capitalism in the classic vein of Weber, Tawney or Groethuysen seems finally exhausted without having resolved the question. But the recent extended historiographic discussion surrounding European proto-industrialization, along with a greater sensitivity born of women's studies, has led to greater interest in subjective or behavioral aspects of social processes formerly considered as objective. The collapse of Marxist certainties has also encouraged a more flexible attitude toward the understanding of class identities and conflict. Accordingly, family structure and patterns of inheritance in Northwestern Europe have been suggested, for instance by Todd, as a major source of such 'social software', when it comes to explaining political systems. In the same way, some analysts, such as von Laue, insist that it has been the export of such 'software' out from this core area that has dominated the last two centuries of world history. In particular, as pointed out by such a doyenne of urban studies as Jane Jacobs, cities and the general dynamic of urbanization have been singled out as the only effective medium in which such 'software' can thrive. Urban rivalries are, therefore, as Rokkan theorized, an excellent indicator of the relation between social tensions of any kind and territorial projections, always the heart of any nationalism. Instead of the usual ideological approach, which easily loses the outsider in the endless thicket of Catalan and Basque local politics and their over-subtle distinctions, it is easier to understand the nature of competing nationalisms through the general perspective of urban growth. The rise of anti-Spanish movements was marked by a visible relation to urbanization and industry, often simplified into a question of 'bourgeois nationalism'. The urban background helps highlight the very real differences between the Catalan and Basque movements (and to a much lesser degree, Galician or Canary Islands' nationalism) in their development during the first half of the twentieth century, as well as the gulf separating their expansion from minor regionalisms in Andalusia, Aragon, Asturias, Extremadura, and Murcia, or even in Castile.

The major cities of the sixteenth century Iberian Peninsula were undoubtedly Seville and Lisbon, urban conduits for the Indies trade. Seville's expansion was clearly at the expense of the towns of northern Castile or even the Basque ports, dependent on the late medieval wool trade. But the Spanish absolutist monarchy was markedly indecisive about establishing its political centre; in any case, it was not Seville. Nor was it Lisbon, which some have argued might have saved the composite monarchy established by Philip II. On the contrary, the "prudent king" preferred to invent a capital out of the fastest growing Castilian city (Madrid) and furthermore to establish his palace outside it (El Escorial). Such a structural imbalance of the

Spanish city system, only changed in the eighteenth century when Madrid's growth, under Bourbon patronage, really took off, leaving behind Seville and any other competitors. The real surprise, however, was the expansion of Barcelona, which came out of comparative urban obscurity to relevance in the second half of the eighteenth century, and by the early nineteenth century, established itself as Spain's major industrial center, on top of its character as a headed commercial port. The Andalusian cities, by Seville, had dominated Spanish Atlantic trade, while northern ports decayed along with the interior. Accordingly, revolutionary liberalism in the Peninsular War, a subject closely connected to the repercussions of European events in an American context, was centered in Andalusia: the constitutionalist center of Spain was Cadiz, from 1810 to 1868. But American independence ultimately ruined Andalusian prospects and the region would become a byword for backwardness by the end of the nineteenth century. In contrast, much of the Atlantic trade was taken over by Basques, while industrialization took hold in Barcelona and its hinterland.

Family structure and inheritance patterns, along with the growth of new forms of organized male sociability were analogous in Catalonia to what has been indicated as the crucial factor in England and the Low Countries, as well as part of central Germany. These elements of 'social software' facilitated the adaptation to industrial production between the late eighteenth and mid-nineteenth century. The Basque family pattern, equally northern but less flexible in its implications for sociability, encouraged greater commercial risk-taking and emigration. As a result, the evolution of an entrepreneurial Basque bourgeoisie came about through a state-wide network, with connections from Madrid or Cadiz to Havana, Manila or Buenos Aires, while the consolidation of a Catalan bourgeoisie, broader based but without as many great fortunes, was linked rather to the development of Barcelona as a great city, soon the only urban center in Spain capable of rivaling Madrid's role as State capital. While Madrid controlled meritocracy and therefore enjoyed a capacity to keep attracting immigrants from all of Spain anxious to progress through political promotion, Barcelona's factories kept pulling in peasants from all the surrounding regions. In marked contrast, neither the Basque Country nor Galicia, nor any other historic region of Spain, developed a pull towards a major capital, capable of concentrating resources and establishing territorial ambitions, in the way that happened in Catalonia. Up to the last decades of the twentieth century, specific sociologies of domesticity and male sociability characterised not only the fact of urban development, but also the highly subjective debate regarding differences in culture and behavior between the regions of Spain.

From the mid-nineteenth century onwards, Madrid and Barcelona were locked in a bitter rivalry over the privileges that allegedly accrued from their relative democratic weightings: from around a quarter million inhabitants in the 1860s, the urban antagonists increased to about a half million by the turn of century, leaving the rest of Spain's cities far behind. By 1931, both cities were the only million-plus cities in Spain, when this was held to be a universal sign of real metropolitan magnitude. Madrid had all the advantages of being official capital. Barcelona, the outstanding economic center, bitterly resented being relegated to provincial status, comparable to minor centers of 20-30,000 inhabitants.

Accordingly, Barcelona was the historic reference point for Spanish federalism. All the so-called 'peripheral nationalisms' tended to look to Barcelona's leadership, since none of the other regions with nationalist movements advanced beyond domestic rivalries between cities for predominance. Although the Bilbao metropolitan area was a serious demographic contender, for example, it never has been anything other than a modest conurbation whose primacy was unrecognized by other Basque urban rivals. Local politics in the Basque country, as in Galicia, Andalusia or the Canary Islands, has been dominated by peer competition between cities. Barcelona's status as metropolitan challenger to Madrid as the capital of centralism in turn encouraged all manner of grand pan-Catalanist dreams among intellectuals, who dreamed of joining all the Catalan-speaking areas of Spain with the Occitanian South of France in a vast cultural revival. Within Catalan politics, this solipsism meant that a basic substratum of 'Catalanism', whatever this meant, was common to a large portion of the political spectrum, despite the seemingly divisive labels, such as federalism, regionalism or separatism.

Barcelona, like Madrid, kept growing through immigration, attracted in one case by economic, and in the other, by state power. But Barcelona's push for pre-eminence became mixed up with the formation of a new cultural market, not just in Spanish, but now also in the Catalan language. As elsewhere in cities that had no recent cultural significance, 'modernism' was a chance for a clean start, with monuments from the past being considered anachronistic. A new cultural beginning, in which everybody kicked off with the same resources and the same style, 'modernism' in theory gave no precedence to old-established cultural centers as opposed to new starters. As a result, Catalan literature and art could be just as good as Spanish literature and art, and the Catalan capital just as imposing as the Spanish capital. Such attitudes came about easily, since Spanish administration was traditionally inefficient, and, precisely because it was inefficient, furthermore tended to be defensively overbearing, aggressive, far more preoccupied with maintaining order than with solving the conditions that nurtured disorder in the first place. Education policy, or its absence, was a prime example of the general mediocrity of state services from the citizen's viewpoint, whereas the Civil Guard served as a counter example of one of the few portions of the administration that worked outstandingly well. With such attitudes widespread, Barcelona became the focus for all discontent, the 'Big City' of contradiction to the state, as much of a beacon for anarchists or republicans as for staunch Catalan nationalists. In a seemingly enduring way, Barcelona was characterized as a center of pluralism. This appearance, however, was only due to the fact that any political solution was conditioned by the essential vagueness of the city's status (i.e., by the contradiction between its metropolitan size and its anomalous nature as no more than a provincial capital). Paradoxically, the looming end of dualism, in the measure that Madrid finally won the urban race with Barcelona and became the unquestioned 'prime city' after the 1970s, could betoken a greater impulse towards more separatist forms in future Catalan politics. According to geographers, the urban systems of minimally durable political spaces are extremely stable: it is considered normal for the capital or 'prime city' to be twice the size of the 'second city', which in turn is twice the size of the third, and so on. In Spain, such proportions would not be achieved until the 1990s, when Madrid has three million inhabitants to Barcelona's million and a half.

VI.   The Paradoxical Failure and Success of Nationalism in Late-Twentieth Century Spanish Politics

The accidental birth of the Franco regime in 1936-39 was arbitrary in the extreme, resulting in a genuine and deep break with the continuity of state practice. The military plotters of the summer of 1936 had only planned a coup; their failure set off a civil war, the prolongation of which led to the need to improvise a new administration, more or less in the fascist mold, when the intention had been merely to take over the old one. The pressure to adjust to the principal, international sponsors of the rebel cause favored Franco over his possible rivals, but the establishment of a personal dictatorship was a complicated, often delicate political process that began in October 1936 and which gave way to a 'New State' only in early 1938. All this meant that Franco, in addition to his republican enemies, faced many opponents in his own camp, especially among the monarchists, happy to overthrow the Republic and the Popular Front but not keen to accept long-term postponement of a restoration. Franco plundered the symbols of the past precisely to be free of responsibilities to immediate political interest groups. His cause, already labelled as 'nationalist' before he rose to absolute pre-eminence, offered generic ideological trademarks that, in the extreme polarization of a civil war, forced those who loathed the republicans to accept his symbolic leadership. The 'New State' became officially *El Estado Español*, neither republic nor monarchy; if anything, Franco claimed it to be an 'Empire'. Strictly speaking, Spain ceased to be so only in 1975 when the dictator's death coincided with the cession of the Western Sahara to Morocco.

Paradoxically, the logic of symbols that accompanied *Franquismo* opened the way to a significant change. Since the central objective of Franco propaganda was to stress Spanish nationalist unity within the confines of the counter-revolution, and accordingly eschew all points of doctrine that could favour opponents within his own ranks, the régime ended up abusing the rhetoric of centralizing statist nationalism of identity to the point of exhaustion. By dint of monopolizing it, Franco turned the inherited 'high' tradition of 'Greater Spanish' discourse into slogans (*Una, Grande, Libre*) which became clichés. Such a political context strongly favored the symbolic expansion of rival, anti-Spanish nationalisms, which could turn Franco messages on their head: if the régime claimed that there had been no civil war but rather the "War of Spain", Catalan or Basque nationalists could answer that it had been just that, an attack by Spain against Catalonia or Euzkadi; if the régime was officially "The Spanish State", then Catalan or Basque nationalists could claim that it pointedly excluded the rival nationalities. This process of symbolic inversion was equally based on the impact of industrial development on Spanish society after the late 1950s.

By the late 1970s, as the Crown, the régime's successors and the opposition sought to find ways towards a political compromise, virtually every region aspired to copy Catalans, Basques and Galicians in their demands, creating a variety of regionalist movements that aped the arguments of these so-called 'historic nationalities'. The heart of the 'democratic transition' consisted of the enthronement of the 'little Spain' tradition as the accepted, even carefully nurtured, philosophy of state, while tolerating the survival of symbolic traits associated with its rival. For these reasons, the move back to a parliamentary system after the death of the dictator permitted an eclectic symbolic settlement, in which all the identities, central and local, were allowed to prosper in an unstable and contradictory administrative reform based on the simultaneous existence of autonomic and centralized institutions. This tendency coincided with some overall European trends, when strongly centralized states such as Italy or France moved towards administrative regionalization in the decades after World War II and 'devolution' remained an ongoing topic in British politics. In the measure that the construction of the European Economic Community could seriously be taken as the reconstitution of an empire in compensation for colonial loss by the major western European states between the 1940s and 1960s, its continued push towards a more profound European Union after the mid-1980s seriously called to question, at least theoretically, the future role of the state and offered obvious potential for regions previously relegated to minor political or administrative functions.

The unwieldy balance between state and regions in Spain, maintained under the long years of socialist rule (1982-96), has created a situation where the expression of identity tends to be far more particularist than statist, the precise opposite of the preceding Franco years. By the mid-1990s, within Spain, it seems unclear who is a Spaniard. While the relative electoral victory of the Popular Party in March 1996 was prepared with an intense campaign of Spanish nationalist rhetoric, directed at younger voters with an explicit rejection of Pujol's brand of Catalan nationalism and of the unending threat of Basque terrorism, the uncertain results forced the right into an uncomfortable alliance precisely with those sectors - Pujol and the Basque nationalists - whose 'disloyalty' right-wing propaganda had, until then, so strenuously denounced. The result is confusion, so that Spanish historians such as Tusell or Álvarez Junco deny that today Spanish nationalism as such even exists.

In conclusion, using Spanish experience as a case study, the central point of this paper has been to show how, in the particular area of nationalist justifications, the accretion of historical vocabularies over time is subject to permanent reuse, with new meanings given to old symbols, images or ideas. The sustained use of the same vocabularies, which build up their store of reference with the passage of time, offers an important insight into the perspectivees of both sides in the renewed debate surrounding nationalism. Nationalist historiography points to the recurrence of patriotic terminology dating back far beyond the French Revolution. This is offered as proof of nationalism, like the family, being a 'primordial' tie in society. Historiography critical of nationalist presumptions has presented the manipulation of messages as a demonstration of the need for diverse 'functionalist' approaches to the understanding of nationalism, many of which stress its bourgeois class definition. This paper would suggest that both are right in part, while being insufficient as global explanations. Inherited arguments do, in fact, reach very far back. But their recurrent use is always subject to changing contexts and therefore new interests. In this sense, the paper has tried to indicate how civil wars, as well as international conflicts, can serve to recast older arguments and adapt them to new social circumstances; civil wars in particular recycle ideas and images and mold them into apparently new shapes. Ultimately, 'civic culture', i.e. stable civil peace, cannot be understood without reference to long-term patterns of recurrent civil conflict. Equally, it has been argued here that the imperial form of the state provides a useful framework for placing apparently modern nationalist phenomena in a longer time span. In general, the implications of territory have scarcely been investigated, at least by historians, unlike geographers. Finally, this paper suggests that urbanization and urban rivalries are a useful but little-used way of studying the territorial aspect and social dynamics of rival nationalisms.

Bibliography

Andreucci, F. & Pescarolo, A. [eds.] *Gli Spazi del Potere*, Florence, 1989.

Almond, G. & Verba, S.   *The Civic Culture*, Princeton, 1963

Anguera. P. et al.,   *Origens i Formació: dels Nacionalismes a Espanya*, Reus, 1994.

Ansprenger, F.   *The Dissolution of the Colonial Empires*, London, Routledge. 1989.

Association des Historiens Modernistes,
      Le Sentiment National dans l'Europe Moderne, Paris, 1991.

Bahamonde, A. & Martínez, J. A.,   *Historia de España siglo XIX*, Madrid, 1994.

Beramendi, X. G. & Núñez Seixas, X.M.,   *O Nacionalismo Galego*, Vigo, 1995.

Bergeron, L. [ed.],   *La Croissance Régionale dans l'Europe Méditerranéene, 18e-20e siècles*, Ecole des Hautes Études, 1992.

Brubaker, R.,   *Citizenship and Nationhood in France and Germany*, Cambridge, Mass., 1992.

Bullón, E.,   *El Concepto de la Soberanía en la Escuela Jurídica Española del siglo XVI*, Madrid, 1936.

Burke, P.,   *The Fabrication of Louis XIV*, London, 1992.

Caro Baroja, J.,   *Las Falsificaciones de la Historia (en Relación con la de España)*, Barcelona, 1992.

Cassirer, E.,   *The Myth of the State*, New Haven, 1946.

Chabod, F.,   *L'Idea di Nazione*, Bari, 1961.

Checa Cremades, F.,   *Carlos V y la Imagen del Héroe en el Renacimiento*, Madrid, 1987.

Cepeda Adán, J.,   *En Torno al Concepto del Estado en la Época de los Reyes Católicos*, Madrid, 1956.

Chamberlain, M. E.,   *Decolonization. The Fall of the European Empires*, Oxford, 1985.

Clavero, B.,   *Razón de Estado, Razón de Individuo, Razón de Historia*, Madrid, 1991.

Di Febo, G. [ed.], "Spagna: Immagine e Autorappresentazione", *Dimensioni e Problemi della Richerca Storica*, 2, Milan 1995.

Doyle, M., *Empires*, Ithaca, 1986.

Duran, E., Gil Pujol, X., Torres Sans, X., et al., "El patriotisme i la monarquia hispànica".*Rercerques 32*, 1995.

Duverger, M., et al., *Le concept d'empire.* Paris, 1980.

Eisenstadt, S.N., *The Political Systems of Empires,* New York, 1969.

Elliott, J.H., *The Revolt of the Catalans,* Cambridge 1963.

Fabre, D. [ed.], *L'Europe Entre Cultures et Nations,* Paris, 1996.

Fernández Albaladejo, P., *Fragmentos de Monarquía,* Madrid, 1992,

Ferarri, J., & Wunenberger, J.-J., [eds.], *L'idée de Nation,* Dijon, n.d.

Figueiredo, F. de, *As Duas Espanhas,* Lisbon, 1959.

Gallagher, J. *The Decline, Revival and Fall of the British Empire,* Cambridge, 1982.

García Pelayo, M., *El Reino de Dios, Arquetipo Político,* Madrid, 1959.

Granja, J. L. de la, *El Nacionalismo Vasco: un Siglo de Historia,* Madrid, 1995.

Guichonnet., P.& Raffestin, C., *Géographie des Frontières,* Paris, 1974.

Hobsbawm, E. J., & Ranger, T., [eds.], *The Invention of Tradition,* Cambridge,1983.

Hobsbawm, E. J., *Nations and Nationalism Since 1780,* Cambridge, 1990.

Jacobs, J. *Cities and the Wealth of Nations,* New York, 1984

Jones, E., *Metropolis: The World's Great Cities,* Oxford, 1990.

P. M. Kennedy, *The Rise and Fall of the Great Powers,* London, 1988.

Koebner, R., *Empire,* Cambridge 1966.

Lalinde Abadía, J., & Pelaez, M. J. et al., *El Estado Español en su Dimensión Histórica* Barcelona, 1984.

Laue, T.H. von, *The World Revolution of Westernization,* New York, 1987.

Linz, J. J., *Conflicto en Euzkadi,* Madrid, 1986.

Lisón Tolosano, C.,	*La imagen del Rey. Monarquia, Realeza y Poder Ritual en la Casa de los Austria*, Madrid, 1991.
Maravall, J.A.,	*El concepto de España en la Edad Media*, Madrid, 1981.
Margadant, T.W.,	*Urban Rivalries in the French Revolution*, Princeton, 1992.
Mayer, A. J.,	*The Persistence of the Old Regime. Europe to the Great War*, New York, 1981.
Morán, M.,	*La Imagen del Rey: Felipe V y el Arte*, Madrid, 1990.
Moreno Fraginals, M.,	*Cuba/España: España/Cuba Historia Común*, Barcelona, 1995.
Nieto Soria, J.M.,	*Fundamentos Ideológicos del Poder Real en Castilla (siglos XIII-XVI)*, Madrid, 1988.
Nora, P. [ed.],	*Les Lieux de Mémoire*, Paris, 1984-1993, 7 vols.
Pagden, A.,	*Lords of All the World. Ideologies of Empire in Spain, Britain and France c. 1500-c. 1800*, New Haven, 1995.
Pagden, A.,	*Spanish Imperialism and the Political Imagination* New Haven, 1991.
Pocock, J.G.A.,	*Virtue, Commerce and History*, Cambridge, 1985.
Porter, B.D.,	*War and the Rise of the State*, New York, 1994.
Ranzato, G. (ed.),	*Guerre Fratricide: Le Guerre Civili in Età Contemporanea*. Turin, 1994

Rokkan, S., & Urwin, D. W. (eds.), *The Politics of Territorial Identity*, London, 1982.

Santamaría Pastor, J.A., Orduña Rebollo, E., & Martín-Artajo. R.,

Documentos Para la Historia del Regionalismo en España, Madrid, 1977.

Sahlins, P.,	*Boundaries: The Making of France and Spain in the Pyrenees*, Berkeley, 1989
Segarra, M.	"Una llengua d'ús estrictament popular" in P. Gabriel (ed.), *Història de la Cultura Catalana*, III, Barcelona, 1997.
Smith, A.D.,	*National Identity*, Reno, 1990.

Snyder, J.,	*Myths of Empire: Domestic Politics and Imperial Ambition*, Ithaca, 1991.
Southworth, H.R..	*Antifalange*, Paris, 1967.
Tilly, C.,	*Coercion, Capital and European States AD 990- 1990*, Oxford, 1990.
Todd, E.	*L'invention de l'Europe*, París, 1990.
Vilar, P.,	*Estat, Nació, Socialisme. Estudis Sobre el cas Espanyol*, Barcelona, 1981.
Williams, G.,	*When Was Wales?*, London, 1985.
Yates, F.A.,	*Astrea: The Imperial Theme in the Sixteenth Century*, London, 1985.

The present paper relies in part on some material previously published in: (1) B. de Riquer & E.Ucelay-Da Cal, "An Analysis of Nationalisms in Spain: A Proposal for an Integrated Historical Model", in J.G. Beramendi, R. Máiz and X.M. Núñez (eds.), *Nationalism in Europe. Past and Present. Actas do Congreso Internacional "Os Nacionalismos en Europa. Pasado e Presente"*, Santiago de Compostela, 1994, vol. II, pp. 275-301; (2) E. Ucelay-Da Cal, "The Nationalisms of the Periphery: Culture and Politics in the Construction of National Identity"; and "Catalan Nationalism: Cultural Plurality and Political Ambiguity" in H. Graham & J. Labanyi (eds.), *Spanish Cultural Studies. An Introduction. The Struggle for Modernity*, Oxford, 1995, pp. 32-39, 144-151; (3) the unpublished texts of lectures given at the Cervantes Institute in London in February 1993 and at the Martin-Luther Universität at Halle in October of the same year. I have also utilized some bits from my articles: "Prefigurazione e storia: la guerra civile spagnola del 1936-39 come riassunto del passato", in G. Ranzato (ed.) *Guerre Fratricide. Le guerre Civili in Età Contemporanea*, Turin, 1994, pp. 193-220, and "La visión de la nación española y de los nacionalismos hispánicos desde la perspectiva catalanista", presented at the conference on Spanish Nationalism at the Fundación Pablo Iglesias in Madrid in October 1995, publication pending. The present text, however, is a complete reformulation of these materials with a new and different general argument.

This essay was written as a working paper for discussion within the framework of a practical exercise in transcultural comparative history: that is, to be presented at a meeting of Spanish and British historians gathered to discuss a similar topic in their respective historiographies without each group necessarily having more than a relative knowledge of the others' speciality. For this reason, I thought it best to adopt an aggressively interpretative mode, it being, to my mind, both easier and much more rewarding to discuss ideas than to contrast facts. Accordingly, the text eschews a more descriptive or narrative approach, for a style frankly closer to historical sociology or political science than to usual historiographic prose. Indeed, the paper proceeds from the notion that much of the historiography dedicated to the investigation of the phenomenon of nationalism is, at least, in a Hispanic context, far from satisfactory in offering comprehensive explanations. Extensive pruning for publication, however, has naturally rendered the essay even more schematic, while changes have been incorporated in the light of the discussion. For reasons of length, no footnoted references have been included; the summary bibliography includes works alluded to in the text, together with others which afford some (albeit contradictory) conceptual insight.

LIBERALISM AND NATIONALISM IN RECENT SPANISH HISTORIOGRAPHY: FAILURE AS SHARED IDENTITY.

ISABEL BURDIEL
(Universidad de València)

Contemporary Spanish approaches to the history of national identity began to develop during the last years of the Franco régime and the early stages of the transition to democracy. Initially the impulse came from the so-called 'peripheral nationalities', especially the Catalans and the Basques. These studies were perceived (by their authors as well as the public at large) as part of a movement of opposition to Francoism and/or as a programme for political democratisation. This political context explains at least three features of the research in question. Firstly, there is the overriding determination to assert the historical existence of identities different from that of Spain. This may have produced an excess of positivist historiography and a neglect of reflection on theory. Secondly, hardly any weight has been accorded to the question of Spanish national consciousness, which only began to be studied from the 1980s. Finally, there has been a lack of a comparative dimension to research on the various Spanish movements.

From the end of the 1980s this scenario has changed substantially, as Ucelay-Da Cal's paper demonstrates. My remarks focus on the insights to be gained by a comparative approach, especially by relating liberalism and nationalism at the level of the state. In this domain research has tended to adopt a 'modernist' and functionalist viewpoint, concentrating on the weakness of national integration in Spain during the nineteenth century. I have sought to raise awareness of a number of topics: the need for more in-depth study of the process of pre-political or non-institutional national self-awareness; 2) the comparative lack of exploration of terms such as 'state' or 'nation', and in general of how language is used to construct national identities; 3) the reification of 'identity' in current usage, despite the insights of recent post-structural thought; 4) the potential inflexibility - and ignorance of historical content - of the contrast drawn between local and national loyalties; 5) the singling out of the Spanish case as a paradigm of 'failure', generally with reference to the failure to achieve an "authentic liberal revolution" during the nineteenth century. The latter is often held responsible for a lack of modernisation or of integration of the masses within a proper nation state.

More recent research and comparisons with other parts of Europe have shed new light on many of these topics. Here the contribution of Professor Ucelay-Da Cal has been particularly interesting, in seeking to situate Spanish national integration and its limitations within a European context. His reflections on the link between nationalism and liberalism suggest the need for a revision of the respective impacts of the two Spanish colonial crises of 1826 and 1898. Though the first was more important in real terms, since a whole empire was lost, it had none of the emotional aspects of the second, despite the lesser sacrifice of territory. The reason is perhaps that in 1826, the feeling was that an absolute monarch was to be blamed, whereas it was a nation that lost Cuba and Puerto Rico in 1898.

This distinction seems fundamental to me for an understanding of the crisis of national identity in 1898, since it highlights a prior development of a sense of nationhood, which must have been more significant than once thought. The perception of 1898 as a disaster clearly demands further research. Firstly, it appears to signal the difficulties of the transition from the politics of the notables to those of the masses - difficulties which Spain shared at this time with other parts of Europe. These can no longer be blamed on an 'incomplete' or failed liberal revolution alone. Secondly, the crisis of 1898 has to be situated in a context in which the national integration of the masses throughout Europe was bound up with imperialism until at least the First World War. Spain proved unable, being a second-rate power, to use imperialism as a factor promoting national integration while delaying the concession of democracy to its citizens at home.

In conclusion, consideration of the obstacles in the path of national integration in Spain may bring out the surprising strength of the 'nation-state' after all, especially when we take account the force of the movements for regional autonomy with which it was confronted. In this regard, it is useful to bear in mind the question of 'double identity', of dual national affiliation, and the ways this can be built up, undermined or restored. This is a topic which, as yet little explored, may have a number of surprises in store.

LIBERALISMO Y NACIONALISMO EN LA HISTORIOGRAFIA RECIENTE. EL FRACASO COMO IDENTIDAD COMPARTIDA

ISABEL BURDIEL

(Universidad de València)

La discusión de la ponencia del profesor Ucelay-Da Cal en el contexto historiográfico actual es una tarea difícil por varias razones. En primer lugar, por la clara voluntad heterodoxa de su posición teórica. En segundo lugar, por la extensión y variedad de los problemas planteados. En tercer lugar por la óptica de análisis, situada en el tiempo largo, que desborda las fronteras de especialización habituales en el mundo académico español. El resultado es una cierta "desfamiliarización" respecto a los ejes habituales de discusión sobre el tema. [1]

Desde finales de los años setenta, el reto de los historiadores profesionales ha sido precisamente el de profesionalizar el análisis histórico de la cuestión nacional. Es decir, elaborar propuestas de reflexión críticas que se alejasen, tanto del nacionalismo español (frecuentemente implícito), como de la subordinación a los proyectos políticos explícitos de los nacionalismos llamados 'periféricos'. Es obvio que el establecimiento de una dicotomía rígida entre historiografía nacionalista e historiografía profesional es un punto de partida problemático y, al menos a primera vista, fácilmente impugnable.

Por una parte, indica una opinión tajante respecto a la relación existente entre la voluntad de asegurar una identidad nacional (sea ésta la que sea) y la subordinación de la perspectiva analítica a supuestos implícitamente esencialistas, organicistas o historicistas. Por otra parte, se sitúa bajo sospecha de reproducir - al servicio del propio nacionalismo - la subordinación analítica que denuncia en los otros nacionalismos. Como se puede observar, la lógica nacionalista de esta argumentación es inevitablemente circular y no falsable. Su interés intelectual es, por lo tanto,

---

1 Entre la abundante historiografia de Enrique Ucelay-Da-Cal, merece la pena destacar: *La Catalunya Populista: Imatge, Cultura i Política en l'Etapa Republicana, 1931-1939,* (Barcelona, 1982). Estas notas tuvieroncomo objetivo situar a los participantes británicos de Seminario en las coordenadas del debate español sobre el nacionalismo. Dada la diversidad de los temas planteados, opté por orientar mis comentarios en torno al naciionalismo español y al liberalismo de siglo XIX. Buena parte de mis reflexiones al respecto forman parte de la discusión teórica del proyecto de investigación GICYT.PB93-0686. Entre las referencia bibliográficas, se han primado aquellas más accesibles a los lectores británicos.

bastante limitado y si hago alusión a ella es porque creo que su presencia en la bibliografía disponible sobre los diversos nacionalismos del estado español sigue sin ser desdeñable.

Ello es producto en buena medida de las condiciones políticas de origen de dicha historiografía, cuando transición democrática y problema nacional se plantearon como problemas políticos e históricos estrechamente vinculados entre sí. En aquellos años, como señala Núñez Xeisas, la investigación al respecto(e incluso el boom de la llamada Historia Local) podían ser entendidas como formas de oposición democrática al régimen de Franco. Lo inquietante, en todo caso, es su pervivencia más o menos disfrazada y alimentada por el españolismo latente que sigue gravitando sobre buena parte de la historiografía más general. No es sorprendente que, en tanto que ambos nacionalismos (central y periféricos) participan de una lógica similar, se "entiendan bien", bloqueando la reflexión a través de la inútil acritud ocasional de algunos de los debates de los últimos años. Mas allá de las consideraciones teóricas de orden general que una situación como ésta suscita, merece la pena destacar el resultado práctico y paradójico de que el gran ausente del panorama de discusión haya sido precisamente el nacionalismo español. A diferencia, por ejemplo, de lo que ocurre con los nacionalismos catalán y vasco, aún hoy sabemos muy poco y suponemos demasiado acerca de sus orígenes y de su evolución histórica. Al menos hasta finales de los ochenta, la discusión tendió a ser tangencial y a descansar sobre supuestos implícitos basados, generalmente, en su materialización circunstancial a través de la ideología franquista. Una consecuencia, de nuevo, de que el llamado 'problema nacional' entrase en la historiografía al hilo de la transición democrática y de la mano de los proyectos nacionalistas periféricos.[2]

Aún así, creo que el panorama actual permite el optimismo, especialmente por el incremento del nivel de reflexión teórica que comienza a sustanciar el extraordinario volumen de información empírica acumulado en los últimos venticinco años. El interés de la ponencia del profesor Ucelay-Da Cal reside, precisamente, en el hecho de señalar algunos de los retos más urgentes que, en estos momentos, afectan a la historiografía crítica sobre los nacionalismos y en afrontarlos a través de una

---

[2] Para una visión general, y al mismo tiempo muy pormenorizada, de la evolución historiográfica hasta mediados de los años ochenta , ver: Nuñez Seixas, X.M.: *Historiographical Approaches to Nationalism in Spain*, Saarbrucken – Fort Lauderdale, Verlag Breitenbach Publishers, 1993.

propuesta de interpretación general del problema. Entre esos retos no es el menor la superación del empirismo y de la fragmentación de los estudios sobre los diversos nacionalismos del estado español a través del desplazamiento de la tensión excesiva (e inútil heurísticamente) entre primordialistas y modernistas. La ponencia que discutimos opta en este sentido por el poco frecuentado (y sumamente arriesgado) análisis del tiempo largo de la génesis de la idea moderna de nacion, buscando comparaciones sistemáticas (no sólo entre los diversos nacionalismos del Estado español) sino entre éstos y los del resto de Europa.

En primer lugar, pues, la declarada vocación modernista del debate actual es uno de los problemas que Ucelay-Da Cal se plantea como tal. Su ponencia resulta aquí especialmente valiosa; no tanto, quizás y una vez más, por los problemas que resuelve como por los que plantea. Entre ellos, me parece oportuno insistir en uno de los más antiguos de la profesión: aquel que suscita el hecho de que el pasado tan sólo puede ser entendido con el lenguaje del pasado al tiempo que nunca es plenamente entendible tan sólo a través de él. Cuando la percepción actual (historiográfica) de una realidad histórica choca con el lenguaje en que esa realidad fue experimentada por sus protagonistas, tan peligroso es asumir acríticamente ese lenguaje como sustituirlo globalmente. 'Patria' y 'Nación'; 'Estado' y 'Lengua'; 'Central' y 'Local', son buenos ejemplos de esas dificultades y del peligro de escamotearlas mediante su utilización ahistórica. En este terreno, tanto el funcionalismo como el esencialismo revelan sus mayores limitaciones analíticas en tanto que sus supuestos de partida y de llegada, en términos de 'función' o de 'nación', no sean revisados eliminando su carga anacrónica.

En segundo lugar, y por lo tanto, a mí me ha parecido especialmente pertinente la reflexión apuntada en torno a dos problemas cruciales y estrechamente relacionados entre sí, cuando no idénticos. Me refiero a los relativos a las nociones de identidad y de lenguaje. Nociones que implican situaciones mucho más fluidas, complejas, e internamente contradictorias, de lo que se suele valorar en un ambiente teórico (el del análisis de los nacionalismos) que parece ajeno a las aportaciones del postestructuralismo y de la nueva historia sociocultural.[3]

---

3 El escaso nivel de reflexión al respecto puede valorarse a través de, por ejemplo, Graham, H. Y Labanyi, Jo:*Spanish Cultural Studies. An Introduction*, , Oxford University Press, 1995.No es casualidad, creo, que la identificación entre lenguaje, identidad y razón fuese realizada por primera vez en términos modernos por el maestro reconocido de Herder, J.G. Hamann, una mente sin

De hecho, en los últimos años, los intentos de elaboración de un esquema general sobre los nacionalismos en el Estado español se han realizado básicamente desde los supuestos de la historia y de la sociología políticas con particular atención hacia el problema de la conformación y la acción instrumental del Estado. Desde ese orden de intereses, se ha prestado una atención muy limitada - como señala Ucelay-Da Cal - al carácter discursivo de las nociones de 'Estado' y 'Nación'. En este sentido, Ucelay-Da Cal recuerda el papel de comodín que desempeña el concepto de 'Estado-nación', el cual evita el analisis de las relaciones existentes entre sus dos componentes mediante la adscripción implícita a una interpretación funcionalista de las mismas. En el camino de esa línea argumental, tiende a perderse el desarrollo histórico de ambos conceptos y las condiciones de su evolución como lenguajes de identidad autolegitimados, históricamente, mediante su supuesta correspondencia política y cultural. Una correspondencia que, en todo caso, se supone contrastable al margen de las operaciones linguísticas que la han creado.

Las promesas de desarrollo en este ámbito que contiene la ponencia del profesor Ucelay-Da Cal no acaban, sin embargo, de cumplirse y el autor empeña sus esfuerzos en otras direcciones. Así, a pesar de sus referencias al problema del lenguaje, la ponencia no ahonda en las condiciones históricas de evolución (desarrollo y quiebras) de los diversos lenguajes nacionalistas excepto para remarcar las continuidades globales. Más aún, y en términos más concretos, desdeña en buena medida el papel fundamental desempeñado por las diversas 'lenguas nacionales'como mecanismos simbólicos de autopercepción diferenciadora. Resulta cuanto menos mencionable (dentro de la perspectiva comparativa que propone la ponencia) el hecho de que todos los nacionalismos fuertes del siglo XIX europeo se hayan basado en una profunda autoconciencia linguística diferencial. La comparación que se apunta en algun momento respecto a Portugal, donde no se desarrollan proyectos nacionales alternativos fuertes al estatal, resulta entonces inadecuada. Es cierto que la trayectoria política portuguesa es muy similar a la española - con tensiones entre lealtades nacionales y locales igualmente importantes. Sin embargo, habría sido necesario recalcar la excepcional unidad linguística del Estado-nación portugués; un caso modélico aludido en todos los estudios

---

duda más.original que la de sus discípulos, vid, Berlin, I., *The Magus of the North: J.G. Hamann and the Origins of Modern Irrationalism* (London, 1994).

generales al respecto. El discurso identitario sobre la lengua -y no tanto la lengua como esencia de identidad - quizás debería haber merecido mayor atención.

Todo ello señala sin duda la dificultades reales de penetrar en la larga génesis (y en la valoracion jerárquica de los materiales multiples) de la idea de nación contemporánea sin caer, al mismo tiempo, en una concepción esencialista de los diversos nacionalismos o en una cómoda adhesión al concepto de Estado-nación. Quizás se entienda mejor lo que quiero plantear a través de uno de los aspectos del debate actual que me interesa especialmente. Me refiero al problema del malogrado nacionalismo español. Un problema que la discusión reciente ha tenido la virtualidad de traer al escenario, asumiendo (al menos implícitamente) que nada (y menos que nada todo aquello que tiene que ver con la formación de identidades individuales o colectivas) es inteligible salvo en sus relaciones.

En el establecimiento de esas relaciones, parece existir un acuerdo básico acerca de la debilidad del proceso de nacionalización español durante el siglo XIX. Una debilidad entendida en términos relativos a la ausencia de un proyecto nacional-estatal español suficientemente integrador; e.g: falta de escuelas, de señas de identidad nacional, carácter discriminatorio del servicio militar, incompleta integración del mercado nacional, irresolución de las tensiones entre localismo y centralismo, falseamiento del proceso electoral y fracaso del sistema parlamentario liberal en su conjunto[4]

Los planteamientos varían según se aborde el tema y la discusión gira en torno al diagnóstico sobre las relaciones entre la debilidad del Estado central y el surgimiento de los nacionalismos periféricos en la España de finales del siglo XIX. Para autores como Borja de Riquer, por ejemplo, fue la escasa eficacia del proceso de nacionalización español, y la desafortunada actitud de las élites españolas, lo que posibilitó la aparición de los proyectos nacionales periféricos. Por su parte, Juan Pablo Fusi, y en buena medida también J. Alvarez Junco, entienden que la dinámica de construcción del Estado contemporáneo en España no reside tanto en la existencia de un nacionalismo españolista explícito como en las operaciones estructurales del largo proceso de adaptación de la maquinaria de gobierno a las fuerzas más bien impersonales del proceso de modernización. Las dificultades de este último proceso - entre ellas, la falta de

---

[4] Una descrpción que, para mi sopresa, tiende a reproducir exactement (en los noventa, y con más fe que investigación) un artículo ya viejo de Juan Linz "Early state-building and the late peripheral nationalism against the state: The case of Spain" en, Eisentdat, S.N. y Rokkan, S. (eds.), *Building States and Nations*, vol II, (Beverley Hill/London, 1973).

democratización y el imperio del orden público sobre cualquier otra consideración - habrían dado lugar a un Estado de centralismo legal pero de localismo real. Un Estado incapaz de producir los mínimos de cohesión y de consenso necesarios para hacer viable una conciencia nacional unitaria.[5]

No intento ser ni siquiera lejanamente exhaustiva porque lo que me interesa recalcar aquí es que bajo todas esas divergencias gravitan acuerdos a mi juicio sustanciales, y profundamente polémicos, que limitan la capacidad de los argumentos esgrimidos. Limitaciones que, en algunos de sus supuestos, enlazan inintecionadamente con los de la historiografía nacionalista periférica y siguen permitiendo conceder relevancia a la explicación canónica procedente de la misma. Según esta última, las cosas sucedieron más bien al contrario: fue la fortaleza irredenta de la identidad nacional vasca, catalana o gallega, lo que minó irreversiblemente los esfuerzos del españolismo dominante, impidiendo establecer históricamente la ecuación política y de identidad entre Estado y Nación. Una ecuación quebrada definitivamente cuando el viejo Estado de la Restauración se demostró incapaz de autolegitimarse mediante la representación de intereses sociales y económicos en cambio muy rápido. El resultado fue 'la expulsión' de las burguesías periféricas a estrategias centrífugas que enlazarían con los sentimientos de pertenencia nacional anti-españoles de la gran mayoría de la población.[6]

Desgraciadamente, el debate no parece capaz (de momento) de despegar de ahí. Como los mismos participantes han puesto de relieve, lo que no sabemos sobre el Estado español, y sobre sus relaciones con los proyectos nacionales español y 'periféricos', es

5 Ha suscitado especial interés la polémica protagonizada por: Riquer, B.: "Sobre el lugar de los nacionalismos en la historia contemporánea española" en: *Historia Social* n.7 (1990); pp.105-26 y "Reflexions entorn de la dèbil nacionalització espanyola del segle XIX en: *L'Avenc*, n.170 (1993); pp.8-15; Fusi, J.P." Revisionismo crítico e historia nacionalista. A propósito de un artículo de B. De Riquer" en: *Historia Social* n.7 (1990); pp. 127-134 y "Center and Periphery, 1900-1936. National Integration and Regional Nationalisms Reconsidered" en: Lannon, F. Y Preston, P.: *Elites and Power in Twentieth-Century Spain*, Londres, 1990; pp.33-40. Ver también: Alvarez Junco, J.: "Redes Locales, Lealtades Tradicionales y Nuevas Identidades Colectivas en la España del siglo XIX" en: Robles, A. (Ed): *Política en Penumbra. Patronazgo y clientelismo políticos en la España Contemporánea*, Madrid, S.XXI, 1961; pp. 71-94. Elorza, A.: Ideologías del Nacionalismo Vasco, 1876-1937, San Sebastián, 1978. Siguen siendo extraordinariamente sugerentes las orientaciones de J.M. Jover, el auténtico pionero de los estudios sobre el problema del nacionalismo español. Ver por ejemplo: "Caracteres del nacionalismo español, 1854-1874" en *Zona Abierta* n.31 (1984); pp.2-22. Disponible en inglés, para algunas de las últimas aportaciones al respecto, ver: Mar-Molinero, C. y Smith, A.: *Nationalism, and the Nation in the Iberian Penisula* Oxford/Washington D.C., 1996

6 Ver, de nuevo, para una visión general, Núñez Xeisas, X.M.: *Historiographical Approaches..*,op.cit.supra. Sobre el caso catalán, resultan ilustrativos los estudios de A. Colomines: *El Catalanisme i l'Estat (1898-1917)*, Barcelona, 1993 y "Buròcrates i Centralistes: Centre i Perifèria en la construcció de l'Estat liberal espanyol" en: *Afers* n.16; pp.471-481.

demasiado. Es demasiado, incluso, como para convertirlo en chivo expiatorio de toda una identidad colectiva construida en torno a la idea de fracaso. Destacaré algunas de las cuestiones que me parecen especialmente objetables.

En primer lugar, el debate sobre "las debilidades del Estado español" concede escasa relevancia analítica (e histórica) a los procesos de nacionalización no institucionales y/o pre-políticos. Lo que implica - de paso - una fijación modélica en el caso francés y en la versión del mismo ofrecida por la obra ya clásica de E. Weber[7]. Obviamente, las dificultades aquí son graves y no es la menor la tautología implícita en el concepto de 'paleonacionalismo' o, en algunos contextos, el abuso explicativo del concepto de 'modernización' que tiende a sustituir el análisis por una teleología modélica, positiva o negativa.

En segundo lugar, me parece problemática la valoración de resistencias regionales a la centralización (real) como formas de peculiaridad española y como evidencias de un tipo de tensión insalvable entre nación y región. Una valoración global que sigue asumiendo la existencia dicotómica de lo que Richard Herr (hace ya demasiados años) llamó la 'pequeña tradición' y 'la gran tradición'. El carácter rígido y ahistórico que, en ocasiones, ha adoptado esa distinción se compadece mal, a mi juicio, con su demostración histórica concreta, en especial por lo que se refiere a su valoración jerárquica y secuencial. Esa dicotomía, además, corre el riesgo de asumir la doble identidad (regional y nacional) como necesaria o potencialmente conflictiva. La inevitabilidad histórica de un momento u otro de ruptura constituye un nuevo tipo de teleología tautológica no avalada por otras y diversas experiencias europeas: Francia, Alemania o Portugal, por ejemplo.

Todo ello debería obligar a recordar y analizar el carácter histórico, cambiante, de las relaciones entre 'lo local' y 'lo nacional'. Los supuestos no analíticos producen en este ámbito resultados muy desconcertantes; por ejemplo, la atribución retrospectiva al federalismo o al carlismo de mediados del siglo XIX (e incluso anterior) de contenidos nacionalistas alternativos al españolismo central. Así, se pasa por alto que lo que estaba en juego en las luchas políticas del segundo tercio del siglo XIX no era la unidad del Estado (o, incluso, la unidad nacional) sino la definición del modelo de Estado y del proyecto nacional global que había de surgir de la revolución liberal. Algo bastante

---

7   *Peasants into Frenchmen. The Modernization of Rural France, 1780-1914*, Stanford University Press, 1977.

distinto. [8] Considero, por lo tanto, sumamente aventurado identificar los proyectos alternativos al del moderantismo finalmente dominante - procedentes o no de las diversas periferias- con formas de nacionalismo "proto". Quizas sea aquí donde la ponencia de Ucelay-Da Cal encuentra mayores dificultades para argumentar satisfactoriamente la transición entre las pertenencias locales (y forales) procedentes del Antiguo Régimen y los nacionalismos periféricos de finales del siglo XIX y del XX.

En tercer lugar, y de forma más general, todo ello confluye en un acuerdo básico sobre el carácter arcáico de la sociedad y del Estado español del siglo XIX y sobre la pervivencia excesiva del Antiguo Régimen político, social y económico. Es decir, sobre la idea del estancamiento en una mentalidad tradicional, sin transformaciones sustanciales o suficientemente importantes, identificada con un modelo clientelar y localista al que se considera inmutable antes y después de la revolución liberal del siglo XIX. Esta última (fracasada, incompleta o incluso impotente) suele ser definida como 'meramente política' en un tono peyorativo que otorga (por razones que no conozco o no comparto) un carácter intrascendente a 'lo político', reforzando (paradójicamente, en algunos casos) la más clásica de las concepciones estratigráficas de la realidad social.

Como ha señalado recientemente Santos Juliá, esa recurrencia del mito del fracaso -de raíz clara en el regeneracionismo español (y españolista) de la generación de 1898 - se ha convertido más en un recurso que en una explicación.[9] Hoy por hoy creo que todas las míticas limitaciones de la revolución liberal española deberían rebajarse sustancialmente en su capacidad explicativa. Es 'una solución' demasiado fácil y demasiado poco atenta al análisis comparado con las revoluciones liberales europeas. Su resultado es una peculiarización excesiva del caso español que, además, no está sostenida ni por la investigación más reciente ni por el debate teórico internacional al respecto.

En este sentido, y para acabar, la valoración en un continuum explicativo por parte del profesor Ucelay-Da Cal de la idea imperial de nación y su crisis a finales del siglo XIX me parece altamente adecuada. Sin embargo, la relevancia otorgada en esa

---

[8] Las espléndidas reflexiones al respecto de Anna Mª García en :"El primer republicanismo. La Barcelona revolucionaria: 1835-1837" verán la luz en breve, demostrando lo que pueden cambiar las cosas cuando desde los aprioris globales se pasa al análisis detallado de la realidad histórica. Agradezco a la autora que me haya permitido la consulta del texto mecanografiado de su trabajo.

[9] El artículo de Santos Juliá: "Anomalía, Dolor y Fracaso de España" en*Claves* (1996); pp. 10-121, constituye eseste ambiente un auténtico soplo de aire fresco.

quiebra de la nación-imperio a la pérdida de las colonias de Cuba y Puerto Rico en 1898 me suscita algunas preguntas finales.

Por ejemplo, en primer lugar, las conexiones (concretas) entre dicha crisis de conciencia y el anquilosamiento del régimen de la Restauración, entendiendo ese anquilosamiento como producto de una dinámica propia no necesariamente implicada en el proceso revolucionario liberal de la primera mitad del siglo. Es decir, como parte de un nudo de cuestiones que permitirían enlazar el proceso de construcción estatal-nacional con el fenómeno europeo general del imperialismo (triunfante o frustrado) del siglo XIX y, a ambos, con los problemas derivados del tránsito de la política de notables a la política de masas en España y en Europa.

En segundo lugar, la necesidad de estudiar el papel del Regeneracionismo en la creación de un españolismo (doliente) entendido como 'problema de España' en competencia (y a veces en extraña simbiosis) con el españolismo más conservador y/o militar de perfil auto-congratulatorio. Entre las multiples posibilidades de ese doble papel no me parece la menor la que ayudó a bloquear la crítica nacionalista a traves de la incorporación (nacionalizadora en terminos españoles) de algunos de sus supuestos y de muchos de sus agravios.

En tercer lugar, la valoración de el porqué de las repercusiones de la crisis colonial/de identidad nacional de 1898 en comparación con otra crisis colonial de mayor envergadura: **la** crisis colonial, en realidad. Me refiero, por supuesto, a la de aquellos años veinte del siglo XIX en que se perdió todo un imperio y España pasó de ser una potencia internacional (aunque debilitada) a una comparsa tulelada e impotente internacionalmente. Quizás merece la pena pensar las implicaciones que, respecto al grado de nacionalización (española) alcanzado, tiene el hecho de que entonces (en 1826) las colonias se sintieran como perdidas por la Monarquía(por el Rey, absoluto) y en 1898 se pudieran sentir como perdidas por la nación (liberal) en su conjunto.[10] ¿Qué nación era esa que sentía la pérdida como tal nación, frustrada en sus expectativas al respecto?. Quiero recordar, por otra parte, que la crisis del Estado en los años veinte era mayor que la del régimen de la Restauración y que a la España de 1826 le interesaban más (económicamente) las colonias americanas que a la España de 1898. ¿Podría la amplitud de esa crisis de conciencia nacional (y sus resultados) hacer pensar

---

[10] A ello alude, J. Alvarez Junco, J.: "Redes locales, Lealtades Tradicionales...",art,cit.supra.nota 5

(precisamente por su amplitud y sus resultados) en un mayor grado de conciencia nacional española (compartida) que la que se ha valorado hasta ahora?

La disparidad entre pérdidas 'objetivas' y 'subjetivas' me parece fundamental para entender la crisis de identidad nacional de 1898 como un fenómeno que requiere un análisis en el corto plazo y en el contexto de la interrelación entre política nacional e internacional. Por una parte, como la expresión de las dificultades del tránsito del liberalismo a la democracia, que España comparte con el resto de Europa y que no pueden achacarse a una 'revolución liberal' incompleta o frustrada. Por otra, como la expresión **nacional** de ese tránsito en un contexto **internacional** en el que la nacionalización de las masas estuvo estrechamente ligada al imperialismo, al menos hasta la primera guerra mundial. El vehículo imperial de nacionalización sin democratización - o con lenta democratización - no resultó posible para una potencia de segundo orden que perdía los restos de su imperio cuando las grandes potencias europeas creaban y consolidaban los suyos.

Para acabar, quizás sería necesario revisar aquí también los supuestos del mito del fracaso y valorar la fuerza histórica indudable de las 'dobles identidades nacionales' (vasco-española, catalano-española, etc) que quizás tan sólo ahora se está quebrando. Precisamente ahora, cuando muchas de las deficiencias achacadas a la debilidad del Estado central ya no pueden mantenerse. Precisamente ahora, después de cuarenta años de nacionalización española militante como no se había conocido nunca y cuando se consolida el régimen democrático más estable y de más larga duración de toda nuestra historia común. Quizás no sea baladí tampoco pensar algo más, junto a las condiciones de debilidad del proceso de nacionalización español, las condiciones de su fortaleza durante el siglo XIX y buena parte del XX. Una fortaleza tanto más sorprendente a la luz de sus debilidades.

DECLINE AND NATIONALISM NOTES ON 17TH CENTURY SPAIN

SALVADOR ALBINANA
(*University of Valencia*)

At the end of 1898 Spain and the USA signed a Treaty in Paris establishing the independence of Cuba and ceding the Philippines, Puerto Rico and Guam to the United States. And so the history of colonial Spain drew to its formal conclusion, after a long period of retreat beginning in the seventeenth and eighteenth centuries.

While the independence of mainland America in 1825 met with relative indifference on the part of metropolitan Spain, the loss of the remaining Caribbean territories was to be perceived as a catastrophe and would serve as a catalyst for the movement known as the 'generation of 98', which began to question the nature of Spain. The events of 1898, then, can be seen as the conclusion of a long series of disasters and problems, whose roots lie in developments in early modern Spain.

The Eternal Debate : Hispanism or Europeanism.

The intellectual questioning in 1898 recalls a similar crisis at the beginning of the seventeenth century, when writers debated concepts such as decline and reform. The recurrent, bitter controversy between europeanisers and traditionalists was really an attempt to come to terms with the reasons for the decline of Spain. Throughout, from the age of the Baroque through the Enlightenment and down to 1898, the same topics are rehearsed. One of these is the question of the relationships between the various bits of the Spanish mosaic - the tension between centre and periphery with the successive moves towards political unity.

The aim of my paper is to explore the sense of terms like decline and reformism as used by historians, and suggest their relevance to the debate on the formation of Spanish national identity. I will limit myself to an analysis of these ideas in their relation to what has been called 'paleonationalism'. The defence of royal dynastic interests in Europe, together with the conquest and subsequent loss of America mark out a period during which relations between the monarchy and its provinces had to be re-defined in the context of a debate about economic and fiscal reform.

In 1492 the new Spanish monarchy acquired territories which would soon constitute the American empire. At this time America did not exist, nor did Spain as such; however, their encounter may help explain how each came to be what it is. After all, the loss of Cuba in 1898 prompted a major analysis by Spanish thinkers of their own country. In the early stages of the encounter, the great imbalance in population and resources between the different parts of Spain, together with their different political traditions, proved to be a fragile basis on which to build dynastic unity and an empire. To some extent, this imbalance could be compensated for by religious unity. Jews and Muslims were expelled, and the reference to Catholicism as a symbol of identity was frequent. We find it even in authors who are sometimes seen as forerunners of nationhood in early modern Catalonia, like the Jesuit Manuel Morcillo, who boasted of the role played by his province in the evangelisation of America. The New World seemed to be a factor for unity: though legally subject to Castile, there was soon enough open territory for all the peoples of Spain.

Decline and Critical Writings
We no longer limit discussion of the decline of Spain simply to economic or military aspects. The reformist writings of the seventeenth century inevitably had much to say about America at a time when separatist tendencies were gathering force there. They were also concerned about the relationship between the monarchy and its constituent kingdoms, and between Spain and Europe at a time when modern science was making its impact felt north of the Pyrenees. The fiscal overtones of the word *arbitrismo* ('reformism') are not the whole story; we need to be aware of other aspects of the debate. Thus, the *novatores* at the end of the seventeenth century marked the end of the complacent Spain of the Baroque, with their emphasise on science and their desire to close the gap between Spanish and European culture.

Europe and America as Catalysts of Spanish Identity.
During the seventeenth century Spanish attitudes shifted from a generally uncritical outlook on the world to one of questioning, with Europe becoming less a foe and more a model to be imitated. Older attitudes can be seen in de Quevedo's *España defendida* (1609), with its stress on Spain's uniqueness. Greater critical awareness, by contrast, can be found in Juan de Cabriada's lament of 1687 about the backward state of Spanish science. His call for an Academy of Science like those in

Paris or London was matched by demands elsewhere for commercial companies in imitation of those of the Dutch. This change of attitude requires further research, but it may have promoted a certain sense of national identity on the part of the Spaniards.

Equally we should pay heed to the impact of America on Spanish culture. There was a tendency to see Spaniards as the 'Indians' of Europe. But we also find both in the Castilian literature of decline (González de Cellorigo, Sancho de Moncada) and in a Catalan optimist like Feliu de la Penya, a perception of America as a source of harm in some respects to Spanish society, especially as regards silver inflation and the drain of manpower abroad.

So we might say that, in reaction to Europe and America, seventeenth-century Spain became more aware of itself collectively - so long as we do not read the present back into the past and imagine that early 'national' identities were mutually exclusive.

By Way of a Conclusion

From the perspective of Spanish nationhood, the seventeenth century left an important legacy to the succeeding age, during which the Bourbon monarchy became closely identified with the Iberian Peninsula, promoting administrative uniformity and laying the basis of Spanish national identity. During the eighteenth century European and colonial problems again seemed to serve as factors promoting integration. The many criticisms of American colonisation penned by Enlightened thinkers, together with Masson de Morvilliers' celebrated denunciation of Spanish backwardness, prompted a literature in defence of Spanish history and culture. At the same time, it sparked off a controversy about Spanish science, which was to run through the nineteenth century and merge with the questioning of the Generation of 1898. We may conclude that much of this debate helped foster a growing awareness of 'Spanishness', while recognising that it was not sufficient to weld Spain together as a nation.

DECADENCIA Y NACIONALISMO. NOTAS SOBRE LA ESPAÑA DEL SIGLO XVII

SALVADOR ALBIÑANA
(Universidad de Valencia)

En diciembre de 1898, España y los Estados Unidos de América firmaban en París un Tratado que reconocía la independencia de Cuba y la cesión a Estados Unidos de Puerto Rico, Filipinas y la isla de Guam. De este modo, se sancionaba el final de la historia colonial española. La España del siglo XIX, ha escrito Roberto Mesa, no era sino una gran potencia de museo, una albacea testamentaria de un imperio reducido a las salas de banderas africanas.[1] Tras las pérdidas de diferentes territorios europeos a lo largo de los siglos XVII y XVIII, y el surgimiento de las repúblicas americanas a comienzos del XIX, concluía ahora una larga etapa de la historia española asociada al dominio más vasto de su experiencia imperial, el americano.

Si la independencia de la América continental - una más, también, de nuestras guerras civiles - tuvo lugar ante una relativa indiferencia en la sociedad y la cultura metropolitanas, por contra, la desaparición de estos vestigios coloniales antillanos será percibida como una catástrofe y servirá de precipitante de la llamada generación del 98. Una generación - no entro a considerar la pertinencia de la discutida expresión de Azorín - que recogerá y acrecentará las reflexiones sobre los problemas de la España de la Restauración iniciadas unos años antes por la abundante nómina de los llamados regeneracionistas. Al mismo tiempo que la pérdida de Cuba - que merecerá la calificación de Desastre - formaliza el llamado 'problema de España' y el estilismo noventayochista, la firma del Tratado de París explica algún texto de urgencia, como el que Henry Charles Lea publica ese mismo año en la revista *Atlantic Monthly* con el título de *The Decadence of Spain*, aireando un término - decadencia - tan polémico como corriente en el vocabulario decimonónico y aún anterior. El hispanista norteamericano, con tono más historiográfico, y los regeneracionistas y noventayochistas, con un acento más ensayístico, coinciden en reflexionar sobre la

---

[1] Roberto Mesa, *El colonialismo en la crisis del XIX español: Esclavitud y trabajo libre en Cuba*, Madrid, Ediciones de Cultura Hispánica, 1990, 2ª edición. Sobre las grandes monarquías coloniales en la época moderna, Anthony Pagden *Lords of all the World: Ideologies of Empire in Spain, Britain and France c.1500-c.1800*, New Haven – London, Yale University Press. 1995.

sombría realidad española de fines del XIX desde una consideración histórica de la experiencia hispánica. Los hechos de 1898 son percibidos como el final - desastroso y fatal - de una larga serie de problemas, males y errores cuyo origen se rastreará en los inicios y en el desarrollo de la edad moderna española.[2]

El eterno retorno: el debate entre hispanismo y europeísmo

La crisis de 1898 activó una reflexión que tiene un evidente aire de familia con aquella otra iniciada a fines del siglo XVI y formalizada a comienzos del XVII en torno a términos como decadencia - declinación o descaecimiento, dirán los autores del barroco - y arbitrismo. Lo que Ferrater Mora, en su trabajo sobre Unamuno, ha llamado el largo y áspero debate entre europeizantes e hispanizantes se concreta en una serie de razones que trataban de explicar el declive español. Razones de muy diversa naturaleza y entidad histórica donde encontramos ingredientes de carácter psicológico - en consonancia con la psicología de los pueblos, tan en boga entonces - junto a otros religiosos, como el dogmatismo, la intolerancia y el espíritu inquisitorial; también demográficos y económicos - la despoblación causada por los sucesivos conflictos bélicos y, en particular, por la conquista y colonización de América, los efectos perversos del oro americano, gastado en consumo suntuario, en sostener conflictos bélicos de alcance dinástico en lugar de ser invertido juiciosa y productivamente; también razones de orden social y político como el raquitismo burgués por mor de la expulsión de los judíos y del fracaso de las revueltas comuneras y agermanadas, el mal gobierno y a la administración deficiente; y, finalmente, de naturaleza intelectual y educativa tales como el aislamiento impuesto por la cultura contrarreformista, el analfabetismo y la fragilidad científica y técnica.[3] Esta simple enumeración pone de relieve la estrecha cercanía que este repertorio de males guarda con los registrados por la literatura crítica del barroco y por su heredera, la del reformismo ilustrado. En tal sentido, puede hablarse de un ciclo entre memorialístico, ensayístico e historiográfico que comenzaría a fines del XVI y culminaría en la

---

[2] La cercanía del centenario de 1898, propiciará, sin duda, una amplia revisión de toda la literatura noventayochista y de la época de la Restauración. Una inteligente consideración del llamado "problema de España", en Santos Juliá, "Anomalía, dolor y fracaso de España", *Claves de Razón Práctica*, 66, octubre 1996, pp.10-21.El artículo de Lea en, *Atlantic Monthly*, 82, 1898, pp.36-46. El presente trabajo toma como punto de partida mi artículo "Notas sobre decadencia y arbitrismo",*Estudis*, 20, 1994, pp. 9-28, si bien considerando los problemas a la luz de la gestación de una identidad tendencialmente española. Concluída esta comunicación, viene a mis manos un trabajo que no me ha sido posible utilizar, Clare Mar-Molinero y Angel Smith (eds.), *Nationalism and the Nation in the Iberian Peninsula.Competing and Conflicting Identities*, Oxford-Washington, D.C, Berg, 1996.
[3] José Ferrater Mora, *Unamuno. Bosquejo de una filosofía*, Madrid, Alianza Universidad, 1985.

DECADENCIA

España de la Restauración. Como problema recurrente y central de ese largo período encontraremos - aunque algo más apagado en el XVIII y comienzos del XIX - el de la siempre difícil relación entre algunos de los componentes del mosaico español, el de la tensión centro-periferia en torno a un proyecto político unitario.

Uno de los más reconocidos miembros del 98, Unamuno, había dado a las prensas algo antes de esa fecha su novela *Paz en la guerra*, evocando un Bilbao liberal y español que, para entonces, ya no lo era tanto. La fundación del Partido Nacionalista Vasco casi al tiempo que la Unió Catalanista aprovaba las bases de la Constitució Regional Catalana, las llamadas Bases de Manresa, eran expresión de la importancia del problema vasco y catalán en la configuración de la España contemporánea. El paroxismo identitario que conoce la España de la Restauración lo pone de relieve la sucesión y convivencia de actitudes muy diversas que no hacen sino recordar la dificultad de acordar qué sea una identidad española. A modo de ejemplo, puede recordarse como junto al casticismo agarbanzado - sarcástica descalificación de Azaña hacia los noventayochistas - aparece el casi metafísico no-ser de España de Ortega y Gasset; el mesianismo hispánico del ya para entonces fascista Ernesto Giménez Caballero, que en su *Genio de España*, publicado en 1932, incluía una "Biblioteca farmacológica de los males de España", y el anhelo democrático de quienes verán como única salida de la crisis el establecimiento de la segunda república, justamente el momento en que parece comenzar a resolverse la cuestión del nacionalismo español y los restantes nacionalismos, en particular el catalán, vasco y gallego. Si ustedes me lo permiten, también podría mencionarse, como expresión de la fiebre de identidad nacional, aquella *boutade* de Pío Baroja, la República de Bidasoa, acogida al lema "Sin moscas, sin frailes, sin carabineros", ejemplo del llamado anarco-aristocraticismo de los autores del 98.[4]

En los orígenes de este largo ciclo que acompaña el declive hispánico se sitúan términos de honda raigambre histórica al tiempo que polémicos como decadencia y arbitrismo, o de más reciente acuñación como Leyenda Negra, nacida con el libro de Julián Juderías, aparecido justamente en 1914.[5] Pues bien, el propósito de mi comentario - lejos de recrear el tono de esencialismo castellano y de psicologismo

[4] Miguel de Unamuno, *Paz en la guerra*, introducción de Juan Pablo Fusi Aizpurúa, Madrid, Alianza, 1988. Véase el dossier "Mites i nacionalisme", en *Manuscrits. Revista d'Història Moderna*, 12, 1994, pp. 173-266.
[5] Ricardo García Cárcel *La Leyenda Negra,. Historia y opinión*, Madrid, Alianza Universidad, 1992.

71

con que el 'problema de España' fue analizado por la literatura finisecular - es apuntar el sentido que términos como decadencia y arbitrismo han adquirido en la historiografía, y sugerir su pertinencia en el modelado de las ideas y actitudes relacionadas con la identidad del conjunto hispánico, en la urdimbre del nacionalismo. No entraré, por tanto, a considerar todo el ciclo, la totalidad de ese largo período que podemos fechar entre fines del siglo XV, cuando despunta y se va fraguando la España moderna, y fines del XIX, con la crisis precipitada por el desastre colonial. Me ciño, por tanto, a comentar algunos aspectos de lo que Ucelay caracteriza como 'paleonacionalismo español', en relación con el problema de la decadencia y de la literatura que da cuenta de ella, y también con la importancia - destacada en su ponencia - del concepto de imperio. En definitiva, la defensa de los intereses dinásticos en Europa perturbará las relaciones entre monarquía y reinos, y un hecho imperial - la conquista y la pérdida de América - acompaña el inicio y final de ese largo ciclo plagado, como se ha dicho, de una literatura a caballo del memorialismo, el ensayo y la historiografía.

En 1492 una monarquía de reciente constitución llega a las tierras que poco después llamaremos americanas. En esa fecha, ha escrito Rubert de Ventós, América no existía, pero tampoco España, y sólo su encuentro explica que ambas llegaran a constituirse en lo que son. A tal punto es cierto - y es oportuno señalar que Elliott, predicando con el ejemplo, ha insistido en la necesidad de no escindir los dos relatos, el metropolitano y el colonial - que un episodio americano servirá de coartada para el examen de la historia española y la reflexión sobre su presente a fines del siglo XIX.[6] La monarquía de todas las Españas, por utilizar la expresión de Diego de Valera en su *Crónica de España*, aparecida en 1481, nace - es bien sabido - con una notable desigualdad y asimetría entre sus grandes componentes iniciales, el castellano, el catalano - aragonés, el vasco y el navarro. Desigualdad territorial y demográfica doblada por distintas tradiciones políticas y una diferente orientación expansiva. La unidad dinástica será un frágil vínculo - aunque vínculo al fin - de un conjunto cuyo desacuerdo original se ha revelado, finalmente, como un problema siempre latente y todavía no resuelto de manera definitiva en la España de hoy.[7]

---

[6] Xavier Rubert de Ventós, *El laberinto de la hispanidad*, Barcelona, Editorial Planeta, 1987, p. 22. La llamada de atención de Elliott no acaba de ser atendida por una historiografía un tanto enclaustrada en las especializaciones académicas.
[7] Pablo Fernández Albaladejo, *Fragmentos de monarquía: Trabajos de historia política*, Madrid, Alianza Universidad, 1992.

DECADENCIA

Desajuste que hará necesario acudir a otros ingredientes comunes, desequilibrio que se intentará menguar apelando a otros elementos identitarios que refuerzen los vínculos del conjunto. Tal será la unidad de la fe, la comunidad confesional, reforzada por la sucesiva expulsión de judíos, musulmanes y moriscos, y la elaboración de una cultura que enfatiza la condición de cristiano viejo. Señala Ucelay en la ponencia que el nacionalismo español y los nacionalismos catalán, vasco, gallego, como los restantes, tienen un orígen común y una también común herencia. En tal sentido, y en relación con la sobreidentidad religiosa hispánica, no es ocioso señalar que el Partido Nacionalista Vasco - como también la organización ETA, años más tarde - se funda el día de la festividad de san Ignacio de Loyola, y que, como ha recordado Jean-Pierre Dedieu, el Título 1º del Libro 1ª de la *Novisima Recopilación de las Leyes de España* (Madrid, 1805), se titula *De la Santa Fe Católica*. La apelación a la catolicidad, como referente simbólico de la identidad, es constante y común. También la encontramos en autores en torno de los cuales Antoni Simón, ha rastreado el surgimiento de una identidad catalana nacionalista en la época moderna. Así, Andreu Bosc quien en el *Sumari, Index o Epítome dels admirables títols d'honor de Catalunya, Rosselló i Cerdanya*, aparecido en 1628, reivindica que en Cataluña se instaló por vez primera en España el tribunal de la Inquisición; o el jesuita Manuel Morcillo que en su *Crisis de Cataluña hecha por las naciones extranjeras* (1685), reclama para Cataluña el mérito de la primera evangelización americana. En el mismo sentido pueden recordarse algunas afirmaciones de Narcís Feliu de la Penya en su *Fénix de Cataluña*, publicado en 1683, cuando al hablar de la nobleza y antigüedad de Cataluña, escribe que "No tiene España raíz más anciana que la de Cataluña, aviendo vencido y arrojado con tanta puntualidad de sus tierras a los moros apartando la ocasión de mesclarse y escurecerse la sangre, por lo que se presia lo más calificado de España en tener su orígen y su raíz fuerte y limpia en este Principado."[8]

Análogo sentido de refuerzo comunitario tendrían las Indias, el dominio colonial - aunque esta observación requiere, sin duda, mayor estudio - que, si bien están jurídicamente vinculadas a Castilla - la pieza que en definitiva hegemoniza el

[8] Jean-Pierre Dedieu, "La défense de l'orthodoxie", en Christian Hermann (coordination),*Le premier âge de l'État en Espagne (1450-1700)*, París, Éditions du Centre National de la Recherche Scientifique, 1990, p. 217. Antoni Simon, "Patriotisme i nacionalisme a la Catalunya moderna. Mites, tradicions i consciències col.lectives", *L'Avenç*, 167, 1993, pp. 8-16.

conjunto - serán territorio franco para los súbditos de la monarquía, con alguna efímera e inicial excepción. En tal sentido, debe recordarse que la crisis de Cuba fue la ocasión para que sectores del empresariado catalán, asociado al comercio azucarero, desplegarán una retórica colonialista que apelaba a imágenes, como las numantinas, que emparentan con los tópicos del nacionalismo español. En relación con América, ha escrito Rubert de Ventós que "España exportó la contrarreforma pero también la concepción federal de los virreyes iniciada por Cataluña, en cuya base el estado patrimonial podía engarzar con el federal, lo que ocurre hasta Felipe II y en cierto sentido hasta Felipe V, gracias a su respeto por las cortes y constituciones de los estados ibéricos como por los usos y tradiciones de los americanos. Quizás por eso, quizás porque en América este espíritu puede prosperar más que en la propia península, concluye el filósofo catalán, resulta que es allí más que aquí el lugar donde muchos conseguimos sentirnos efectivamente españoles".[9]

Puede decirse, por tanto, que la unidad dinástica, la unidad de la fe y, en cierto sentido, la común posesión y explotación americana, han sido los elementos aglutinantes y, por lo mismo, celosamente protegidos de un territorio político y cultural donde siempre ha resultado laborioso aquilatar la homogeneidad y su oponente, el impulso exclusivista. Bennassar en su estudio sobre los testamentos de los monarcas de la casa de Austria ha destacado el carácter de *leit-motiv* que tiene la recomendación hecha al sucesor de mantener por encima de todo la continuidad dinástica, el carácter inalienable del patrimonio dinástico, y el tribunal de la Inquisición, un organismo, en suma, que actuaba sin cortapisas en todos los dominios de la monarquía y, por tanto doblemente homogeneizador. Por último, podría añadirse otro elemento cohesionador asociado al primero que he mencionado, si bien este percibido negativamente. Me refiero a la servidumbre de las guerras dinásticas, en particular al aventurerismo habsburgo en Europa, que espoleará la siempre latente tensión entre centralismo y centrifugismo. Tensión que encontramos en la España del XVII, tanto en sentido anticastellano - rebelión de Cataluña - como en el contrario. La escenografía y el programa pictórico - reconstruído y bien estudiado por Elliott y Brown - que Olivares diseña para el Salón de los Reinos del Palacio del Buen Retiro, sería la mejor expresión simbólica del propósito del valido para que Felipe IV acabara

---

[9] Xavier Rubert de Ventós, *El laberinto...*, p. 103.

con la titulación fragmentada - que reconoce el carácter multinacional de la monarquía - y se proclamará llanamente rey de España. Empeño que debía comenzar con la llamada Unión de Armas, cuyas virtudes ensalza, precisamente, un cuadro de asunto americano - *Toma de Bahía*, pintado por Juan Bautista del Maíno - en el que se relata la reconquista de un enclave del litoral brasileño gracias a la acción concertada de castellanos y portugueses.[10] Por el momento, como bien saben ustedes, no se pondrá fin a la titulación seriada. Habrá que esperar un tiempo para ver rotulado un monarca como rey de España; será José Bonaparte, rey de España y de las Indias, antes de que lo haga, entrado ya el XIX, Isabel II.

El programa nacionalista de Olivares - en cuya época, como ha recordado Fernández Albadalejo, se reeditan las *Excelencias de la Monarquía de España*, de Gregorio López Madera - fracasa por el momento y la monarquía hispánica conoce a lo largo del XVII un notable desajuste entre la corona y los reinos. Tensiones en Andalucía, el País Vasco, Sicilia, rebelión de Cataluña, erosionada en sus territorios en beneficio de Francia, segregación de Portugal, y fuerte impulso a la americanización de las Indias en un momento en el que va emergiendo la conciencia criolla[11]. No son los únicos episodios de un siglo de crisis y decadencia en el que puede apuntarse, como hipótesis necesitada de mayor investigación y estudio, que en su desenlace parece reforzarse la cohesión identitaria del conjunto hispánico.

Decadencia y literatura crítica

No resulta fácil defender ante ustedes, en este Seminario Anglo-Hispano, la pertinencia de un término como decadencia, que en cierto sentido emparenta - como señaló Alain Milhou - con la estructura 'destrucción/restauración' común a la cultura europea, aunque también profundamente hispánica. Término polémico que ha encontrado en la historiografía británica atentos estudiosos y sólidos argumentadores del *Decline of Spain*. John Elliott, que ha utilizado la palabra ampliamente, considera que oscurece las cosas más que aclararlas, y Stradling la calificó de "vague and hackneyed phrase", insistiendo en la necesidad de establecer cronologías diferenciadas entre lo político y económico. Pero ha sido Henry Kamen - que lo

---

[10] Bartolomé Bennassar, "Un état, des états", en Christian Hermann (coordination),*Le premier âge*..., pp. 69-86. John Elliott y Jonathan Brown, *Un palacio para el rey. El Buen Retiro y la corte de Felipe IV*, Madrid, Revista de Occidente-Alianza, 1981.
[10] David A. Brading, *Orbe indiano. De la monarquía católica a la república criolla, 1492-1867*, México, Fondo de Cultura Económica, 1991. Ruggiero Romano, *Coyunturas opuestas. La crisis del siglo XVII en Europa e Hispanoamérica*, México, El Colegio de México-Fondo de Cultura Económica, 1993.

califica de mito histórico - quien de manera más sostenida, frontal y radical ha criticado tal concepto. A juicio suyo se trata de un término que nace de prejuicios políticos emparentados con la Leyenda Negra, cuya competencia explicativa apenas si alcanza el problema de la decadencia imperial y que ha actuado como elemento distorsionador al confundir el ascenso y declive imperial con el ascenso y declive de España. La palabra, opina Kamen, generaliza una recesión que tan sólo afectó a determinados sectores de la economía castellana y parte del supuesto de un esplendor o bienestar anterior que no acaba de encontrar por parte alguna. Lo más que podemos admitir - concluye - es que hay una etapa de crisis que podemos fechar de manera aproximada entre 1580 y 1660, y que se explica mejor por el carácter dependiente y subordinado de la economía española.

Ciertamente, el debate ha servido para quebrar la imagen de una decadencia económica y política en la que no se introducían demasiados matices geográficos y cronológicos y que identificaba, de manera estrecha, el imperio con España, y a ésta con Castilla. No obstante, la descalificación no ha encontrado mucho eco en la historiografía hispánica como ha precisado Domínguez Ortíz en fechas recientes. A mi juicio, el témino es adecuado y las cautelas de Kamen son acertadas, o lo son en mayor medida, sólo a condición de identificar decadencia, economía y hegemonía imperial; solamente si lo utilizamos desde un punto de vista exclusiva o acusadamente económico. Y en tal sentido, considero que debemos tratar de menguar esa identificación tan estrecha, dándole al concepto un mayor sentido, un alcance más amplio.[12]

Existe, qué duda cabe, una notable preocupación económica en la literatura del siglo XVII, pero esa literatura no sólo convive con la preocupación por el retroceso hegemónico en Europa, con el paso de España a potencia de segundo orden o con las sucesivas derrotas militares, también lo hace con problemas americanos - en un momento que las Indias extreman su tendencia centrífuga - con la crisis del modelo de relaciones entre monarquía y reinos, y con el *décalage* entre la cultura hispánica y la del resto de Europa, en un momento en el que se formaliza la nueva ciencia, la ciencia moderna.

---

12 Para la referenciàs bibliográficas sobre los términos decadencia y arbitrismo, vease Salvador Albiñana, "Notas sobre decadencia y arbitrismo", *Estudis*, 20, 1994, pp.9-28

DECADENCIA

¿Puede utilizarse 'decadencia' como un concepto literario?, pregunta Kamen, para señalar la parodoja de tal palabra en el llamado Siglo de Oro. Un historiador de la literatura diría que la decadencia literaria se produjo tan sólo en el siglo posterior a la decadencia económica, en el XVIII. Contradicción, concluye, que resulta de intentar forzar un concepto para aplicarlo a hechos que no lo respaldan. Ciertamente, la noción de decadencia no colisiona con el esplendor literario o con una excelsa nómina de pintores, pero es que no tendría por qué hacerlo. Nada tiene que ver la existencia y percepción de una situación crítica con la calidad de las expresiones simbólicas - no es necesario recordar como la crítica Europa del primer tercio de este siglo alumbró una incesante y rica actividad en el dominio de las artes y las letras. Y también puede recordarse como la observación de Kamen es pertinente para el ámbito literario en lengua castellana y que, precisamente, los historiadores de la lengua catalana - con otro alcance, desde luego - también han hecho uso del término decadencia para referirse al retroceso del catalán como lengua culta desde comienzos del siglo XVI.

No pretendo abusar del término decadencia y entronizarlo como concepto clave en torno del cual vertebrar buena parte de la historia española moderna y contemporánea, como ya hicieran los liberales y los noventayochistas, pero eso no desmiente que, a mi juicio, en el XVII tiene un sentido más amplio que el económico, territorial y castellano y que, en otros ámbitos, como por ejemplo el cultural y científico, se mantiene vigente hasta comienzos del siglo XX.

Estrechamente asociado a decadencia encontramos la otra palabra recurrente del vocabulario del XVII, arbitrismo. Se trata de términos solidarios que comparten además cierto carácter polémico, equívoco y, quizás el segundo de ellos, algo insuficiente, sobre todo si con él pretendemos dar cuenta de escritos alejados de la primera e inmediata preocupación económica. Ciertamente, si convenimos que lo económico no es lo único que debemos asociar a la noción de decadencia habrá que admitir que con sólo los arbitristas - en su acepción hacendística y económica - no damos noticia de cuantos reflexionan con sentido crítico sobre la sociedad, la política y la cultura. Tanto Michael Gordon como Elliott han advertido contra una explicación que sobredeterminara la economía. Más recientemente, Christian Hermann, ha recordado como el pensamiento político del XVII no sucumbe al reduccionismo económico y que su nota más fecunda es la de una perspectiva que reúne realidades institucionales, económicas y sociales. No sugiero entablar una disputa nominalista, tan sólo, señalar que bajo la palabra arbitrista se reúnen especies muy variadas y que si bien en su inicio el arbitrio es un término relacionado con lo fiscal y lo económico, ese sentido primero no debe invadir todo el campo de reflexión en torno a la decadencia. En definitiva, o consideremos la noción de arbitrismo de un modo más amplio, o - lo que parece quizás más ajustado a la realidad del XVII - debemos estudiar más y mejor otras voces que, más alejadas de la problemática económica o imperial, escriben con sentido crítico sobre la realidad de la España del barroco.[13]

Esa mengua o retroceso de lo económico obliga también a revisar la cronología que solemos manejar; esa literatura, incluso la que tiene un perfil más económico, no desaparece con el reinado de Felipe IV, se mantiene, si bien algo decrecida, a lo largo de la época de Carlos II, al tiempo que deja de ser predominantemente castellana. Diferentes autores - Vilar, Kamen, Molas o Pérez García, entre otros - han ido mostrando la existencia de un importante grupo de autores, de procedencia menos castellana que la anterior, entre quienes aparecen intereses de signo pre-ilustrado, vinculados al movimiento novator, un grupo que desde preocupaciones culturales y científicas, intentará salvar las distancias de la cultura española con la europea, rompiendo con el tono mesiánico y autocomplaciente de autores anteriores.

Europa y América, precipitantes de la identidad española.
Recordando a Ferrater, aludía antes a la disputa entre hispanizantes y europeizantes. Si calificaba la disputa como el eterno retorno es porque algo de eso se verifica también en el pensamiento del siglo XVII, en una cultura en la que se opera el tránsito de una percepción autocomplaciente a otra más crítica, donde Europa deja de ser una rival, un modelo antagónico, para erigirse en modelo y norma, en anhelo. Dicho tránsito - que puede ilustrarse en el contraste de diferentes textos y autores - también actuaría - y también lo sugiero *ex hipotesi* - en el sentido de ir soldando la identidad hispánica.

---

[13] Michael Gordon, "Morality, reform and the empire in seventeenth century Spain"*Jl Pensiero Politico*, XI, 1978, pp. 3-19. John Elliott, "La decadencia de España", *España y su mundo, 1500-1700*, Madrid, 1990. Christian Hermann, "L'arbitrisme: un autre état pour une autre Espagne", Christian Hermann (coordinateur), *Le Premier Âge de l'État*. . . pp. 239-56.

Estudiando los orígenes de la ilustración española, en torno al movimiento de los *novatores*, François López ha aludido al cambio de percepción de la realidad europea, o dicho de otro modo, a la modificación de la propia imagen que se verifica en sectores de la cultura española a lo largo del XVII. Cambio que la conduce del predominio de la autocomplacencia, que López ilustra con un autor como Francisco de Quevedo, a la autocrítica dictada por el utilitarismo moderno, que identifica con el médico pre-ilustrado Juan de Cabriada. Quevedo, como bien saben ustedes, es una de las plumas más aceradas y sarcásticas de la literatura castellana, y uno de los autores - sus críticas a los catalanes en torno a la crisis de 1640 son bien conocidas - donde el proyecto español más se confunde con el castellano. Celoso defensor de los enemigos de la monarquía - con frecuencia protestantes - su pluma no conoce desmayo. En 1609, "cansado de ver el sufrimiento de España", escribe su *España defendida* para salir al paso "de tantas calumnias de extranjeros". La airada réplica de Quevedo, que trata de enfatizar la singularidad cultural hispánica frente a lo común europeo, también debe situarse en el contexto del acoso libelista antihispánico que tendrá en los Países Bajos, como ha recordado García Cárcel, uno de sus centros editoriales más activo. Por lo mismo, Holanda, que introduce en América la primera sinagoga al ocupar la isla de Curaçao y logrará afirmar su independencia frente al imperialismo hispánico, será objeto permanente del denuesto y la sátira del vigoroso escritor castellano. Si traigo a colación el ejemplo de Holanda - más tarde dirá Cadalso de los catalanes que "algunos los llaman los holandeses de España" - es porque será invocada, con frecuencia, como ejemplo a seguir por buena parte de la literatura memorialista del último tercio del XVII.[14]

Ese modo, tolerante, y ya relativista desde el punto de vista confesional, de referirse a los restantes países europeos van cambiando a lo largo del XVII. Puede recordarse el muy citado lamento admirativo del médico Cabriada, al reconocer la marginación española del proceso de aparición de la nueva ciencia, de la ciencia moderna, y solicitar la creación de una Academia de las Ciencias en Madrid: "¿Porqué...no se fundará en la Corte del Rey de España una Academia Real, como la ay en la del Rey de Francia, en la del de Inglaterra, y en la del señor Emperador?" se pregunta. Encontraríamos otros ejemplos similares en los que un genérico 'norte' de

---

[14] José Cadalso, *Carta Marruecas. Noches lúgubres*, edición de Joaquín Arce, Madrid, Cátedra, 1978, Carta XXVI, p. 151.

Europa no es ya el lugar del hereje y del enemigo. Pero no es sólo en el ámbito de la ciencia o la técnica donde localizamos esa actitud. García Cárcel ha hablado de escepticismo pragmático al referirse a la pérdida de beligerancia contra Francia, a comienzos del reinado de Carlos II; y Jover y López-Cordón han rastreado la mengua del determinismo providencialista en la publicística del barroco. ¿Cómo explicar ese tránsito?, se preguntó hace unos años François López; ¿de qué modo se opera esa transición en el pensamiento español? ¿En qué momento se va abriendo paso la idea de que era necesaria una autocrítica?[15] ¿En qué sentido - podríamos añadir - esa crisis de la conciencia, por utilizar la expresión hazardiana, interviene en el modelado de la identidad o identidades nacionales hispánicas?

El médico Cabriada, al que me acabo de referir, escribe también en su obra: "Que es lastimosa y aún vergonzosa cosa que, como si fuéramos indios, hayamos de ser los últimos en percibir las noticias y luces públicas que ya están esparcidas por Europa". El lamento de este científico recurriendo a un símil americano - y la imagen de los españoles como indios de los europeos es un tópico que ya encontramos en el *Memorial* de Luis Ortíz, mediado el siglo XVI, y más tarde en autores como Gracián, que se refiere a España como las "Indias de Francia" - permite también hacer un comentario referido al ámbito colonial[16]

Es sabido que América sin dejar de ser vista como espacio utópico, como geografía mítica en la que todavía es posible alcanzar Eldorado, es crecientemente invocada - y así lo han señalado López-Cordón y Elliott - como causa de algunos de los males que afligen a la monarquía, en particular por el efecto perverso de la riqueza metálica americana y por la sangría demográfica.

De esa doble percepción metropolitana de la realidad colonial son ejemplo algunos de los grandes nombres del arbitrismo. "De cómo la república de España de su gran riqueza ha sacado suma pobreza", escribe González de Cellorigo hacia 1600 en su *Memorial de la política necesaria y útil restauración a la república de España*; con idéntico propósito, y de manera más rotunda, Sancho de Moncada concluye algo después que "La pobreza de España ha resultado del descubrimiento de las Indias

---
[15] José María Piñero, "Juan de Cabriada y el movimiento novator de finales del siglo XVII. Reconsideraciones después de 30 años", *Asclepio*, XLV-1, 1993, pp. 3-53. *François Lopez, Juan Pablo Forner (1756-1797) et la crise de la conscience espagnole au XVIIIe siècle* Bordeaux, 1976.
16. Escribe Ortíz que es vergüenza y grandísima lástima de ver y muy peor lo que burlan los extranjeros de nuestra nación que cierto en esto y en otras cosas nos tratan muy peor que a indios",*Memorial del contador Luis Ortíz a Felipe II*. Valldolid, 1 de Marzo 1558, prólogo de José Larraz, Madrid, Instituto de España, 1970, p.30.

DECADENCIA

occidentales"; y Pedro Fernández de Navarrete, en su *Conservación de monarquías*, de 1626, titula uno de sus discursos "De la despoblación de Castilla por los nuevos descubrimientos y colonias", haciendo de América la segunda causa - la primera habría sido a su juicio la expulsión de judios y moriscos - de la depresión demográfica castellana.[17] Pero tales juicios no son privativos de la época de Felipe III, cuando se formaliza el género arbitrista. Así, Feliu de la Penya en su ya citado *Fénix de Cataluña* habla del "origen y causa de los aumentos antiguos y descaecimientos presentes del Principado de Cataluña", señalando - junto a la 'desasistencia' del monarca que Feliu justifica por la vastedad de los dominios - una razón que hace común: "Otra también he entendido fue la causa y orígen incierto del infeliz estado, no sólo de Cataluña, si de toda España, que fue la falta de gente (olvido los que salieron en las expulciones de Iudios y Moros, que no hazen falta en tan Cathólica Provincia) los que han salido y salen continuamente para las Indias y nuevo mundo...que aunque gloriosamente la aclaman Señora, dexan despoblada España". A fines del XVII y desde Cataluña encontramos idénticos argumentos a los esgrimidos por el quejumbroso y victimista memorialismo castellano.

Estas referencias a autores de procedencia y preocupación diversa creo que pueden ser ejemplo - debo insistir que falto de mayor estudio - de cómo a lo largo del XVII el contraste y el impacto de lo europeo y de lo americano en el pensamiento y la sociedad española, parecen jugar un papel que refuerza la conciencia comunitaria entre los integrantes peninsulares de la monarquía hispánica, favoreciendo el modelado del llamado 'paleonacionalismo' español. No obstante, en el equívoco ámbito del nacionalismo en los siglos XVI y XVII, más cercano a solidaridades complementarias que excluyentes, debemos prevenirnos contra insensibles deslizamientos presentistas o ideologizados. Ciertamente, el texto al que acabo de hacer referencia, el de Feliu de la Penya - un autor que a juicio de Antoni Simón representa un austracismo españolista compatible con la reivindicación patriótica catalana - puede ser leído como expresión de un catalanismo que juega la baza del posibilismo austracista, o como manifestación de una identidad distinta, que bien podemos llamar 'española'.

---

[17] María Victoria López-Cordón, "Dall'utopia indiana all maledizione dell'oro: L'America nel pensiero spagnolo del XVI e XVII secolo", *Dimensione e problemi della recerca storica*, 1, 1991, pp. 29-57. Véase también, John Elliott,*Illusion and Disillusionment: Spain and the Indies*, London, 1992.

A modo de conclusión

"Pero en la monarquía de España, donde las provincias son muchas, las naciones diferentes, las lenguas varias, las inclinaciones opuestas, los climas encontrados, así como es menester gran capacidad para conservar, así mucha para unir." Son palabras de *El Político Fernando* de Gracián, autor en quien es frecuente ese género del cotejo entre naciones y regiones, y aparecen al tiempo que estalla la revuelta catalana.[18] Ciertamente, las naciones eran diferentes y las inclinaciones opuestas pero parece que en el siglo XVII, en el contexto de la primera fuerte crisis del modelo de relación entre monarquía y reinos, sale reforzada la identidad colectiva hispánica. Cataluña, desinteresada del proyecto imperial europeo de la monarquía, titubea unos años pero además de no escindirse, se integra en el proyecto político de la monarquía.

El desenlace del XVII es, desde el punto de vista de los intereses de un nacionalismo español *ante litteram*, la mejor entrada en el XVIII, un siglo que identifica mejor la monarquía de España con la geografía peninsular, en el cual el nacionalismo borbónico ampliará el grado de uniformidad y españolizará en mayor medida el conjunto. Feijoo que distingue entre el amor a la patria - como sinónimo de española y afecto positivo - y la 'pasión nacional' - calificada de 'peste' y asociada al arraigo regional - afirmará en su *Defensa de la agricultura*, que escribe, con frase que se diría de Unamuno, "porque el descuido de España me duele". Es explicable, por tanto, que fuera un escritor protegido por la monarquía.[19]

También ahora, en el Setecientos, problemas europeos y coloniales parecen actuar como integradores: las críticas de buena parte de la ilustración europea hacia la colonización americana y la famosa requisitoria de Masson de Morvilliers forzarán una respuesta reivindicativa de la historia y de la cultura española, creando al mismo tiempo, una polémica - la de la ciencia española - que recorre todo el siglo XIX y se acabará encabalgando con los problemas suscitados en el 98.[20] Por diferentes razones y en torno a determinados hechos y problemas - común percepción de una situación

---

[18] Baltasar Gracián, *Tratados Políticos*, texto establecido, prólogo y notas por Gabriel Juliá, Barcelona, Louis Miracle, 1941, p.312.
[19] Para el siglo XVIII, puede verse, Roberto Fernández (editor), *España en el siglo XVIII: Homenaje a Pierre Vilar*, Barcelona, Crítica, 1985, y Antonio Morales, "El Estado de la ilustración", en G. Gortázar (ed.),*Nación y estado en la España liberal*, Madrid, Noesis, 1994, pp. 15-75.
[20] Sobre la llamada polémica de la ciencia, E. y E. García Camarero, *La polémica de la ciencia española*, Madrid, Alianza Editorial, 1970; los autores la inician con Feijoo, aunque bien pudiera incluirse a los novatores, a los pre-ilustrados.

de crisis y decadencia, retroceso cultural y científico en relación con Europa, coincidencia en la explotación americana, españolización borbónica - a lo largo de los siglos XVII y XVIII el conjunto hispánico tiende a homogeneizarse, aunque tal impulso, quizás, es más el resultado de una incitación exterior que de un acuerdo interno, surgido de los propios reinos. Se verifican, de este modo, algunos de los rasgos del modelo explicativo que plantea el profesor Ucelay en su ponencia. No obstante, los evidentes signos de una identidad que podemos llamar creciente y tendencialmente 'española' en el Antiguo Régimen son, sin duda, un requisito necesario, si bien parece - como la crisis de la Restauración se encargará de recordar - que no suficiente.

NACIONES, PROVINCIAS Y REGIONES: UNA PERSPECTIVA ESCANDINAVA

PETER ARONSSON
(*Universidad de Växjö, Suecia*)

Resumen

Desde una perspectiva escandinava, conectar la historia nórdica por medio de un conflicto entre Inglaterra y Castilla en una batalla política de carácter simbólico llevada a cabo en el Consejo de Basilea (1432-49) es un buen punto de partida para ciertas reflexiones comparativas sobre los siguientes temas: las nación, las provincias y las regiones. Las cuestiones que inmediatamente se plantean, aunque sólo a manera de esbozo, son las siguientes:

¿Qué nación?

Las regiones naturales o históricas permanecen, en gran medida, como si no fueran problemáticas, a pesar de las luchas y enfrentamientos que se nos dan a conocer diariamente en ellas. Ucelay-Da Cal distingue entre 'estado' y 'nación' - un principio dinástico y jurídico confrontado con otro derivado de la comunidad y de la cultura. Se trata del universalismo frente al particularismo, de España, por ejemplo, frente a Castilla o Cataluña.

En Inglaterra, el caso parece ser más complejo y hallarse quizás 'resuelto' hasta cierto punto gracias a la flexibilidad del concepto de 'Gran Bretaña' en ciertos momentos de su historia. Como sabemos, tal ambigüedad no es siempre el caso, pero sí que lo es en la mayoría de las regiones históricas. Los términos son conceptos que se prestan, en cada época histórica, a ser 'interpretados', ofreciendo un cierto abanico de posibilidades para la consolidación de una jurisdicción y poder territorial. Crean un grado de flexibilidad que pudiera ayudar a la maniobra do los políticos, y evitar así la lucha armada.

Miremos nombres como 'Escandinava' o 'Norden', y la equivalencia que pueden tener en el ámbito geográfico con las Islas Británicas o Península Ibérica, y en el político-ideológico con Gran Bretaña y España. Mi tesis es que la nación 'nórdica' y su cultura histórica desempeñan un papel importante en el desarrollo do los estados nórdicos actuales.

Existen una cultura, religión, economía y estructura social nórdica, que hubieran podido servir como base para la construcción de una nación. El hecho de no haber cuajado tal nación puede ser visto como un ejemplo de 'fracaso'. Sin embargo, su fragmentación política se produjo sin la ruptura cultural característica de muchas zonas del mundo. A diferencia del caso español, nuestros nacionalismos regionales sí que lograron sustituirse al concepto más amplio de nación. En esta evolución, tuvieron un papel significativo las guerras civiles tanto como los escritos de los historiadores.

¿Qué nacionalismo?

¿Cómo armonizar las ideas de Ucelay-da Cal sobre los inicios del paleonacionalismo con la orientación reciente de la historiografía hacia los cambios producidos en el siglo XIX? ¿Se trata de una evolucíon o de dos cosas distintas? ¿Es otra cosa el nacionalismo español o inglés del ochocientos en relación con sus antecedentes?

1. Habrá que preguntarse, primero, si debemos hablar de 'protonacionalismo', ya que el término de por sí sugiere un continuidad entre la edad moderna y la contemporánea. El nacionalismo contemporáneo, creado por la movilización del pueblo dentro de una sociedad democrática, clasista y de masas, ¿no habrá de ser considerado como un fenómeno nuevo?

2. Cuando se utilizan y se vuelven a repetir términos culturales e históricos, lo importante es saber hasta qué punto esto refleje, efectivamente, una continuidad de conceptos. Habrá que saber si el repertorio de términos es lo bastante amplio como para permitir todas las posibilidades, o si bien deja lugar a tan sólo una gama reducida de 'naciones' posibles.

3. Hay que recalcar la importancia del derecho en el antiguo régimen. Hasta bien entrada la época moderna, las leyes parecen enmarcar la identidad de los distintos pueblos escandinavos. La ciudadanía tuvo su expresión en los códigos, los cuales se veneraban como absolutos, aun cuando el derecho se administraba a través de distintos tribunales. El rey tenía la responsabilidad suprema, considerándole legítimo, sin embargo, en la medida en la cual mantenía las costumbres. Por lo tanto, el

'patriotismo' se basaba no sólo en la lealtad hacia la dinastía sino tambíen hacia las leyes.

4.   En los casos de Suecia, Noruega y Finlandia, la idea moderna de nacionalismo y la de identidad nacen en una cultura más rural que urbana.   Estos países experimentaron una urbanización e industrialización muy tardías en comparación con gran parte de Europa, y las ciudades apenas influyeron en el desarrollo demográfico hasta la Primera Guerra Mundial, ni en las ideas culturales hasta mucho después de la Segunda Guerra Mundial.   Además, tanto la industria como el urbanismo se desarrollaron en gran medida en el campo, en pueblos que se industrializaron en torno al ferrocaril o al molino.

<u>¿Qué conceptos?</u>
    La disyuntiva estado-nación es un tópico de la política, tanto en la investigación como en la práctica.   La etnicidad representa un resurgir del factor racial, un concepto ya obsoleto en una época en la que la cual la 'cultura' se ha convertido en la metáfora clave de los que buscan el progreso de la humanidad.

    Quizás nos sea útil empezar, por lo tanto, con un concepto más abierto, como es él de region, sin olvidar el papel del estado como elemento integrante en su formación.   Nos hace falta no sólo situar en su contexto histórico el sentido de palabras como 'nación', 'estado' o 'comunidad', sino buscar su capacidad de movilación como mitos o conceptos.   Poedemos aprender de los geógrafos, para quienes la 'región' se define desde varias perspectivas, como estructura, función o potencial.

<u>¿Qué método?</u>
    Habrá que pensar en las entidades que queremos comparar, si son estados o no. ¿Es mejor comparar Suecia con Inglaterra o con Gran Bretaña, con España o con Castilla? Suecia logra integrar sus territorios ocupados tras 1660; pero ¿sería útil comparar la minoría sueca en Finlandia, por ejemplo, con los Vascos? ¿Puede ser más útil, quizás, enfocar las 'fuerzas dinámicas' de que nos habla Ucelay-Da Cal - es decir, las guerras civiles? El concepto, sin embargo, presupone lo que intenta explicar - la unidad que luego se fragmenta. Desde una perspectiva nórdica, la historia de Escandinavia está caracterizada por una larga guerra civil; pero no si - como suele ser

el caso - partimos de la base de los estados actuales. Por supuesto, se puede combinar ambas perspectivas.

Al fin y al cabo, quizás no debemos tomar como nuestro punto de partida un territorio como tal. El objetivo del estudio será explicar comó llegan a formarse tales territorios, tanto si son estados como regiones. Entonces, podemos investigar más la propia evolución de su cultura histórica. De ahí podemos enfocar su cultura política, que forma un nexo complejo con la evolución de la comunidad política, a través de guerras, retórica revolucionaria, instituciones, educación de la juventud. No debemos pasar por alto, tampoco, el papel de los politicos, que saben crear imágenes de legitimidad, compensando la subyugación con la integración del súbdito.

NATION, PROVINCES AND REGIONS: A SCANDINAVIAN PERSPECTIVE

PETER ARONSSON

(*Växjö University, Sweden*)

1. Nordic arguments in Basel in 1434

The bishop of Växjö from 1426, Nicolaus Ragvaldi, later Archbishop of Sweden, was at the Council of Basel (1431-49) in 1434 to discuss the urgent demands for reform, fighting back heresy and a possible unification with the Greek Catholic Church.

As often is the case in international negotiations, the formal obstacles, centred on the important issue of honour and power, were a major obstacle to getting started. The important question about seating required a considerable amount of attention, starting with the quarrel between the English and Castilian delegates. To the distress of many northern European legates, England lost the case. One of the arguments used by the Castilians was their ancient connection to the mighty Goths. This provided the Nordic bishop with a tenuous thread, which he eagerly picked up in order to make his own protest. Ragvaldi deplored the fact that the delegates had started to quarrel about seating procedure, distracting attention from the church and the holy matters under consideration. But he could no longer keep quiet when all the others were boasting about the supposed glory of their own kingdoms. The Gothic thread provided by the Castilians was readily woven into a fantastic history of the glory of the Goths, who were placed in the north by the authors of antiquity and could be further located in Götaland and Svealand, which were called Sweden by those same authors. The Finns were the basis of the tribes of Langobards, Burgundians and the Huns; Wends and Saxons came from the same northern nation - remarks made to give the rest of the northern European delegates something to think about and keep them from further pretensions. However, Ragvaldi concentrated on the Goths in his oration and certainly found enough successful battles, conquests and glorious dynastic relationships with the Persians, Greeks, Romans, before he eventually arrived at their conquest of the Iberian Peninsula. All these triumphs prepared, of course, the way for their conversion to Christianity and their subsequent crusades on behalf of that faith. He concluded rhetorically: What kingdom is older or more powerful than ours?

The case was clear: Ragvaldi and his mission should have the pre-eminent seat - or at least, not to be presumptuous, the second best. The arguments used were the mythical-historical glory, antiquity and age of the kingdom and also the date of conversion to Christianity. Alfonso de Cartagena gave the all-too-quick and ingenious answer: 'why should we honour those Goths who languidly remained seated in their cold country more than those brave people leaving for glorious journeys, eventually settling in Spain?' The Nordic protest was utterly unsuccessful, at least in the short run.[1]

Connecting Nordic history via a conflict between England and Castile in a symbolic political battle fought with historical arguments seems an appropriate starting-point for some comparative reflections on the topic of nation, provinces and regions from a Scandinavian perspective. The questions that immediately arise, and can, of course, only be hinted at here, are:
1. What nation?
2. What nationalism?
3. What concepts?
4. What method?

1. What Nation? State and Nation in Scandinavia - a more problematical distinction than usually thought.

'Natural' or historical regions are still to a large degree accepted without much questioning as a subject or concept, though the news bulletins carry daily reports of struggles over their territorial definition. Professor Ucelay-Da Cal draws a distinction between statehood and nation: a dynastic and legal principle set against one more embedded in community and culture - universalism versus particularism, Spain as compared with Castile or Catalonia.

In England, the situation seems to be more complex, though perhaps 'resolved' to some extent by greater ambiguity surrounding the concept of Britain, successfully invoked at various times. This ambiguity does not apply in all cases, but it affects many historic regions. Names are concepts, which at each moment or another in the past may serve as a gateway to the establishment of power and

---

[1] Ragvaldi became Archbishop in 1438 and died ten years later. My translation from Thorsten Petersson, " Växjöbiskopen Nils Ragvaldssons tal on goternas fornbragder på kyrkomötet I Basel", *Hyltén-Cavalliusföeningens Årsbok*, 1945, pp. 169-87.

jurisdiction over a given territory. If flexible enough, they may provide a framework within which political action can take place without provoking civil war.[2]

So will Scandinavia or *Norden* serve as a counterpart to the Atlantic Archipelago or the Iberian Peninsula, or to their political expressions, Britain and Spain?

In whose name was Bishop Ragvaldi speaking, beyond that of the church? The ruler at the time was Bogislav, rechristened Erik of Pomerania in order to give him a proper Nordic aura, head of a Scandinavian union that was seriously threatened by a rebellion in central Sweden at the time the protest was being delivered in Basel. Ragvaldi, in other words, was the spokesman of a ruler engaged, from his coronation in 1397, in that early attempt to build a Nordic state, the Union of Kalmar, which would eventually fall apart around 1520.

The violent revolt of 1434 has variously been described as a Swedish-nationalist uprising/war of liberation, an aristocratic, bourgeois or proletarian revolution, or an anti-state, anti-fiscal upheaval concerned to safeguard local autonomy. The prejudices of the writer and of his epoch seem to count for more in this regard than any careful reconstruction of the ideas and aspirations of those involved. Traditionally the disintegration of the Nordic political system from around 1520 and the subsequent consolidation of Swedish and Danish states have been commonly depicted as liberation - at least for Sweden - from foreign rule; but the process could just as well be interpreted as a continuation of civil wars between competing regions. If the Nordic nation is taken as the basis of analysis, then we are dealing with recurring civil conflict between the fourteenth and seventeenth centuries, with a gradual shift away from armed confrontation by the eighteenth century.

In addition to Norway, Denmark and Sweden, Iceland often boasted of belonging to the exclusive group of nation-states that actually lived up to the idea of one people, one country and one state, statements that were constantly repeated during the nineteenth century. Although there sometimes seems to have been a recognition of the Scandinavian peninsula as a natural or desirable territory for co-operation, it has been until quite recently the very *late* nation states of Denmark (1864/1920),

---

[2] See John Morrill's contribution in this volume; Reinhardt Korselleck,*Futures Past: On the Semantics of Historical Time*, (Cambridge, Mass., 1985); *Critique and Crisis and the Pathogenesis of Modern Society* (Oxford, 1988).

Norway (1814/1905), Finland (1809/1917) and Sweden (1809/1905) that are regarded as the natural and desirable shape of states in the region.[3] Is this unproblematic?

Let me just state that I think there are fewer differences between Scandinavia and other European countries in regard to regional questions than one might think. The following list provides a few examples of this to add to the lessons already drawn from the medieval epoch:

- the 'federal structure' in the Middle Ages is quite mainstream in its regional complexity.

- the ambition of *Dominium mare baltici* held by both Denmark (also with Atlantic ambitions) and Sweden creates two aspiring multinational empires, in principle very much like Spain, England or later Prussia - only less successful ones.

- the Swedish conquest of southern Scandinavia and Jämtland (which had strong 'federal/national' tradition itself within Norway/Denmark) in the seventeenth century created a potentially 'British' situation.

- the Danish - German conflict over Schleswig and Holstein lived on until 1920.

- the Finnish question. Finland was an integral part of the Swedish kingdom until 1809, with a definite majority of Finnish-speaking subjects, taken over by Russia as an archduchy, leaving a large minority of Finnish-speaking subjects in Sweden and an even larger minority of indigenous Swedish-speaking subjects in Finland. This provided a good reason for conflict in Finland, which broke out first as cultural movements and then in 1918 as a civil war.

- The Union between Sweden and a reluctant Norway in 1814, which was dissolved quite peacefully in 1905, mostly by political means and with only irresolute sabre-rattling.

---

[3] Øystein Sørensen and Bo Strath (eds.), *The Cultural Construction of Norden*, (Oslo, 1997), Uffe Østergård,*Europas Ansigter: Nationale stater og politiske kulturer I en ny, gammel verden.* (Copenhagen, 1992).

- The Lapps, an international minority in the north of Scandinavia, are often overlooked owing to their small numbers.

To summarize: a fairly ordinary European experience could be depicted as regards the potential region-national complications in Scandinavia. What might need explanation is why this heritage of potential injustices for most of the provinces was not utilized for aggressive nationalist purposes in the age of nationalism. It is my argument that a *Nordic* nation and historical culture are important factors in the process of building the Nordic *nation-states*. The argument can be developed in several directions, few of them hitherto explored because respect for present-day borders has been part of Nordic political correctness among historians.[4]

There is a common Nordic culture, religion, economy and social structure that makes a Nordic nation-building project a real alternative. The Nordic case can be looked upon as 'one of those that did not make it', if we are looking for the creation of a greater nation-state. But it did mean that changing territorial boundaries within the Nordic community were not the kind of cultural ruptures they tended to be in many other areas. Of course it was easier to choose the optimal mixture of violence and assimilation in this kind of context. In contrast to the Spanish case, regional nationalisms *did* succeed in replacing the Nordic one. The outcome of the civil wars *and* national historiography played important parts in promoting that outcome.

2. What Nationalism?

How do Professor Ucelay-Da Cal's suggestions regarding early modern paleo-nationalism square with recent historiographic developments? Are the two kinds of nationalism quite different, or does one feed into the other, as the use of terms proto- or paleo-nationalism might suggest? Max Weber and Ernest Gellner, among others, link the rise of nationalist movements to the onset of modernisation; but then what are the forces behind proto-nationalism?[5]

---

4. Some historians have dwelt upon this perspective. Harold Gustafsson, "Statsbildning och territoriell integration. Linjer I nyare forskning, en nordisk ansats samt ett bidrag till 1500-talets svenska politiska geografi" *Scandia*, 1991:2, J Gidlund & H.S. Sörlin, *Det europeiska kaljdoskopet* (SNS, 1993).
5. The literature is immense. For a few examples, see J. Hutchinson and A.D. Smith (eds.), *Nationalism*, (Oxford, 1994); E. Gellner, *Nations and Nationalism* (1983) (Blackwell, 1993); E. Hobsbawm and T. Ranger (eds.), *The Invention of Tradition*, (CUP Canto, 1992); and on the Scandinavian issue, Sven Tägil (ed.), *Ethnicity and Nation Building in the Nordic World*, (Southern Illinois University Press, 1995); E.L. Lönnroth, K. Molin and R. Björk (eds.) *Conceptions of National History*, Proceedings of Nobel Symposium 78, (Berlin, 1994).

When Professor Ucelay-Da Cal is discussing twentieth-century Spain, his remarks on the development of cities and resulting patterns of migration might suggest an explanation in terms of modernisation. But his real emphasis is on 'civil war', broadly interpreted, or the momentum of state-building and reactions to it.

I think there is a useful insight to be gained by looking at institutions and historical memory as tools of nation-building. Historiography creates a store of cultural attributes, which can then be drawn upon when required, for different kinds of community-building. It has recently been suggested that Sweden's involvement in the Thirty Years' War is impossible to explain in terms of a rational calculation of self-interest. Erik Ringmar argues that the construction of a glorious tradition and demands for military honour are the motives which were eventually allowed to override the better judgment of statesmen. The fact that the strategy was successful for a period of time suggests how a state can consolidate its power through mobilising ideas and emotions, as well as more material assets like cannon and taxation.[6]

There are some problems of the continuity-thesis that seem to apply to both Britain and Spain:

1.   The first question is whether the prefix of proto- in the term proto-nationalism is valid, since it appears to suggest the continuity of a complex phenomenon. If modern nationalism is created by popular mobilization within a democratic, mass and class-bound society, is this not really to be regarded as a new phenomenon? What was the social base for, or function of, paleo-nationalism? Is it possible to make a distinction here, in line with a suggestion by Ringmar, between the contribution of historiography and history itself?

2.   Where we find cultural and historical elements being reused, as often is the case, the question is how important this is as a sign of continuity. Is the repertoire rich enough to support *any* project, or does it put serious institutional restraints on what type of nationalism could be developed?

3.   More specifically I would like to stress the importance of law in the *ancien régime*. Well into early modern times, the adherence to a specific law seems to have

---

[6]   E. Ringmar, *Identity, Interest and Action: A cultural explanation of Sweden's intervention in the Thirty Years* War (Diss, Cambridge, 1996).

been the most important identifier in Scandinavia. The law codified the way people related to each other and was regarded as absolute, although justice could be implemented by many different institutions. The king was responsible for and was regarded as legitimate as long as he upheld the law. So 'patriotism' seemed to centre on the law and not simply on dynastic loyalty. To what extent is this the same in the other areas under discussion here?

4.   For modern nationalism and identity in Sweden, Norway and Finland at least, rural and not urban cultural elements are of overwhelming importance. Urbanization and industrialization were extremely late from a European perspective, and did not dominate demographic development until World War One, nor cultural ideals until well after World War Two. Furthermore, both industry and urbanization were to a large extent developed in the countryside in small railway or mill-centred industrial communities. It was not clear even to a progressive elite that an agrarian society was obsolete around 1900. Denmark with its intensive small-scale husbandry seemed to prove there was an alternative way to modernise.

Ragvaldi's story, referred to above, was immediately reused in an important ideological context as an introductory part of the new edition of the Law Code of King Kristoffer in 1442. The story of the Nordic nation, developed by Ragvaldi and early historiographers of the Reformation period, took on further trappings later. Johannes Magnus, Ericus Olai and students of the Icelandic sagas from the seventeenth century provided a historical context in which each nation (and its historians) found a way to discover itself as the most Nordic country. Ragvaldi is cited in the sixteenth book of Johannes Magnus' magnum opus *Historia de Omnibus Gothorum Sveonumgue Regibus* published in Rome for the first time in 1554, and in Swedish in 1620. The intention of the bishops was to use the story the same way as the Castilian delegate a hundred years earlier did, to criticize the weakness of the contemporary Nordic ruler.[7]

---

[7]   Petersson, "Växjöbiskopen Nils Ragvaldssons". On the utilisation of the gothic legacy, see J. Nordström,*De yverbornas ö: Sextonhundratalsstudier*, (Stockholm, 1934); Bernd Henningsen in "The Swedish Construction of Nordic Identity"*The Cultural Construction of Norden*.

From the seventeenth century, a common Nordic heritage was constructed more forcefully by combining that legacy with the newly discovered Saga material to create a more authentic, ancient and self-contained Nordic identity which was still mainly utilized in the European arena at a time and place where there was a need for grandeur and powerful images. The main products in the age of Sweden's great power status were meant for foreign diplomats and compiled by Erik Dahlbergh, *Suecia Antiqua et Hodierna* while Olof Rudbeck wrote *Atlantica (Atland eller Manheim)* for the world of scholars.[8]

It required more than a century before that legacy was used in the discovery of the people. German insights led to the development of *Volkskultur*, a popular or common culture where all the states began to think of themselves as the true Nordic descendants of the heroic, strong and yet egalitarian pagan culture - the Nordic culture. In the nineteenth century, this approach flourished and even became political hard currency when there was a continental threat of any kind, as from Prussia towards Denmark over Holstein, and has continued down to today's movements against the European Union.

I would argue that this followed and follows the same rationale underlying the arguments advanced by Ragvaldi, although today we tend to honour an egalitarian social structure and proto-democratic cultural traits rather than glorious massacres on the battlefield. That rationale is the projection outward of an identity based on images and experiences of what we are. The myths of the past are nowadays well-known by everyone - not only by a handful of learned scholars. But this may have been the case already before modernization brought cheap mass communications within reach.[9]

It is important to realise that this heritage was not only put to work on a Nordic or state level. It could and was also used for regional cultural movements, trying to politicize within a national framework a *de facto* legal, political and cultural regionalism at a sub-state level. A regional culturalism arose at the latest in the seventeenth century. Here the historical writings of Ragvaldi were used once more. The name of the province 'Småland' was, according to Peter Rudebeck,

---

[8] G. Eriksson, *The Atlantic Vision: Olaus Rudbeck and Baroque Science*, (Canton, Mass., 1994) and Gunnar Broberg (ed.), *Gyllene Äpplen: Svensk Idéhistorik Läsebok*, (Atlantis, 1991), pp. 270-319.
[9] If this really is the case or just a matter of surviving sources is a matter of legitimate questionning. H. Nordmark,". . . iag har wägen banat" – *PetterRudebeck och hans historia, Scripta Minora. Uppsatser och rapporter från Institutionen för humaniora*, Högskolan I Växjö, nr 8 (1991); Lars-Olof Larsson, *Historia om Småland*, (Växjö, 1975).

Ridgothaland. The home of the Goths was not Nordic, not Sweden but the province of Småland! And this was used in practice to defend the regional custom of equal inheritance on behalf of both male and female children in the seventeenth century. Later on the argument was 'nationalized' to pursue the same norm but now within a liberal framework. And in the age of nationalism, popular roots were an asset upon which self-confidence and museums, but not political demands for regional self-government, could be built. Regional self-government was already accessible within existing political institutions.[10]

The self-confidence of local and regional culture was manifold and partly institutionalized in a communal movement that had existed on a local scale at least since the sixteenth century and as an important ideological bridge to modernity in the nineteenth. Jurisdiction was performed with a large amount of popular and symbolic participation at a regional level.[11] Until the late seventeenth century, foreign policy took place at a regional and local level, to some extent without consulting authorities.[12] Paradoxically, all this seems rather to have helped the state, at least in the long run, to assimilate the regions into national instead of regional political movements. The best examples from Sweden are the creation of the great folkloristic museums, *Kulturen*, *Skansen* and *Nordiska museet*, which all theme regional culture based on provinces as the basis for national culture. Sweden *is* a regionalised culture, it should be stressed, though it is called Nordic, not Swedish.[13] The creation of regional culture became a necessary intermediary between local community and national identity while the Nordic stereotype was invented, reinforced and used in a European context.

As mentioned earlier, the regional importance of urbanization is no doubt significant. Recently the position of Jutland between a weakened Copenhagen and a steadily growing Hamburg has been emphasized as one of the important factors in the development of regional political dynamics in nineteenth-century Denmark. So too

---

[10] H. Nordmark, "Den Svenska Historien och Historia i Småland. Petter Rudebeck och farbrodern i Uppsala, . . . och fram träder landsbygdens människor. . ." *Studier i nordisk och smålandsk historia tillägnade Lars-Olof Larsson på 60-årsdagen den 15 november 1994* (Växjö, 1994). P. Aronsson, "Swedish Rural Society and Political Culture: The Eighteenth and Nineteenth-Century Experience", *Rural History*, vol. 3, 1992:1, pp. 41-57. Of course there was also some violence in Nordic politics, but after the sixteenth century it was rare and had no regional implications as far as we know.

[11] E. Österberg, "Social arena or theatre of power: the courts, crime and the early-modern state in Sweden",*Maktpolitik och husfrid: Studier i internationell och svensk historia tillägnade Göran Rystad*, (Lund, 1991).

[12] Larsson, *Historia*.

[13] K. Arcadius, *Museum på svenska: Länsmuseerna och kulturhistorien*, (Stockholm, 1997).

has the impact of rural culture in the other Nordic countries as a striking feature of their development down to World War Two.

Regionalism can be politicized in opposition to state-nationalism, but also exploited in order to reinforce a national culture. The division of labour between different academic disciplines plays an important part here. To sum up, I would suggest that since the nineteenth century historians have tended to overlook the significance of regions, while anthropologists have focused on their folk-cultures as something inherent and natural (thus removing them from the political arena), and geographers have concentrated on the function of regions as the building-blocks of an integrated welfare state.[14]

3. What concepts?

The state-nation dichotomy is much discussed in research and practical politics. Ethnicity stands for a revival of the racial aspect, an otherwise obsolete concept in an age in which culture has developed into the central metaphor of a constructivist approach in the humanities.

Professor Ucelay-Da Cal says: 'State is a discourse, a kind of language with a mesmerizing effect'.[15] Yes, and it is worth mentioning that the Austrian physician who gave his name to the concept, F.A. Mesmer, lived between 1734 and 1815, the age in which there was an important restructuring of such concepts as state, nation and society in order to cope with the increasing complexity of society bureaucratic centralisation. The use of the concept before and after that brief moment in history, the later eighteenth-century, has at least in Sweden and perhaps particularly so there, *merged* the concepts of nation, state and society into one politically viable vision, that of a kind of welfare-state. Projecting this understanding on the past leads to serious error.[16]

The nucleus of all early-modern meanings of the state is *a specific and concrete ordering of things as in a household*. The Swedish word is until the

[14] My own arguments concerning regions are mostly drawn from P. Aronsson, *Regionernas roll i Sveriges historia*, ERU rapport 91 (Fritzes, 1995) which is available in a brief summary in English in "The Desire for Regions: The Production of Space in Sweden's History and Historiography", *Institut für Europäische Regionalforschungen, Interregiones* 1994:4. For complete references I refer to these texts.
[15] See Ucelay-Da-Cal, in this book, p.14.
[16] P. Aronsson, "The possibilities of conceptual history 'from above' and 'from below': Reflections on the concept of samhälle 'society' in Sweden, 1700-1990", *Historia a Debate, tomo II, Retorno del Sujeto, Actas del Congreso Internacional "A historia a debate" celebrado el 7-11 de julio de 1993 en Santiago de Compostela*, ed. Carlos Barros (1995), pp. 237-60.

seventeenth century more connected with the household and the concrete provisions made for its support, rather than with an abstract judicial concept, and it does not refer to political governance over a given territory. This closeness and similarity between the concepts of household and state can be seen further in contemporary literature on the economy, in the old broad meaning of the word *Oeconomia*, and is apparent in the rhetoric of the old Vasa kings.

Scholarly research has even argued that there was a more explicit and reinforced household ideology in the eighteenth century.[17] Only at the end of the eighteenth century did the territorial aspect of central government and bureaucracy reach a qualitative level where the abstraction and holism of a modern concept of the state could be used without serious misunderstanding.[18] The discontinuity should not be overemphasized - the metaphor of the household, its connotations of reciprocity and division of labour for the common good, continues until well into the twentieth century.[19] Nationalism in this interpretation should be seen as a more democratic form of State/household metaphor than was possible in the older dynastic context.

In the contemporary debate in Europe during the last decade, we have often seen warnings about blurring the difference between the nation as utopian community (sometimes in the conceptual rediscovery of 'civil society'), and the state as the real political unit. But I would argue from an investigation of the use of the Swedish concept for state, *stat,* that it has, as its nucleus, a root metaphor of household as an image of community *and* authority. This is a continuous feature of our modern history even when other dimensions of the concept are switched from the dynastic principle to that of community. The abstract division between state and society never developed strongly in Swedish discourse or practice.

---

[17] Tex Per Brahe, *Oeconomia*, ed. J. Granland and G. Holm (1971); H. Horstbøll, "Cosmology and Economics: Discontinuity and Continuity in Economic Conceptions on the Market for Popular Prints in Denmark During the Seventeenth and Eighteenth Centuries", *Scandinavian Economic History Review, 1989:2;* Per-Arne Karlsson, "Housekeeping Ideology and Equilibrium Policy in Eighteenth-Century Sweden", *Scandinavian Economic History Review, 1989:2,* K. Johansson & M. Ågren, "Economiska brott och egendomsbrott", *Normer og sosial kontroll i Norden ca. 1550-1850, Rapport II till det 22. Nordiske historikernøte* (Oslo, 1994).

[18] P. Frohnert, *Kronans skatter och bondens bröd: Den lokala förvaltningen och bönderna i Sverige 1719-1775,* (dess Stockholm, Lund, 1993).

[19] L. Trägårdh, "Varieties of Volkish Ideologies: Sweden and Germany 1848-1933", in B. Stråth (ed.),*Language and the Construction of Class Identities,* (Gothenburg,.1990).

More generally one could perhaps argue that there were two features of dynastic state-building which provided material for different aspects of nineteenth-century development: the way the empire extended feudal, dynastic links to other territories; and secondly the patriarchal household modernizing as a reflection of the nation in the form of an extended family. Only the potential of the latter was readily utilized in Scandinavia, whereas both were more intrinsically part of the national history of the Iberian Peninsula and the Atlantic Archipelago.

The division of labour between history proper and other disciplines of cultural history is part of the game. If it is one of the subjects for study by history proper, a given territory can acquire an aura of political legitimacy. Why is it that we tend to describe thoughts at a regional level as 'popular culture' when they are ideologies at state level? Feelings are local, strategies and symbols are central; reaction is local, initiative is central. Maybe this is the case in practice but I have the feeling (it is no more than that) that it might be the perspective of historians employed in the services of the state or the nation is at work here with serious, unwitting repercussions on theory.

It might be useful to start with a more open-ended concept like the region and use it more generally to include the states as some of the more successful actors in the territorial regional arena. Obviously we need concepts that help us not only to deconstruct an established nation, state and community but to appreciate the connotations and implications that made them so powerful as descriptive and mobilizing concepts. It might be helpful to consult the wide-ranging debate on 'space' and region in human geography, where there are many suggestions for definition using functional, structural, instrumental or constructivist approaches to region as an analytical tool. My favourite is Anssi Paasi's because of its combination of subjective and institutional aspects of territorialization. Within the framework of a focus on regional identity, Paasi distinguishes carefully between 'regional consciousness' which refers directly to people's experiences, and 'the identity of the region', which finds expression in the institutions (in a broad sense) that are formed by a historical process. It is the latter process that leads to regionalism, while the former connotes ties to a place.[20]

The following elements, or 'interacting stages', are included in the creation of 'regions', the transformation of social spaces into 'real', objectively perceived entities, although not necessarily in chronological order:

- the conception of the existence of a territorially distinguishable space.
- the territory as a conscious conceptual form, with symbols being associated with its space.
- the formation of institutions such as laws, organisations, language systems, etc.
- the region's occupation of a place in a system of regions, externally recognised and legitimate.

4. What methods? Some comparative remarks.

What entities are we to compare: states: Sweden with England, or an unsuccessful Britain or Spain or Castile? Sweden successfully integrating its occupied territories from 1660: the Swedish-speaking minority in Finland with the Basques? Or are we to compare the dynamic forces as suggested by Professor Ucelay-Da Cal, i.e. civil wars? The concept itself presupposes what it is designed to explain. It begs the question and presupposes a unity disturbed or created in the process. Scandinavian history is marked by civil war in a Nordic perspective, but lacks it to a large degree if the later nation-states are the starting point, as is usual in the historiography. Of course, with an even broader concept of institutional politics as regulated 'war' one could re-examine the way various regions came into being.

Perhaps we should not use territories and their history as a starting point. As Professor Ucelay-Da Cal states: it is easier to discuss ideas than contrasting facts.[21] If territorial regionalization, both at an inter-state and intra-state level, is the general object of study, comparative reflection has to take account of historiography, or rather historical culture and its dynamics and logic to a larger extent than hitherto. From there we could move on to political culture - which is part of the moulding of the political community and the way in which interaction is created and channeled

---

[20] A. Paasai, "The institutionalisation of regions: a theoretical framework for understanding of the emergence of regions and contstitution of regional identity", *Fennia* 164:1 (1986), 131-5 and A. Paasi, *Territories, Boundaries and Consciousness*, (Chichester, 1995).
[21] see Ucelay-Da Cal above, p.13.

institutionally (civil war, revolutionary rhetoric, jurisdiction, education). Thirdly but no less importantly, political skill has to be taken into account. We need to emphasize the capacity of the political leaders not only to create legitimate images but also real policies to balance integration and subjugation.

By doing that, we might as historians add something significant to the general theories put forward by sociologists and political scientists such as Charles Tilly, Max Weber, Ernest Gellner and Adam Smith. One of the rewards might be that we would find more striking similarities in the case of the Iberian Peninsula, the Atlantic Isles and the North than are apparent at first sight. In a way I would argue that this is the kind of analysis Ragvaldi attempted in Basel, with the material, methods and interests that were current at that time. What historical context we are playing within now - or perhaps more often, is playing with us - I do not dare start exploring at this stage.

LOS VALENCIANOS Y ESPANA: LA BUSQUEDA DE IDENTIDAD

JAMES CASEY
(*University of East Anglia*)

Esta comunicación trata de la evolución de la región valenciana y su sentido de identidad desde la época de los árabes hasta nuestros días. El reino de Valencia se originó en 1238 como resultado de la Reconquista cristiana; sin embargo, muchos moros permanecieron allí después de esta fecha, constituyendo un tercio de la población total cuando se llevó a cabo su expulsión final, en 1609. Después de 1238, el reino se fue integrando gradualmente a la corona de Aragón, esa fachada mediterránea de la Península Ibérica a la que estaba unida por lazos comerciales y movimientos de población. Sus lazos con Cataluña explican, de manera específica, la aportación excepcional de Valencia, en la baja Edad Media, a la lengua y cultura catalanas, pese al hecho de que gran parte de su población interior fuera de habla aragonesa o árabe. El 'dualismo' de la sociedad valenciana, del cual nos da cuenta el historiador valenciano Joan Reglà, se mantenía bajo control gracias a un código legal único (los *Furs*) e instituciones políticas comunes, que le daban a Valencia un sentido de orgullo colectivo en su tradición de gobierno fuerte pero al mismo tiempo libre.

La unidad de la mancomunidad empezó a agrietarse hacia el final de la Edad Media, con el incremento de las tensiones sociales: entre la Iglesia de la Contrarreforma y los moros, y entre la ciudad de Valencia y los señores feudales, cuyos intereses los fueron acercando progresivamente a la corte española, alejándolos así de Valencia. Los acontecimientos que propiciaron el cambio definitivo fueron la gran revuelta popular de 1519-22 contra los nobles (las Germanías) y la expulsión del pueblo morisco en 1609. Ambas medidas fortalecieron la posición de la corona. La expansión del Estado fue un rasgo señalado del período de los Habsburgo (1516-1700), en el que los jueces de la corona empezaron a invalidar los *Furs* en beneficio de una mejor gobernabilidad. Fue bajo el famoso ministro de Felipe IV, el Conde-Duque de Olivares (1622-43), cuando se empezó a adoptar el sistema de la "Unión de Armas", que exigía que Valencia ayudara a España de manera permanente en materia fiscal y militar y dejara de considerarse a sí misma como un reino autónomo. Un largo proceso de cambio de actitudes en este sentido desembocó en la crisis originada por una revuelta popular en Valencia en 1705-7, durante la Guerra de Sucesión española, que le dio a Felipe V la oportunidad de abolir las leyes e instituciones independientes de la región.

Las viejas ideas del derecho de los valencianos a su autogobierno siguieron saliendo a la superficie durante el período de los Borbones (1700-1808), reforzadas ahora por un interés literario creciente en la cutura y las tradiciones regionales por parte de los representantes valencianos de la Ilustración. Con el hundimiento del Antíguo Régimen en 1808, al igual que en otras partes de España, se puso de manifesto, con el Carlismo, la adhesión conservadora a los valores de la religión y la tradición. Esto constituyó una especie de protonacionalismo, ensalzando la belleza del pasado medieval y los *Furs*, pero con el objetivo de proporcionar un baluarte contra el gobierno centralista de Madrid, de carácter liberal y anticlerical.

Al mismo tiempo, dentro del movimiento romántico europeo de principios del siglo XIX, estaba surgiendo una *Renaixença* cultural; sin embargo, ésta no se convirtió en un nacionalismo moderno al estilo catalán. La última parte de esta comunicación se encarga de examinar el porqué de esto. Parece que las élites valencianas compartían más los valores de sus homólogos castellanos que los de la burguesía barcelonesa, más industrial y progresista. Asímismo, no se permitió que la defensa de la tradición pursiera en peligro la jerarquía social. Mas bien, el movimiento de reforma en Valencia se asoció, alrededor de 1900, a la influencia dominante del novelista Blasco Ibáñez, que combinó el compromiso con el pueblo con una predisposición en contra del regionalismo, que podría aumentar el poder de los curas y patrones. Son estas tensiones contrastadas las que hacen de Valencia un caso de estudio tan interesante, al ser una región con una lengua y cultura arraigadas, pero que sin embargo no consiguió desarrollar un movimiento nacionalista fuerte.

THE VALENCIANS AND SPAIN: A SEARCH FOR IDENTITY

JAMES CASEY
(*University of East Anglia*)

The definition of a national identity has generated much fruitful debate among students of Spain and her history. Commenting on the tragedy of the Civil War of 1936-9, Pierre Vilar wrote: "It is almost as if those peoples which have seen their history come to an abrupt halt take their revenge by writing about it."[i] Arriving in Barcelona in 1927 to do research on the human geography of the land formed by the Pyrenees and the valley of the Ebro, he became aware that his study could not be completed without an analysis of the people, their culture and historical traditions. As he pointed out in the introduction to his classic history of Catalonia (1964), a landscape is the product of an interaction between the material and moral environments. It both creates and reflects patterns of human solidarity, which may be called 'patriotism' and in certain circumstances may coalesce into narrower and sharper form : nationalist movements.

One of the continuing features of Spain has been the strength of the *patria chica*, the regional homeland. The French traveller Barthelémy Joly commented on it already in 1604 : "Among themselves the Spaniards are bitterly divided, each preferring his own province to that of his fellow and , pushing their desire to be different to an extreme, make more of their nations than we do in France."[2] Joly is using the word 'nation' here in its medieval sense, of a group of people distinguished by race, language or custom but united by religion or political allegiance. The centrifugal force of the Spanish 'nations' poses something of a question. As Menéndez Pidal, doyen of the historiography of Spain, has pointed out, neither geography nor culture will quite explain it. The peninsula was admittedly one of the most incommunicable terrains in pre-industrial Europe, carved up by its famous sierras into valleys and plains, with no navigable rivers to link them together. But the nations of Spain straddle the mountains (Catalonia, Valencia) and turn their backs on the possibility of riverine communication (Portugal and Castile, linked by the Duero and Tagus, bitterly divided by history and culture). Meanwhile, the centuries-long wars of reconquest of the peninsula from the hands of the Arabs (711 - 1492 A.D.)

fostered an American-style pattern of migration of peoples, so that, compared with France or Italy, Spain is "the Latin country in which the diversity of tongues is the least, relative to the size of the territory."[3] Anyway, language would not explain the early formation of the Spanish kingdoms - not Navarre with its mixture of Latin-dialect and Basque, nor León, which always incorporated Galicia (tied by language to Portugal).

The focus of this paper is on Valencia, one of the autonomous communities within Spain at the present day. As its greatest modern writer, Joan Fuster, put it in his pioneering study of 1962, "There is a question which we have always asked ourselves at some time or another: what are Valencians? what are we, the Valencians?"[4] He described a process of Castilianization, political and cultural, which had been going on for centuries, but which had stopped short of the complete absorption of a very distinctive Mediterranean people. Valencia presents itself on the map as a ring of mountains, created partly by the break-up and fall of the high Castilian tableland to the sea, enfolding bits and pieces of coastal plain. It had been welded into a polity under Arab masters in the central Middle Ages. From 1021 two kings carved out dominions in this territory, after the collapse of the great Caliphate of Cordoba, which had maintained the old unity of Iberia, created by the Romans and Visigoths. One emir arose in Valencia itself, and another in Denia, sharing jurisdiction over what we would now recognise as the Valencian lands. In further internecine struggles, the emirate of Denia was absorbed by that of Murcia. The Christian reconquest of the thirteenth century was complicated by the fact that the Murcians surrendered to the king of Castile (1243), while the north of Valencia was occupied by the Catalans and Aragonese under their great monarch, James I. The latter's triumphal entry into the city of Valencia in 1238 is the official birthday of the modern community, though it was not until 1305 that Alicante and its hinterland would be separated from Murcia and joined to it. This new frontier corresponded to some extent to linguistic reality, since Alicante had been settled by Catalan, not Castilian speakers. But the political frontier did not follow the nationality of the settlers exactly, and it was blurred even further in the nineteenth century when, for reasons of administrative convenience, the Castilian speakers of Villena (1836) and Requena (1851) were attached to the provinces of Alicante and Valencia respectively.

The human geography of this frontier territory was as complex as its physical counterpart. In the first place, large numbers of Berber peoples - Arabic-speaking and Muslim in religion - were allowed to live on in what had been their homeland. Christian resettlement was slow and not completed until after 1609, when the native population was finally expelled. It numbered at that time approximately 125,000 people, as compared with some 250,000 Christians. The latter had filtered down over the centuries from their places of origin - Catalan speakers occupying the mountainous borderland with Catalonia and the coastal plains as far south as Alicante, Aragonese speakers settling in the hill country along the roads leading south from their mountain homes. This human movement probably consolidated itself over many generations. The novelist Blasco Ibáñez describes the lure of the Mediterranean lowlands for the Aragonese peasantry in the nineteenth century: "To head for Valencia was to follow the path of riches, and the name of the city would come up in all the conversations of the poorer Aragonese families during those evenings when the snow lay on the ground and they huddled round their smoking log fires..."[5] A quick look at the *Libros de Avecindamiento*, the registers of citizenship accorded to selected immigrants to the city of Valencia before about 1600, would suggest that, in the 1590s at least, these came to a large extent from the hill country to the north - the Maestrazgo, Teruel, Aragon, and beyond there the Pyrenees and the Massif Central. Catalan speakers would have made their way in chiefly by sea - from the Balearic Islands, not least. The Crown of Aragon was still, therefore, a human as well as a political unity. The dynastic union with Castile had made less impact. A petition of Requena (later to be incorporated in the province of Valencia, as we noted above, but then very much part of the kingdom of Castile) to the Cortes of 1629, noted that Valencia was the nearest big town with nunneries where it could place its daughters. But it warned of the drain of currency 'abroad' in dowries and lamented "the unhappiness of the nuns themselves at having to live among people of a different nation (*nación estraña*)."[6] Meanwhile the guilds of Valencia had various discriminatory tariffs against outsiders: the silk weavers charged fees of six Valencian pounds for the master's diploma to the sons of existing masters, thirty-six to other natives of the kingdom of Valencia, sixty to other "Spaniards" and eighty to outright foreigners.[7]

In his study of the trade of Valencia under Philip III (1598-1621), Alvaro Castillo has brought out well the importance of the Mediterranean Sea in giving a certain unity to the fractured coastline. The metropolitan city gathered into itself, as it were, threads of exchange running north to Catalonia and Languedoc and out to the Balearic Islands. The landlocked highlands of Aragon sent down their wheat to Tortosa at the mouth of the River Ebro, their timber to Vinaroz, for onward trans-shipment to Valencia.[8] Sicily, part of the old Crown of Aragon in the later Middle Ages, supplied Valencia with a third of her wheat. Somewhat more remote, perhaps, were Castile (important as a supplier of Atlantic fish) and Portugal (spices). Castile linked up with Valencia more by way of Alicante, from where merchants would freight the goods on to the big city, and overland, selling mutton on the hoof and buying precious panniers of silk. But whereas the Aragonese herds wintered in the Valencian lowlands, the Castilians did not.

Much more research needs to be done into the whole pattern of human migration and exchange of goods in this area. But the emergence of a kingdom in Valencia in the Middle Ages was surely above all a result of political rather than economic considerations. The Aragonese barons, who had constituted the feudal cavalry with which James I conquered Valencia from the Moor, wanted to incorporate their conquests into the kingdom of Aragon. The creation of a separate polity was largely the work of James, an authentic representative of the emerging concept of royal sovereignty, allied to Roman law, which one can find in other parts of medieval Europe at this time. James' struggle against feudal indiscipline is memorably preserved for posterity in his memoirs, the *Libre dels Fets*, one of the great documents of medieval kingship. In 1239 he endowed his new conquests with a political personality through the issue of a code of Roman law, which was revised and published in definitive form in 1271 as the *Furs*. This document became the bedrock of Valencian identity and historical memory. It gave Valencia a single law, coinage, system of measurement, and a single official calendar, constituting "the real beginnings of the kingdom of Valencia."[9] In practice it would take many more generations before the Aragonese barons or the Muslims (who had been guaranteed their own law) would accept the new arrangements.

Indeed, the struggle to impose the *Furs* came to acquire enormous significance in its own right, forging the personality of Valencia in an interesting way during the later Middle Ages. The city of Valencia came to define itself as the bulwark of good government against feudal indiscipline, sometimes in alliance with the monarchy, but occasionally having to call to order those kings who seemed ready to betray their own God-given authority. The chronicle of King Peter the Ceremonious (1336-87) recalled how his father and step-mother had been humiliated by the legendary Vinatea, magistrate of the city of Valencia, when they had proposed giving away part of the royal domain as a fief for Peter's step-brother. The Queen, protesting that in her native Castile Vinatea would have been sent immediately to the block, was reprimanded by her husband: "Dear queen, our people is free and not subjugated like the people of Castile...for we look upon them as good vassals and companions."[10] This freedom of the Valencians was consolidated by the sheer financial strength of the great maritime city - to whose merchants the political theorist Francesc Eiximenis (1340-1409) penned a notable hymn of praise as the backbone of the commonwealth. It was embodied in the classic institutions borrowed from James I's Catalan homeland - a strong parliament (*Corts*) and a system of municipal government which allowed considerable power to merchants and guilds.

The hegemony of the city in a feudal hinterland was reflected in the supremacy of Catalan as a vehicle of culture and government, eclipsing Aragonese and, of course, Arabic. Indeed, most medieval Catalan literature was actually written in Valencia. James I had ordered it to be used as the language of administration instead of Latin as early as 1264, and the Aragonese-speaking towns gradually followed this lead during the fourteenth century, employing Catalan in official documents. The official birthday of the kingdom was celebrated as 9 October 1238, when the mosques of the chief city were reconsecrated to Christian worship ten days after the king had accepted its capitulation. The official sermon at the annual commemoration was always given in Catalan, even after the language had gone into decline as a literary medium.

The kingdom of Valencia at the end of the Middle Ages - in her 'golden age' of the fifteenth century - reposed on a somewhat uneasy equilibrium between a dynamic city state and a feudal, semi-colonial hinterland. A leading historian of early modern Valencia, Joan Reglà, has talked of a 'dualism' - a fluctuation from age to age in the relative weighting of one side or the other in the Valencian balance.[11] Certainly, after the union of Castile and Aragon, with the rise of Habsburg imperialism and the Castilian model of absolute monarchy and religious intolerance, the Valencian 'city state' seemed doomed, like so many of its counterparts in early modern Europe. One of the symptoms of decline from the Renaissance onwards was the eclipse of the Catalan language. The development has sometimes been seen as inevitable, with the rise of Castilian as the language of the court and of a lively culture, increasingly diffused through the medium of print. But the medium of expression can hardly be divorced from the content. Castilian served as a vehicle of ideas about life and society which came from the particular religious, crusading and voyaging traditions of its people. As Joan Fuster has suggested, the Castilianisation of Valencia from the Renaissance onwards reflected a wider problem: the failure of the local elite to maintain that spirit of enquiry which had distinguished it in previous centuries.[12] Valencia was to produce in Juan Luis Vives (1492-1540) the last great flowering of her old genius. Vives, though an exile in northern Europe for most of his life (his family were Jewish converts and pursued by the Inquisition), reflects the vigour of a distinguished group of Renaissance scholars within Valencia itself. These men - Oliver, Conquers, Furió Ceriol, among others - desired to apply the moral lesson of the Scriptures and the Classics to the reform of man and society. But their Spain followed another path: obedience to a Castilian monarchy and a Castilian-inspired church.

The reasons for this development are, of course, too complex to be explored fully in the present short paper. But one may note that the great revolt of 1519-22 in Valencia, the *Germanías* or 'Brotherhoods', sought for the last time to enforce the hegemony of the city state over its feudal and Moorish hinterland. The collapse of the revolt strengthened the moral authority of the nobility within Valencia - an authority dangerously dependent, though, on the support of the crown. It was the Catholic Kings, protagonists of the Counter Reformation, who now imposed on the Valencian lords the forcible conversion to Christianity of their Moorish peasantry and - when that did not work - the expulsion of these same peasants to North Africa (1609). The Valencia which was taking shape in the sixteenth century was far removed from the city state of the Middle Ages. It is, indeed, the development of the state itself which was to be a feature of the new age, shaping other kinds of social relations and the religious sanctions used to bolster these.

One of the most significant Valencian political theorists of the time was Tomás Cerdán de Tallada, member of a local gentry family and a magistrate of the Valencian Audiencia or high court. His great work of 1604 on "Rules of State" was concerned to strengthen the authority of his master, the king, for the good of all Valencians. He drew a distinction between the 'commonwealth' and the 'state'. While the former represented the self-governing corporate institutions of a loosely federated society - guilds, towns, lordships - and was regulated by the traditional laws or *Furs*, the state was very much the king's 'estate' : the patrimony and the corps of servants on which the king could rely to adjust anomalies in the society at large. The king worked by equity rather than law, interpreting the 'spirit' of the *Furs* for the good of all. This defence of an absolute monarchy rested on the belief that society was suffering the malaise of forces of disintegration. Cerdán identified at least two in his own day: a new materialism, fostered by the growth of a money economy, which was leading to unbridled individualism and a breakdown of moral cohesion, and, allied to this, the spread of religious heterodoxy which threatened to overturn all hierarchies.[13]

Cerdán's vision was unnecessarily apocalyptic, but his emphasis on a new policing of the citizen by the forces of the state captured a major shift in the structure of the European polity. Taxation, the army, the courts of law were beginning to give European 'nations' more material frontiers than they had had in the Middle Ages. The most visible symbol of Valencia as a state was, after all, the handsome Renaissance palace of the *Generalitat* - the 'Generality of the Kingdom' - set up to administer the standing taxes required for the defence of the community. Defence was traditionally the king's business, but from the middle of the fourteenth century the cost of warfare had outrun the resources of the Crown of Aragon. Parliament - the Corts - was needed so often to supplement the deficit that it eventually had to establish permanent customs duties. Separate from the tolls which belonged to the royal patrimony, these duties were to be administered by a standing committee of parliament, the *Diputació de la Generalitat*, drawn equally from the estates of clergy, nobles and towns. The principle of the collaboration of all in collective self-defence was taken further in the course of the sixteenth century, with the building of a series of coastal towers against the Barbary corsairs and of a militia to patrol them. Administering its own taxes, the *Generalitat* went on in the sixteenth century to assume wider responsibilities for public welfare - protection against plague or famine, subsidising of fiestas, paying for deputations of protest to the king against infraction of the *Furs*.[14] In other words, a fiscal state was beginning to emerge in the little kingdom around the time of the Renaissance. The only question was who would actually control it.

The Corts, composed of representatives of the three estates (clergy, nobles and towns), were supposed to ratify changes in laws or taxes, and each king had to come to Valencia at his accession to swear to uphold the *Furs*. The sessions were always a forum for expression of the great 'love' which united a monarch and his people. The dynastic union with Castile did not seem to make an immediate difference here. The Valencians told 'their' prince, the Emperor Charles V, of their gratitude for his chivalric endeavours against France and for his defence of the Catholic faith against German Protestants and Ottoman Turks. The Corts of 1585 were profuse in their expressions of devotion to Philip II, on whose life "depends the whole welfare not only of Your Majesty's own kingdoms and monarchy but rather of Christendom as a whole and the universal church."[15]

But, underneath the rhetoric, one could detect the tension which was soon to call into question the nature of the state itself. In the first place the Corts were only prepared to offer Philip II 100,000 Valencian pounds for his "outstanding and heroic enterprises" - a free grant out of their love and not because they were obliged to give him anything (as they were fond of stressing). But this sum had not changed over the last hundred years, during which time prices had quadrupled. The problem came to a head in the early seventeenth century as an increasingly bankrupt monarchy looked around wildly for funds to stave off the disintegration of its power in Europe. The printed memorial distributed by Olivares to the Corts of 1626 spoke of the need for a more permanent arrangement - a 'Union of Arms' between the different provinces of the empire. If Valencia merely gave what it chose, then the Spanish Monarchy would be less secure than a shifting alliance of sovereign states. Even Venice, he noted, had to enter into firmer commitments for its own security: how could Valencia be different? In a secret memorandum of 1624 Olivares had followed through the logic of this line of thinking. His master, Philip IV, must aim to become king of 'Spain' - that is, "reduce the kingdoms which now make up Spain to the state and laws of Castile." The customs barriers were an impediment to economic development; the right of the provinces to be governed only by native sons was a recipe for bad government.[16]

There were two issues here. One was the point made by Cerdán de Tallada that good government required a strengthening of royal authority. The other was whether that authority could be exercised by Valencians within Valencia. Cerdán de Tallada was aware that Madrid was now the *patria común* (common fatherland) of all the different peoples which owed allegiance to the crown ; but he was concerned - like his fellow Valencian and previous constitutional theorist, Furió Ceriol (1559) - that the Valencians should be well represented in the councils of the king and that for most local matters Valencians be subject to Valencian magistrates. The example he gave of Christ being referred for judgment by Pilate to the Jewish king Herod may not have been particularly illuminating, but the drift of his thought was clear enough.

There were sufficient tensions building up within the Baroque state to make it apparent that the old constitutional arrangements could not go on indefinitely. The growing weight of Catholic orthodoxy and court culture gave the Valencian elite a certain openness to Castilian influences, which helped lay the basis of later political change. Between 1580 and 1620 Valencia became the setting for some of the finest Castilian-language poetry and plays, written and read by an elite which was in harmony with courtly ideas of order and hierarchy. The outstanding history of the kingdom composed at this time by Gaspar Escolano (1610-11), parish priest and member of a patrician family, reflects a certain dualism of the Valencian tradition: a pride in order and good law, combined with an interest in the heroism of the old feudal families.[17] There is patriotism here: an attachment to the landscape and the institutions of a beloved homeland. But there is also, perhaps, a certain distrust of popular disorder and a respect for hierarchy, which would make it easier for the patricians and nobles among whom Escolano lived and worked to identify with their fellows in Castile than with their underlings nearer home. The historian of the

Generalitat, Martínez Aloy, tracing the decline of the Valencian Corts and the rise of the power of the monarchy over this period, blamed the lack of social cohesion within Valencia itself. The revolt of the *Germanías* had badly frightened the patricians, while the existence of the Inquisition made it difficult, "in any debate over infringement of the old laws, to call into question the authority of the king."[18] It was in the name of good government that Philip V (1700-46) eventually abolished the autonomy of Valencia in 1707. The Valencians, like the Catalans and Aragonese, had given a hostage to fortune by backing the Habsburg candidate in the War of the Spanish Succession - which did not endear them to Philip. But the protest of the local elites that they had been loyal to the Bourbons all along and had been fighting off yet another social revolt by their peasantry and lower classes (while true, up to a point), could not change the king's mind. The real issue, as expressed in his decree of 1707, was "my desire to reduce all the kingdoms of Spain to a common pattern of law, usages, customs and courts, all equally administered by the laws of Castile, which have won such praise and acceptance throughout the world."[19]

A common view is that Valencian patriotism went into decline during the eighteenth century, as the people concentrated on the economic advantages of union with Castile and a more efficient administration. The old lobbying for privileges was, however, still to be found. In 1760 the Valencian representatives at the swearing of Charles III as king of Spain, joined their colleagues from Barcelona, Zaragoza and Mallorca in protesting against the 'Castilianization' of Spain. The Castilians claimed that there should be one law -their own - for the peninsula since it was united under one ruler, they alleged. But let them remember the example of the human body, a harmonious integration of very different parts. Just as the Indians of America were given preachers who understood the native tongues, so the Catalans and Valencians were entitled to have their native clergy. And the Castilians were taking an unfair proportion of the offices in the Monarchy as a whole.[20]

This was an old voice which had been heard as early as 1412, when the Valencians had protested that they were not getting enough appointments compared with the Catalans to the household of the kings of Aragon.[21] But a rather different kind of patriotism was taking shape in the age of the Enlightenment, reflecting the changing composition of the local elite. The old feudal nobility had very often migrated by 1700 - indeed by 1622, to judge by a complaint of the city of Valencia - to the court. Those who took their place were wealthy farmers and professionals. Typical of the new elite was the leading figure of the Valencian Enlightenment, Gregori Mayans (1699-1781), who from his home town of Oliva maintained a lively correspondence with his peers in the rest of Spain and Europe. As Joan Fuster has suggested, there was a diffusion of reading and writing on a vaster scale than before beyond the walls of the city of Valencia to small-town elites scattered over the kingdom of Valencia as a whole. Such men were beginning to explore in their writings the material and cultural characteristics of the common people among whom they lived. And they were encouraged in this task by a government in Madrid which now believed that the prosperity of the state depended on the welfare of the common man. The Valencians of the later eighteenth century threw themselves with enthusiasm into the task of exploring the geography and history of their region. Marc Antoni Orellana (1713-1813), Joaquín Lorenzo Villanueva (1757-1837), Antonio Joseph Cavanilles (1757-1837), are only a few of those regenerating an awareness of the Valencian landscape and monuments.

Such men were not nationalists and Valencia to them was just one part of Spain. Gregori Mayans was interested in republishing the Catalan classics of the Middle Ages, but he had no wish to use the Valencian language in his own writing, which was aimed at the regeneration of Spain as a whole. But there was an alternative tradition alive in eighteenth-century Valencia, which owed much to Montesquieu perhaps, and which conceived of progress as a return to native founts of law. The respect for tradition, the belief in law as a manifestation of the genius of a people, would manifest itself in reaction to the desire of the enlightened elites for the creation of a new Spain. It was in 1808, with the Napoleonic invasion of Spain and the collapse of the old regime, when a blueprint had to be worked out for the future, that a major debate began about the nature of the regions and their historical traditions. Against the majority of his Valencian colleagues at the reforming Cortes of Cadiz, the deputy Francisco Javier Borrull (1745-1838) advocated that true progress could only be achieved by drawing upon the traditions of the past - that is, by resurrecting the medieval *Furs*, which embodied guarantees of both order and liberty.[22]

The ideas of Borrull were not totally incompatible with those of the liberals. The Romantic temperament of the early nineteenth century drew in Spain and Europe on the philosophy of the Enlightenment, as well as reacting in some degree against it. It emphasized the study of the natural environment and the understanding of the individual in relation to that environment. Its interest in history could be both a search for stability, as with Borrull, and also an invitation to the betterment of the common man. Thus an important milestone in the Valencians' understanding of their past was to be provided by the liberal politician Vicente Boix (1813-80) in his classic three-volume history of the region, published in 1845.[23] As he explained in his introduction, his aim was to provide an insight into the turbulent upheavals of his own day and to save from oblivion the crumbling institutions of a glorious past.

Nostalgia for that past was reflected from the 1830s in the revival of the Valencian language as a vehicle of culture. It was undergoing something of a renaissance anyway with the politicization of the revolutionary age. Liberal journals like *El Mole*, founded in 1837, appealed to the man in the street in the language of conversation - a Valencian much corrupted by Castilianisms and without literary pretensions. The cultural renaissance or *Renaixença* was much more self-conscious. As its first poet, Tomás Villarroya (1812-56), wrote: "In your praise (Valencia) I shall open my lips/And intone a song which comes down from heaven,/In the forgotten language of my ancestors,/Which is sweeter then honey." It was mostly a section of the middle class which threw itself into the new movement, reviving the medieval 'Floral Games' in 1859, at which poets would read hymns of praise to the glory of the Valencian past, its saints, warriors and dutiful peasants. The greatest figure in this group was Teodor Llorente (1836-1911), founder of the conservative newspaper *Las Provincias* (1865) and a rather fine Catalan-language poet. The curious divorce between his political support for the conservative governments in Madrid and his poetic recreation of the lost world of *Furs* perhaps corresponded to the caution of the small landowning-class which dominated Valencia in the nineteenth century. His colleague, Ferrer Bigne, penned a criticism of the more overt politicization of Catalan nationalism in 1874: "Do not seek to splinter the planks of our History,/ For hate and rancour never come from noble hearts" [24]

Undoubtedly Valencia failed to move from a quite rich cultural *Renaixença* to a political nationalism of the Catalan kind, and the reasons are complex and interesting. The southern kingdom did not experience the social transformations of her northern neighbour during the nineteenth century : Valencia lacked the industrial bourgeoisie and working class of Barcelona. On the other hand, such economic development as there was - a tremendous increase in the plantation and export of citrus fruits - rather drove the Valencian middle classes towards free trade and against the protectionist tariffs demanded by Catalan manufactures. Valencia was torn, as it were, between cultural sympathy with the Catalan past and profound antipathy towards Catalan politics. There was, indeed, a certain regional identity beginning to emerge among the Valencian bourgeoisie. One of its most influential spokesmen was Faustí Barberà, whose essay of 1910 on "regionalism and Valencianism" drew a distinction between the Spanish 'state' and the "very different nationalities", marked out by language and history, of which it was composed.[25] The Valencians must guard against a new 'absolutism' from Madrid, more dangerous that that of 1707 because based now in theory on parliamentary liberties. His invitation to the study of Valencian history was very much in tune with the great wave of publication of old chronicles and regional monographs around this time, which were laying the groundwork for much academic study in our own time. The treatise of Martínez Aloy on the Generalitat, cited earlier in this paper, is just one example of a new desire on the part of the traditionalist middle class to make the Valencians aware of their past.

That past was interpreted by the conservative middle classes as a harmonious blend of liberty and order, based on the solidarity of the local community. As a philosophy it had certain affinities with the Catholic corporatism then gathering ground in Europe, with its distrust of wild capitalism and the godless state. To work as a political ideology it would have to make a sufficiently broad appeal to the various groupings in Valencian society. But it faced a challenge here in that there was an alternative agenda available - that of the Left. Constantí Llombart (1848-93) was the heir, in a sense, of Vicente Boix and the liberal Romantics of the earlier part of the century. For him, true democracy would mean creating a Valencian community aware of its own traditions. Founder of the *Rat Penat* ("The Bat"), the club and newspaper which adopted as its title the emblem of James I, founder of the Kingdom, in 1878, he was eager to see the educated classes write not only troubadour-style poetry for themselves but also good theatre for the ordinary people. The latter went to see comic sketches written in colloquial Valencian anyway, and Llombart's aim was to incorporate this popular culture with a more intellectual exploration of life as a Valencian. This cultural programme had enormous political implications and never really got off the ground. Instead, the old spectre of Valencian history, social division, returned to haunt its present. The hero of the people around 1900 was the great novelist Vicente Blasco Ibáñez (1867-1928), editor of the influential journal *El Pueblo* and republican politician. While some of the best pages of literature describing the Valencian people come from his pen, he was bitterly anti-clerical and anti-establishment. The programme of the *Rat Penat*, increasingly associated with Llorente and the 'medievalists' rather than with Llombart, seemed to him a waste of time. While it was admirable to study the past, "obstinately to recreate ruins is an archaeological pastime, a dead thing", and a selling of the common man into the hands of a reactionary, clericalist bourgeoisie.[26]

In a sense, twentieth-century Valencia has been trying to come to terms ever since with this twin legacy, of conservative localism and radical cosmopolitanism. Blasco Ibáñez may have been a diversion, in the sense that from Boix through to Llombart and beyond to Blasco Ibáñez's bitter rival and fellow republican, Rodrigo Soriano, there has always been a radical tradition within the region committed to a better understanding of the local community. But the Valencian experience reminds us that language and history are not necessarily unifying forces, and that national self-awareness requires to be built on firmer social and political foundations.

[1] Pierre Vilar, *Catalunya dins l'Espanya Moderna* (4 vols., Barcelona 1964), I, p.32.
[2] "Voyage en Espagne, 1603-4", *Revue Hispanique,* XX, (1909), p. 618.
[3] Ramón Menéndez Pidal, *Los Españoles en la Historia* (Madrid 1959, new edn.1971),p.147.
[4] *Nosaltres els Valencians* (Barcelona 1964),p.13.
[5] *Arroz y Tartana* (1894, new edn. Madrid 1967),p.28.
[6] *Actas de las Cortes de Castilla*, 48 (1929),p.385-6.
[7] Luis Tramoyeres Blasco, *Instituciones Gremiales: su origen y organización en Valencia* (Valencia 1889),p.218-21.
[8] *Tráfico Marítimo y Comercio de Importación en València a Comienzos del Siglo XVII,* (Madrid 1967).
[9] Manuel Sanchis Guarner, *La Ciutat de Valencia* (Valencia 1972), p.83.
[10] Ibid.,p.90.
[11] *Aproximació a la Història del País Valencià*(Valencia 1968),pp.115-43.
[12] Joan Fuster, *La Decadència al País Valencià* (Barcelona 1976).

[13] Tomás Cerdán de Tallada, *Veriloquium en Reglas de Estado* (Valencia 1604).

[14] José Martínez Aloy, *La Diputación de la Generalidad del Reino de Valencia* (Valencia 1930).

[15] *Cortes Valencianas del Reinado de Felipe II*, ed. Emilia Salvador (Valencia 1974), p.152, "Offerta de la Cort" 1585.

[16] *Memoriales y Cartas del Conde Duque de Olivares*, ed. John H. Elliott and José F. de la Peña, vol. 1. (Madrid 1978), documents 4 and 9.

[17] *Década Primera de la Historia de Valencia*, 1610-11 (facsimile edn., 6 vols., Valencia 1972).

[18] *La Diputación*, p.354-5 ; cf. p. 285-6.

[19] Cited in Sanchis Guarner, *La Ciutat de València*, p.347.

[20] Joan Reglà, *Introducció a la Història de la Corona d'Aragó* (Palma de Mallorca 1973), p.174-6.

[21] Fuster, *Nosaltres*,p. 125.

[22] Manuel Ardit Lucas, *Revolución Liberal y Revuelta Campesina* (Barcelona 1977), p.188.

[23] Vicente Boix, *Historia de la Ciudad y Reino de Valencia* (3 vols., Valencia 1845).

[24] Alfons Cucó, *Aspectes de la Política Valenciana en el Segle XIX* (Barcelona 1965), P.8-9. Cf. Ramir Reig, "La invenció de València", *Afers* 31 (1998) pp.569-85.

[25] Cucó., p.27-8.

[26] Cucó, p.54-5.

CATALONIA AND SPAIN

JOAN-LLUÍS MARFANY
(*University of Liverpool*)

A very distinctive use of the term *la terra* is evidence of the existence of a strong paleo-nationalism in early modern Catalonia, which in turn reflects the existence of well-developed state institutions. The fact that it remained the language of those institutions saved Catalan from the fate of most other similar languages in the European monarchies of the period and provided a further strengthening factor for that paleonationalism. After the same institutions were lost, together with the laws of the land, in 1714, following defeat in the War of Spanish Succession, Catalan paleo-nationalism appears to have died out. It did linger, however, even if in a self-suppressed form, so that, when in the nineteenth century Catalan liberals eagerly joined in the building of the Spanish nation, it resurfaced strongly to tinge their own idea of Spain. Catalans, led in this by their industrial bourgeoisie, were prepared to sacrifice many things in the endeavour, including the written use of their own language, but they also insisted on incorporating their own historical myths (many of which were highly anti-Castilian) in the common national mythology and even wanted to give them pride of place. This was totally unacceptable to a Spanish nationalism which had always been based, since its distant origins in the imperial paleo-nationalism of the Habsburg monarchy, on the confusion between Spain and Castile. Catalans, however, felt justified in their pretensions by the not unreasonable belief that Catalan industry alone could provide the material basis and the leading impulse for the transformation of Spain into a modern, fully-fledged nation. The resulting conflict, aggravated by the clash of interests between industrial Catalonia and agricultural Spain, proved the decisive stumbling block in the building of the Spanish nation.

CATALUÑA Y ESPAÑA

JOAN-LLUÍS MARFANY
(University of Liverpool)

Incluso estrictamente en lo que cae dentro del estrecho marco fijado a mi propia intervención, la ponencia del profesor Da Cal está tan llena de ideas interesantes, provocativas incluso, que me resulta difícil decidir por dónde empezar. Mi principal reserva tal vez sea que, aun cuando estoy de acuerdo que "las formulaciones patrióticas se remontan a mucho antes que la Revolución Francesa," en mi opinión es más que fórmulas y argumentos lo que, en el caso español, se hereda de ese pasado. En este sentido, me parece que su ponencia tiende a menosvalorar la importancia de un paleonacionalismo - para usar su propia terminología - específicamente catalán que trasciende de mucho los límites de los otros particularismos contemporáneos y que constituye por ello uno de los factores más cruciales en el proceso de formación del estado-nación español.

Para estas cosas siempre he tenido gran fe en el método, de tiempo preconizado por Pierre Vilar, de observar con cuidado los cambios que se producen en el sentido de ciertas palabras clave, no tanto en los textos jurídicos o institucionales o en la teoría política como, dentro de lo posible, en el uso común.[1] En lo que al nacionalismo respecta, el cambio fundamental tiene que ser el desplazamiento semántico que se da en la palabra 'nación', del viejo significado etimológico de "la gente nacida en un mismo territorio" - el cual puede variar entre un pueblo y medio mundo - a la designación del propio territorio en su congruencia perfecta con la gente que lo puebla, con lo que se implica lo 'natural' de su organización en estado soberano. Es un desplazamiento que se puede seguir muy bien en el uso inglés del siglo XVII (por ejemplo, en los diarios de Samuel Pepys o el cuáquero George Fox), pero que también se puede rastrear, si bien en formas más implícitas, en otras partes y otros textos - en Montaigne, sin ir más lejos.[2] Yo no he visto la palabra 'nación'

---

[1] Pierre VILAR, "Patrie et nation dans le vocabulaire de la guerre d'Indépendance espagnole",*Annales Historiques de la Révolution Française* (1971), 503-34 (versión española en*Hidalgos, amotinados y guerrilleros* [Barcelona: Crítica, 1982], 211-52) y *Assaigs sobre la Catalunya del segle XVIII* (Barcelona: Curial, 1973), 133-71.

[2] Es interesante observar cómo evoluciona en Pepys la vacilación entre 'the state', 'the kingdom', y 'the nation' como sinónimos: en los últimos años del diario, a medida que Pepys se siente cada vez más identificado con el estado del cual es alto funcionario y a medida que crece su I insatisfacción con el rey y la corte, 'the nation' se convierte con muccho en el término más

usada en este segundo sentido en la Cataluña de la época moderna (aunque es verdad que ni yo ni nadie nos hemos dedicado a comprobarlo sistemáticamente), pero hay una antigua, y muy distintiva, expresión política, *"la terra"*, *"la tierra"*, que había adquirido allí, para el siglo XVII, unas claras connotaciones que transmiten la misma idea de congruencia, entre nación, en el sentido etimológico, y territorio, legitimadora de la soberanía política - o por lo menos de una participación en ella. *"La terra"* había venido siendo de tiempo la manera abreviada de referirse, según los casos, a la comunidad de los súbditos, a su representación en los tres brazos de cortes, o a la institución administradora de sus intereses en los intermedios entre cortes, siempre sobre todo en contraposición a *"el Rei"* y en frecuente sustitución - lo cual no deja de tener ya su interés - de las fórmulas más correctas, técnicas o incluso oficiales, podríamos decir, de *"el General"* o *"la Generalitat"*, *"els Braços"*, y *"la Diputació del General"*[3]. Pero en el curso del siglo XVI y principios del XVII, a medida que se enrarecía la relación entre las instituciones provinciales y la monarquía, también el término se fue identificando más claramente con el binomio "territorio+gente", hasta que, al llegar la guerra de 1640 a 1652, se hizo intercambiable, en la propaganda antifilipista, con "la patria", por Cataluña, claro está. El término, además, no quedaba confinado al vocabulario de las instituciones o de la literatura política, sino que entró en el uso corriente, donde en ocasiones adquirió claras connotaciones clasistas: *"Visca la terra!"* fue el grito de la muchedumbre cuyo tumulto en las calles de Barcelona señaló el comienzo del conflicto. Iba a ser también, años más tarde dentro del mismo siglo, el grito de guerra de la rebelión campesina.[4]

---

frecuente. Fox, por su parte, usa repetidamente la expresión "the four corners of the nation" y habla de ir a Escocia y a Irlanda – pero no, significativamente, a Gales – en términos de trasladarse a "otra nación".

[3] Ejemplos, sobre todo del primer caso, en el proceso de corte de la *Cort General de Montsó 1382-1384* ed. I.J. Baiges i Jardí *et al.* (Barcelona: Generalitat de Catalunya, 1992), 81, 91, 136, 174, 187, 188, 189, y 230. Es posible que el primero de dichos usos deba explicarse ante todo por la indefinición constitucional del estado catalán, que hacía imposible o incómodo el uso de términos más "técnicos" como reino o principado, aunque este último fuera habitual. De todos modos, el tema está por investigar y pudiera ser que el paso del sentido primero (= la universidad de los súbditos) al segundo (= los Brazos de Cortes) y al tercero (= la Diputación) constituyera ya un cambio histórico con implicaciones políticas (los ejemplos que yo tengo más presentes datan de la guerra civil de 1462-1472 y proceden del dietario de la Diputación, enemiga del rey). Para todo lo relacionado con las instituciones catalanas, véase Víctor FERRO, *El dret públic català. Les institutions a Catalunya fins al Decret de Nova Planta* (Vic: Eumo Editorial, 1987), especialmente, para lo que aquí interesa, pp. 19-24, 188-89, y 246-47.

[4] Sigo en todo esto los trabajos pioneros de Xavier TORRES i SANS, "Nacions sense nacionalisme: pàtria i patriotisme a l'Europa de l'Antic Règim", *Recerques*, 28 (1994), 83-89, "Pactisme i patriotisme a la Catalunya de la Guerra dels Segadors", *Recerques*, 32 (1995), 45-62, y "Dinastismo y patriotismo en la Cataluña de la Guerra de los Segadores: el testimonio de un zurrador barcelonés", de próxima aparición en *Actas de la IV reunión científica de la Asociación Española de Historia Moderna*. Véase también Lluís ROURA, "Un petit món en una província: el concepte de nació referit a la Catalunya del segle XVII", *L'Avenç*, 199 (1996), 6-11. Para el uso en asociación con rebeliones campesinas, Pierre VILAR, "Continuïtat històrica de la consciència nacional catalana", en su *Estat, nació, socialisme* (Barcelona: Curial, 1981), 60-80, esp. 72-74; Henry KAMEN, "Una insurrecció oblidada del segle XVII: l'alçament dels camperols catalans de l'any 1688",*Recerques*, 9 (1979), 11-28; Llorenç, FERRER i ALÓS, "L'avalot de les Faves a Manresa. Un moment de la revolta de la terra a Catalunya el 1688",

Para lo que aquí nos interesa, sin embargo, lo importante es el vínculo original - y, creo yo, fundamental - entre el concepto y una serie de 'constituciones' e instituciones políticas consideradas como "las propias" de una cierta gente. Lo que estoy intentando decir es que era porque los catalanes habían desarrollado, para el comienzo de la era moderna, algo muy parecido ya a un estado, aunque fuera imperfecto en razón de la casi permanente ausencia de su cabeza natural, por lo que también habían empezado a desarrollar un cierto sentimiento de lo que tal vez podríamos llamar ya nación.[5] Este no era, insisto, un mero particularismo tradicional que se interponía en el camino de un progresivo paleonacionalismo español, sino *otro* paleonacionalismo, alternativo y rival.

Este paleonacionalismo tenía una manifestación cultural que en cierto modo iba a ser la más permanente y a desempeñar un importante papel por sí misma. El profesor Da Cal escribe que "en la medida que el castellano era la lengua de la burocracia, los otros idiomas hablados pasaron a ser casi exclusivamente vehículos de expresión de las clases inferiores, de interés sobre todo para los clérigos interesados en garantizar la catequización y la ortodoxia dogmàtica y práctica de los campesinos," lo cual es absolutamente cierto, siempre y cuando se ponga todo el énfasis en las palabras iniciales. Porque, a diferencia de lo que ocurría en los otros antiguos reinos, en la Cataluña de los siglos XVI y XVII la lengua no sólo de la burocracia, sino de las instituciones en general, tanto laicas como eclesiásticas, siguió siendo la catalana. La alta cultura sí que estaba (casi) tan castellanizada como en las otras provincias, pero en Cataluña el catalán continuaba siendo, por decirlo con un anacronismo muy práctico, la lengua oficial. Esta asociación con las instituciones hizo de contrapeso al prestigio del castellano como lengua de la corte y garantizó que, incluso entre las clases más altas, la mayoría de los catalanes no vieran ninguna necesidad de

Recerques, 11 (1981), 125-35; y Jaume DANTÍ i RIU, *Aixecaments populars als Països Catalans (1687-1693)* (Barcelona: Curial, 1990).

[5] Lo indicó ya Pierre VILAR, *La Catalogne dans l'Espagne moderne*, 3 vols (Paris: S.E.V.P.E.N., 1962), I, 448-55 y *Estat, nació, socialisme* (Barcelona: Curial Edicions, 1982), 60-72. Véase también Núria SALES, *Els segles de la decadència. Història de Catalunya IV* (Barcelona: Edicions 62, 1989), 53-59 y 99-103. S. SOBREQUÉS VIDAL y J. SOBREQUÉS CALLICÓ, *La guerra civil catalana del segle XV*, 2 vols (Barcelona: Edicions 62, 1973), I, 260, ven ese sentimiento muy claro en el conflicto entre Juan II y la Generalitat y es cierto que en los *Dietaris de la Generalitat de Catalunya. Volum 1. Anys 1411 a 1539*, ed. Lluïsa Cases i Loscos et al. (Barcelona: Generalitat de Catalunya, 1994) la institución rebelde se refiere constantemente a sí misma como representante de todo el Principado o de "la terra". Pero no veo nada que justifique la afirmación de Francisco ELÍAS de TEJADA, *Las doctrinas políticas en la Cataluña medieval* (Barcelona: Aymá, 1950), 268, de que en el uso que hacen entonces los catalanes de "nación" se advierte ya "la superación del primitivo valor etnográfico de la palabra"

abandonar su propio idioma, salvo en determinadas circunstancias y para propósitos muy concretos.[6]

No sabemos prácticamente nada de lo que ocurrió con este paleonacionalismo en el curso del siglo XVIII. Por un lado, parece claro que la mayoría de los catalanes (si se me perdona la vaguedad) se adaptaron con bastante rapidez a la pérdida de sus instituciones y leyes, en un proceso grandemente facilitado por los cambios económicos que, en la segunda mitad del siglo, empezaron a empujar a la sociedad catalana hacia el despegue industrial. Es incluso razonable suponer, sobre todo a la luz de lo que iba a suceder a principios del siglo siguiente, que un considerable, y creciente, sector de la población catalana se sintió conquistado por la idea de la nación española y empezó a tomar parte activa en la creación de un sentimiento nacional español.[7] Y sin embargo, al mismo tiempo, hay pruebas de que la derrota de 1714 fue experimentada como el, en los anacrónicos términos del título del clásico sobre el tema, "fin de la nación catalana" y que este sentimiento, con la correspondiente amargura perduró a lo largo de todo el siglo.[8] El profesor Da Cal nos hace notar con toda razón el "viejo bagaje [ideológico] austracista" reciclado para uso antifrancés en las guerras de 1793-1795 y 1808-1814, pero no es sólo de austracismo de lo que deberíamos hablar: era el viejo paleonacionalismo catalán el que volvía a levantar cabeza.[9] Déjenme citar unas frases de una *Exortació zelosa als catalans* hecha (en catalán, obsérvese bien) en 1795 por el corregidor de Cervera, ante la invasión de las tropas de la Convención:

---

[6] El tema está por estudiar a fondo, pero, en espera de la continuación de la *Història de la llengua catalana* de Josep M. Nadal y Modest Prats, contamos con algunas aproximaciones e indicaciones uótiles en Núria SALES, *Senyors bandolers, miquelets i botiflers* (Barcelona: Empúries, 1984), 207-19; idem, "El catal, llengua no decadent", en *Història dels Paisos Catalans*, coordinada por A. Balcells (Barcelona: Edhasa, 1982); idem, *Els segles de la decadència*, 434-38; Henry KAMEN, *The Phoenix and the Flame* (New Haven/London: Yale University Press, 1993), 362-73; J.S. AMELANG, *Honoured Citizens of Barcelona* (Princeton, N.J.: Princeton University Press, 1986), 190-95, y Josep FONTANA, *La fi de l'Antic Règim i la industrialització (1787-1868)*. *Història de Catalunya*, V (Barcelona: Edicions 62, 1988), 93-97.

[7] J. MERCADER, *Els capitans generals (segle XVIII)*, 2a ed. (Barcelona: Vicens Vives, 1980), 94-95; VILAR, *La Catalogne*, I, 158-61, 670-79, 704-10, II, 555-66, y III, 559-66 y *Estat, nació socialisme*, 74-77.

[8] .Salvador SANPERE y MIQUEL, *Fin de la nación catalana*, (Barcelona: L'Avenç, 1905) ; SALES, *Senyors bandolers*, 143-44: y *Els segles de la decadència*, 431-34; Enric MOREU-REY, *El "memorial de greuges" del 1760* (Barcelona: Edicions d'Aportació Catalana, 1968); Ernest LLUCH, "La Catalunya del segle XVIII i la lluita contra l'absolutisme centralista. El Proyecto del Abogado General del Público de Francesc Romà i Rossell", *Recerques*, 1 (1970), 33-50. Los dietarios y misceláneas del barón de Maldá contienen también frecuentes muestras de ese sentimiento. La persistencia del odio a la Ciudadela construida por orden de Felipe V es otra de sus manifestaciones.

[9] Ángel OSSORIO y GALLARDO, *Historia del pensamiento político catalán durante la guerra de España con la República Francesa*, 2a ed. (Barcelona: Grijalbo, 1977), 117-31, 151-79, y esp. 195-202 y 252-61; Lluís ROURA i AULINAS, *Guerra Gran a la ratlla de França* (Barcelona: Curial, 1993), 135-36; Ferran SOLDEVILA, *Història de Catalunya*, 2a ed. en un vol. (Barcelona: Alpha, 1963), p.263-95.

Que, per ventura, ara que defensas una causa tan sagrada [es decir, la de la religión] *serás menos valent que al principi de aquesta centuria, quant purament* per interessos de la terra *combatias ab aqueix mateix enemic; quant li feyas pérdrer un numerós exércit en lo Ampurdà, lo escarmentabas debant las murallas de Gerona, lo atacabas a cos descubert, obligant-lo a deixar los puestos més fortificats, y, sitiant-lo, finalment, lo precisabas a rendir-te plazas fortíssimas que ocupaba en esta província?*[10]

Lo significativo es que fuera precisamente un tan emblemático representante de la Nueva Planta borbónica (o quizá incluso sus superiores jerárquicos) quien sintiera la conveniencia de apelar al recuerdo reprimido: quiere decir que el recuerdo estaba vivo y que todo el mundo lo sabía. Hay que añadir que el texto se dirige repetidamente a los catalanes, siempre como tales y nada más, exhortándoles a defender el territorio catalán y aduciendo para ello adecuados ejemplos de la historia de Cataluña. También hace uso abundante del término "la patria." El que no sale ni una vez, en cambio, es España.

Esa ambigüedad, sin duda alguna querida, se explica muy probablemente por el deseo de llegar a todos los sectores de la sociedad y en especial a los más bajos, que son siempre aquellos en los cuales confía el poder cuando de luchar se trata. En la literatura política dirigida a círculos más elevados la resurrección del paleonacionalismo catalán se presenta paradójicamente de la mano de algunas de las más tempranas manifestaciones de puro nacionalismo español, combinación que será habitual en el discurso del liberalismo español con base en Cataluña en su prolongada lucha por terminar con el Antiguo Régimen. Los liberales catalanes invitaban constantemente a sus compatriotas a abrazar su causa porque al hacerlo serían fieles a sus "catalanes antiguos, más amantes de la libertad" de lo que lo eran ellos mismos y porque, después de un "siglo de ignominia", la Constitución venía a vengar el viejo

---

[10] Reproducida en Josep M. LLOBET i PORTELLA, "La Guerra Gran contra la França revolucionària vista des de Cervera (1793-1795)", en *Església i societat a la Catalunya del segle XVIII* (Cervera: UNED, 1990), II, 287-290, en la p.287. El énfasis es mío. Se trata, en realidad, de la versión catalana de la proclama publicada en el *Diario de Barcelona* del 8-XII-1794 y reproducida fragmentariamente por OSSORIO, *Historia del pensamiento*, que da otros ejemplos semejantes en las pp. 203-06. Ignoro si la iniciativa de darla en catalán fue del propio corregidor Doyle o de alguna autoridad superior y si se aplicó a otros corregimientos.

agravio de 1714 y a "restituir" a los catalanes "al goce de nuestra antigua imprescriptible libertad".[11]

Esta es la triste paradoja de la desgraciada historia de la construcción de la nación española: el principal obstáculo a ella fue, no como quisieran los historiadores nacionalistas de uno y otro bando, un renacimiento de sentimiento nacional catalán que opusiera nación catalana a nación española, sino, al contrario, la entusiasmada adopción del nacionalismo español por parte de los catalanes. Lejos de ser, como se suele suponer, el primer despertar romántico y literario del nacionalismo catalán, la llamada Renaixença, el resurgimiento ochocentista de la literatura catalana, fue simplemente un vacío gesto simbólico compensatorio del mayor sacrificio que los catalanes estaban dispuestos a hacer y hacían en el altar de la común nación española: el de su propia lengua como vehículo de todo lo que no fuera asuntos domésticos y vida de relación no formal.[12] El problema, en realidad, era que los catalanes, encabezados por su burguesía, no sólo estaban dispuestos a sumarse a la construcción de la nación española, sino que querían estar al frente de ella y reclamaban para sí el papel principal en la empresa. Lo cual quería decir, y ahí estaba el escollo, darle una marcada orientación catalana. Los liberales catalanes aceptaban los mitos históricos básicos y los símbolos del nacionalismo español naciente (Numancia, el Cid, los comuneros, Lepanto, Bailén, Zaragoza), pero se empeñaban en añadir a ellos sus propios mitos nacionales, no sólo subsumiéndolos en una nueva mitología común, sino poniéndolos en lugar delantero.[13] El profesor Da Cal menciona "la nueva mezcla de nacionalismo español que servía a todas las opciones y dominaba la literatura, la retórica política, e incluso los nombres de las calles..." Pero ¿servía ese nacionalismo

---

[11] Las palabras citadas son de un suelto firmado O.A.U. y de Ramón MUNS y SERIÑÁ, "Observaciones sobre la antigua Constitución de Cataluña, leídas en una Sociedad literaria particular el día 11 de julio de 2820 [sic]", ambos en *Diario Constitucional*, 21-VIII-1821 y 17/18-VII-1820, respectivamente. Otro ejemplo del mismo tenor en Alberto GIL NOVALES, *Las sociedades patrióticas (1820-1823)*, 2 vols (Madrid: Tecnos, 1975), I, 286n. Esta combinación de patriotismo catalán y nacionalismo español ya se daba en Capmany, como ha señalado más de una vez Pierre Vilar, por ejemplo en "Estado, nación y patria en las conciencias españolas: historia y actualidad", en *Hidalgos*, 271-72. Para los años treinta formaba parte esencial de la ideología liberal al nivel más popular, como se puede ver por el anónimo diario *Successos de Barcelona (1822-1835)*, ed. J.M. Ollé Romeu (Barcelona: Curial, 1981), esp. 118, 129-30, y 181.

[12] Quien lo dude, que lea, o relea con ojos limpios de prejuicio, los discursos pronunciados por el presidente Milá y Fontanals y el secretario Bofarull en el episodio más fundamental y definitorio de esa *Renaixença*, los Juegos Florales fundacionales de 1859. Pueden verse en *La Renaixença. Fonts per al seu estudi* (Barcelona: Univesitat de Barcelona/Universitat Autònoma de Barcelona, 1984).

[13] Así, para excitar a los barceloneses a la defensa del régimen constitucional en peligro, tanto se invoca el recuerdo de Numancia (por ejemplo, en el himno patriótico cantado en el baile de máscaras dado en el teatro de la Santa Cruz el 6-II-1823 o en el título de "Numantinos Barceloneses" que encabeza la lista de "los ciudadanos que se hallen decididos a perecer antes que a ver dominar en la libre Barcelona tanto los enemigos interiores como los esteriores" [*Diario Constitucional*, 7-II y 23-I-1823]) como lo de las Vísperas Sicilianas, el príncipe de Viana, y la Guerra de los Segadores (por ejemplo en el "Artículo comunicado" firmado N.Z. en *Diario Constitucional*, 24-II-1823).

de veras a todas las opciones? Tomemos el caso de los nombres de las calles, puesto que de ellos hemos hablado. ¿Dónde se encuentra esa nomenclatura al servicio de la construcción de la nación? No por cierto en Madrid, donde las calles ochocentistas llevan nombres de políticos contemporáneos, sino en Barcelona, donde se apreciaba como es debido la importancia de la mitología en el nacionalismo. Sólo que en Barcelona los mitos españoles compartidos eran relegados a la periferia oriental del moderno Ensanche, donde la urbanización no era más aún que un lejano proyecto: Padilla, Lepanto, Dos de Mayo. Las mejores posiciones, en la zona adyacente a la ciudad vieja, quedaban reservadas a la celebración de las gloriosas instituciones del propio pasado "nacional": Gran Vía de las Cortes Catalanas (así, en castellano, naturalmente), Diputación, Consejo de Ciento.[14] Peor aún: el gesto de buena voluntad hacia los mitos comunes era más que contrapesado por el bautizo de calles en posición mucho menos marginal, hacia el límite occidental (y una incluso en el mismísimo centro), en recuerdo de algunos de los mitos más característicamente anticastellanos del repertorio histórico catalán: Claris, Casanova, Villarroel, el Conde de Urgel inicuamente despojado en 1412 de su legítima herencia real por la castellana dinastía de los Trastámaras.[15]

Una tan desfachatada, provocativa, inyección de mitología catalana era sencillamente inaceptable para un nacionalismo español que, desde sus lejanos orígenes en el paleonacionalismo imperial hispánico del siglo XVI, se había basado en la confusión de España y Castilla, español y castellano, encarnada en el nombre mismo de la lengua "nacional".[16] Una lengua que los catalanes, como ya he dicho, estaban más que dispuestos a reconocer efectivamente como nacional,[17] sin por ello

---

[14] La única excepción es la calle Pelayo, en la frontera entre la vieja ciudad amurallada y el nuevo ensanche. La de Trafalgar, en posición parecida, y las de Bailén, Gerona, y Bruch, en pleno Ensanche, pertenecen ya a la mitología nacional común -- y las dos últimas con marcado acento catalán.

[15] La nomenclatura de las calles del nuevo Ensanche fue encargada en 1863 por el Ayuntamiento al entonces cronista oficial, Víctor Balaguer. Véase Lluís PERMANYER, *Història de l'Eixample* (Barcelona: Plaza & Janés, 1990), 101-02.

[16] La confusión era ya denunciada o fomentada (e incluso defendida) en el siglo XVI. Véase H.G. KOENIGSBERGER, "Spain", en *National Consciousness, History and Political Culture in Early-Modern Europe*, ed. O. Ranum (Baltimore/Londres: The Johns Hopkins University Press, 1975), 163-72 y I.A.A. THOMPSON, "Castile, Spain and the Monarchy: the Political Community from 'patria natural' to 'patria nacional', en R.L. KAGAN-G. PARKER (eds), *Spain, Europe and the Atlantic World. Essays in Honour of John H. Elliott* (Cambridge: Cambridge University Press, 1995), 125-59.

[17] "¿Peraqué voler cultivar la llengua cathalana, si la de tota la nació es la castellana, la qual debem parlar tots los que nos preciam de verdaders espanyols?" (J.P. BALLOT, *Gramática y apología de la llengua cathalana* [1813], ed. facsímil de Mila Segarra [Barcelona: Alta Fulla,. 1987, xxiv-xxv) ; "Basta decir que la lengua castellana es la lengua de la Nación,' (de un anuncio del colegio regentado por el presbítero Manuel Casamada, en *Diario Constitucional*, 21-VIII-1821); "...considerada literariamente la lengua catalana, se puede cultivar sin abandonar por esto los esfuerzos que como españoles debemos hacer para conocer la lengua nacional" ([A. de] B[OFARULL] , "La lengua catalana", *Diario de Barcelona*, 1-VIII-1854, rep. en A. de BOFARULL, *Estudis lingüístics*, ed. J. Ginebra [Barcelona: Alta Fulla, 1987).

dejar de negarse tozudamente - y esto también era inaceptable - a permitir que su propia lengua degenerase en *patois* y muriese de muerte natural.[18] No les importaba vivir en un estado paradigmático de diglosia, pero no estaban dispuestos a adoptar el español como lengua familiar y de la vida diaria.[19]

No les guiaba, a los catalanes, el afán de fastidiar y provocar. Había una gran presunción, claro está, en su deseo de colorear tan fuertemente a la nación española de catalanidad, pero era una presunción que derivaba del justificado convencimiento de que estaban, después de todo, a la cabeza de la construcción de la nación. ¿No era acaso Cataluña, como se ha dicho alguna vez, la fábrica de España? ¿No era la industria catalana lo único que podía hacer a España "rica y fuerte"?[20] Siempre y cuando, naturalmente, fuera objeto de la necesaria protección. Pierre Vilar escribió hace años ya unas páginas espléndidas sobre cómo la dialéctica puesta en marcha por esta serie de polaridades (Cataluña industrial-Castilla agrícola; proteccionismo catalán-librecambismo "castellano") multiplicó los equívocos y abrió una zanja, abismo al final, entre unos y otros.[21]

Y sin embargo exigir a los catalanes, como se les exigía, que olvidasen su propia identidad también era pedir gollerías. Su paleonacionalismo había alcanzado en la época moderna un estado de desarrollo demasiado avanzado para que pudiera desvanecerse fácilmente. Y no se trataba simplemente de recuerdos y sentimientos. El profesor Da Cal ha subrayado, muy acertadamente una vez más, la importancia de la rivalidad entre Madrid y Barcelona en relación con lo que aquí estamos debatiendo. Pero el rechazo del estatus de mera capital de provincia para Barcelona y la idea que

---

[18] Que es lo que, para un ilustrado liberal de la época como Wilhelm von Humboldt, debía ser el destino de toda lengua que hubiese dejado prácticamente de escribirse. De ahí su sopresa al ver que no ocurría así con el catalán: véase su*Diario de un viaje a España*, trad. Miguel Ángel Vega (Madrid: Cátedra, 1998), 243-44.

[19] Aunque parezca mentira, nadie ha estudiado hasta hoy esta importantísima cuestión. No cabe duda alguna, sin embargo, que, si bien entre la nueva clase dirigente de la Cataluña ochocentista, las más o menos doscientas "buenas familias" estudiadas por Gary McDonogh (*Good Families of Barcelona* [Princeton, N.J.: Princeton University Press, 1986], esp. 115-,22), la castellanización fue casi (pero sólo casi) total, para el resto de los catalanes dirigirse oralmente a un compatriota (si no era desde la cátedra o la tribuna) en otra lengua que la propia fue siempre (y sigue siendo) incómodo y sencillamente ridículo. Pero al mismo tiempo la diglosia llegó a ser, a partir de mediados de siglo, prácticamente universal y completa: los mismos que no sabían hablarse sino en catalán, no tenían inconveniente en escribirse, incluso las cartas más íntimas, en castellano.

[20] Es el título del libro del secretario de la Junta de Comercio barcelonesa, Bonaventura Gassó:*España con industria, rica y fuerte* (1816). "Cataluña, la fábrica de España" es el que se dio a la exposición conmemorativa de la fundación de la primera fábrica de vapor en Barcelona (existe catálogo con el mismo título y textos de J. Nadal y J. Maluquer de Motes [Barcelona: Ajuntament de Barcelona, 1985]). Pero la identificación absoluta entre industria catalana y prosperidad española es constante desde los primeros momentos de la industrialización, como puede verse en los textos reunidos en*Protecció, ordre i llibertat. El pensament i la política econòmica de la Comissió de Fàbriques de Barcelona (1820-1840)*,ed. A. Sánchez (Barcelona: Alta Fulla, 1990.

[20] VILAR, *La Catalogne*, I, 143-58. Sé que simplifico, lo cual es inevitable dada la limitación de tiempo y espacio. Pero no hay duda de que, en este terreno, la burguesía industrial marcó la pauta para el resto de la sociedad catalana, que la siguió por este camino sin demasiada dificultad y sin excepciones: el carlismo catalán nunca fue anti-español, sino todo lo contrario.

los catalanes se hacen de ella como, en cierto modo, su propio Madrid, su propia capital, no es un fenómeno estrictamente ochocentista, sino arraigado en la historia e ingrediente fundamental del paleonacionalismo catalán. La expresión "la terra", antes mencionada, se usa a menudo, en textos del XVI y XVII, en contraposición a *"la ciutat"* o *"la vila"*. A veces esto corresponde simplemente al contraste entre "villa y tierra o campo," entre Puigcerdá y la Cerdaña, por ejemplo, o entre Tarragona y su Campo.[22] Pero a menudo la expresión *"la ciutat i la terra"* hace referencia al Consejo de Ciento barcelonés y la Diputación, vistos como las instituciones política gemelas fundamentales de Cataluña.[23] Y del mismo modo que, a partir de este significado, *"la terra"* tiende a adquirir las connotaciones "nacionales" a que antes me he referido, *"la ciutat"* también toma visos de representación, de capitalidad, "nacional". Pero no únicamente con carácter simbólico: Barcelona seguía siendo, pese a todo, el centro de la economía catalana y el lugar de residencia de la mayor parte de su clase dirigente y, más importante aun, el título de "ciudadano honrado" de ella era el primer peldaño en la escala de la condición noble para todos los catalanes que a ella aspiraban - y para ellos solos.[24]

A medida que fue creciendo la frustración de los catalanes por no poder desempeñar el papel director en la construcción nacional, el interés en esa misma construcción fue disminuyendo y el sentimiento catalanista aumentando.[25] Ayudaba al proceso el crecimiento del sector terciario de la economía y, con él, de una burguesía profesional y una pequeña burguesía de trabajadores de cuello blanco - o mejor sería decir duro. Su más clara manifestación es la evolución de la cuestión de la lengua. Perjudicados, en la competencia por plazas en una administración pública en expansión, por su pobre manejo del español hablado, estos burgueses y pequeños burgueses experimentaban por otra parte con particular acuidad, dado su relativamente elevado nivel cultural, lo absurdo de su esquizofrenia lingüística. Y así

---

[22] Ejemplos en *Dietari de la fidelíssima vila de Puigcerdà*, ed. S. Galceran Vigué (Barcelona: Fundació Salvador Vives i Casajuana, 1977), passim; Ezequiel GORT i JUANPERE, *El treball i la festa* (Reus: Edicions de Carrutxa, 1995), 18; *Dietaris de la Generalitat*, I, 107.

[23] Varios ejemplos muy claros (las autoridades locales piden el asesoramiento de "la ciutat i la terra") en *El Llibre Verd de Vilafranca*, ed. J. Vallès i Cuevas *et al.* (Barcelona: Fundació Noguera, 1992), I, 284, 341, 385, 421, 424, 518, y 531.

[24] AMELANG, *Honored Citizens*, 24-101.

[25] No hay que olvidar tampoco que Cataluña vivió políticamente durante la primera mitad del siglo en casi permanente estado de excepción, lo cual fue siempre experimentado por los catalanes como un trato opresivo y discriminatorio. Para todo el proceso de frustración y alejamiento, véase FONTANA, *La fi de l'Antic Règim*, 453-64.

empezó, a partir de la década de 1870, un fuerte movimiento de rechazo del estado de diglosia existente y de restauración del catalán al pleno uso oral y escrito.[26] Y esta era la situación para 1900. Como dice muy bien el profesor Da Cal, "un substrato básico de catalanismo [...] era compartido por un amplio sector del espectro político". Era esta - y no el nacionalismo catalán propiamente dicho, que en este contexto es casi una irrelevancia - la principal razón de la frustración del proceso de construcción de una nación española. La mayoría de los catalanes no eran nacionalistas catalanes, pero tampoco eran nacionalistas españoles. El estado español y su propia pertenencia a él eran realidades de la vida aceptadas con más o menos entusiasmo o resignación, pero sobre todo con indiferencia. Todos sabían que eran españoles, pero muy pocos se sentían tales con un mínimo de intensidad. No, en cualquier caso, de por sí. Necesitaban, para suscitar en sí mismos el sentimiento de su españolidad, algún vehículo ajeno: la solidaridad de clase para los obreros, la fe en un republicanismo de tonalidades utópicas para las clases medias y os trabajadores de cuello duro, el miedo a perder los privilegios del poder y la riqueza para la clase dirigente, solidaridad, fe, y miedo compartidos en cada caso con sus homólogos españoles.

---

[26] La fundación, en 1870, de la sociedad "La Jove Catalunya", nombre de obvias resonancias mazzinianas, constituye la fecha inicial más clara de ese movimiento. Véase la antología de textos del mismo título, ed. Margalida Tomàs (Barcelona: Diputació de Barcelona/Edicions de la Magrana, 1992)

FORMACION DEL ESTADO

JOHN MORRILL
(Selwyn College, Cambridge)

PRESENTACÍON POR COLIN DAVIS

La distinguida carrera profesional de John Morrill, uno de los historadores más destacados de Inglaterra en la edad moderna y de su "dimensión británica", empezó con un estudio pionero del condado de Cheshire durante la Guerra Civil Inglesa. A continuación escribió un trabajo de síntesis sobre el papel desempeñado por las provincias y el provincialismo en la crisis inglesa hacia mediados del siglo XVII. *La revuelta de las provincias* (1976/1980) sigue siendo una de las obras más influyentes sobre esa época. Desde entonces, su investigación se ha orientado hacio dos temas conexos: en primer lugar, la exploración de la Guerra Civil Inglesa a través de su dimensión religiosa y su relación con los demás reinos de la corona británica; en segundo lugar, respondiendo a la llamada de John Pocock sobre la necesidad de estudiar la historia 'británica', está explorando el marco de posibilidades de tal empresa.

Su ponencia comienza con un bosquejo de la situación fragmentada del llamado 'Archipiélago Atlántico' (término elegido en preferencia al de las "Islas Británicas" por respeto a las sensibilidades irlandesas) a comienzos del siglo XVI, una fragmentación con cierta dimensión administrativa, lingüística, jurídica y geopólitica a la vez. Sin embargo, en cada uno de los cuatro reinos – Inglaterra, Irlanda, Escocia y Gales – existía un núcleo con la pretensión y la capacidad de formar un estado. Para Morrill, los doscientos años siguientes son caracterizados en parte por la expansión del poder de cada núcleo hacia su propia periferia, y por la del núcleo inglés hacia los demás.

En esta evolución se puede distinguir cuatro etapas de importancia especial. Con la Reforma protestante (1534-1547) Enrique VIII reclamó para sí el poder supremo dentro de su reino, y también logró la incorporación de Gales dentro del sistema administrativo inglés. Entre 1603 y 1610, a pesar de la unión dinástica entre Inglaterra y Escocia en la persona de Jacobo VI y I, la integración jurídica y política deseada por el mismo rey no se pudo conseguir. Luego, con la Guerra de los Tres

Reinos (1639-60), se llegó a la intervención de cada uno en los asuntos de los demás, con una ferocidad y una pretensión sin precedentes. Durante un breve período hacia mediados del siglo, gracias a las conquistas llevadas a cabo por Cromwell, Inglaterra se hizo con el control de los cuatro reinos, creando la posibilidad de un Archipiélago unido. Sin embargo, con la restauración de los Estuardos en 1660, se desbarató todo, abriéndose nuevas posibilidades luego con la caída de esta dinastía en 1688. Otro conquistador, esta vez un príncipe holandés, echó la base de la unión aceptada en 1707 por los Escoceses (mediante capitulaciones favorables para ellos), aunque la conquista despiadada y la expropiación de los Irlandeses hicieron que ellos no integraran el Reino Unido hasta 1801.

Mucho de estos cambios de formas y relaciones constitucionales eran motivados por lo que Morrill llama la "ruleta dinástica," como por la necesidad de asegurar la Reforma protestante, algo controvertida, en los distintos reinos. En su conclusión, por lo tanto, el autor se pregunta cuál ha sido el impacto de tales acontecimientos sobre la percepción que tienen de sí mismos los habitantes de estas Islas. Sugiere que para los Ingleses llegó a ser los mismo - como lo es hoy dia - llamarse inglés o británico. Los Galeses y los Escoceses podían reivindicar a la vez su condición de galés o escocés y británico, sin renunciar a la diferencia. Los Irlandeses se sentirían más bien ajenos, pero los llamados 'Anglo-Irlandeses' miraban favorablemente la Gran Bretaña como el poder que podía garantizar su hegemonía. Resumiendo toda esta complejidad, Morrill vuelve a replantear la necesidad y la utilidad de la 'demensión británica'.

STATE FORMATION AND NATIONHOOD
IN THE ATLANTIC ARCHIPELAGO 1500-1720

JOHN MORRILL
(Selwyn College Cambridge)

In 1500 there was very considerable political, linguistic and cultural fragmentation within the constituent parts of the Atlantic archipelago[1] - an archipelago consisting of the island of Britain with the clusters of islands off its southern, western and northern coasts, and of the island of Ireland.

There were, within this archipelago, two monarchies - the recently-established Tudor royal house of England and the well-established Stewart royal house of Scotland - the principality of Wales (held by the English Crown), many Lordships, including those held by the English Crown (e.g. Calais), and from the English Crown (the Marcher Lordships of Wales outside the Principality, and those bordering the Scottish frontier) or from the Scottish Crown (such as the Lordship of the Isles incorporating much of the Western Highlands and the Western Isles - the Lordship also contained an extensive area of North East Ulster, held from no-one). In addition to all this there were a series of semi-autonomous or entirely autonomous regions. These included much of Ireland, many parts of the Highlands, and the Isle of Man.

To add to the confusions the English royal house spasmodically claimed feudal suzerainty over Scotland. It did so mainly in order to legitimate interference during the regular royal regencies in Scotland, so that the Tudors can be said to have had some sense of themselves as Kings of Britain. However, to complicate things in yet another way, all rulers of England laid claim to be kings of France. This did not mean that they saw Calais, the final vestige of their medieval Imperium, as part of their kingdom of France - Calais sent representatives to sit in the English Parliament right up to its capture by the French in 1558; but it did mean that they treated the land reclaimed or 'liberated' by Henry VIII during his reign - such as Tournai in 1514 - as part of the "separate kingdom" of France with its own insignia, laws and privileges.[2]

---

[1] The more familiar title is the British Isles; and this is a term much used by the modern British but resented by the modern Irish. The term "Atlantic archipelago" was coined by John Pocock and is used here because it prejudges no issues and is, in fact, more evocative of the fragmentation I wish to describe than is the term "British Isles".

[2] See C.S.L. Davies, "Tournai and the English Crown, 1513-1519" *Historical Journal* 41/1 (1998),pp. 1-26.

Indeed, it seems possible that it was not so much the incorporation of Wales into an enlarged 'English' kingdom between 1536 and 1543 or the creation of the Kingdom of Ireland (allowing Henry VIII to assert jurisdiction and title to the whole island of Ireland) in 1541 which transformed the English 'British' enterprise, but the loss of Calais, the final continental toehold in 1558.

In 1500, the writs of the Kings of England and Scotland probably ran in less than half the land mass of the archipelago and were acknowledged by perhaps sixty percent of the inhabitants of the archipelago. In England itself, the royal writ did not run in the Palatines of Chester or Durham, although the King as Elector Palatine in Chester issued writs in that name to similar - not identical - effect (he could not, for example, levy direct taxes, and fugitives pursued on royal writs from neighbouring counties could not be arrested in Cheshire unless a new writ in the name of the Elector Palatine was issued). In Durham, much of the King's authority was vested in a warlike series of Bishops, with consequences similar to those in Cheshire. Throughout the country, there were substantial Liberties in which specific jurisdictions and powers were reserved from the officers of the Crown - the sheriffs of Suffolk could not enter or act in two huge liberties of St Audrey and St Edmund, which restricted them to service in less than half the area of the county.

To look at it from another perspective, representatives from most but not all of England sat in the English Parliament - the exceptions being those Palatine counties of Cheshire and Durham - and those counties not represented paid no parliamentary taxes to the Crown. There was no Parliament in and no parliamentary representation from Wales (until 1543). Meanwhile, the Scottish Parliaments regularly contained representatives of the Lowland shires and burghs only; while the Irish Parliament contained only representatives of the area known as the English Pale. Taxation outside these areas was unknown.

Linguistic boundaries followed, in a ragged way, political ones. Varieties of the English language were spoken by a simple majority of the inhabitants of the archipelago. There were very strong regional variations, and people of the north and the south had great difficulty in communicating with one another (unless they were amongst the ten per cent of adult males who were Latinate); but what were recognisably varied forms of English were spoken by a majority of the inhabitants of

England with the major exception of the inhabitants of Cornwall, where there remained many speakers of Cornish, akin to Welsh and Breton.[3] A heavily inflected version was spoken by Scottish lowlanders and many English Borderers (a reminder that the ancient Anglo-Saxon kingdom of Northumbria straddled what is now the Anglo-Scottish border), and something more akin to Lowland English prevailed in the English Pale in Ireland. On the other hand probably one third of all the inhabitants spoke only one or more of several Celtic languages: the Gaelic tongues of the west and north of Scotland and of the north, west and south of Ireland, and the Brytonnic tongues of Wales and Cornwall. Traces of other languages - Norse and Manx, for example - were still to be found in isolated pockets in Britain and its island groups.

There was also a fundamental divide between two legal, social, institutional and popular cultural worlds. The first was the Anglo-Norman world - to be found in much (not all) of England, in Lowland (not Highland) Scotland, in the Marcher Lordships, but not the Principality of Wales, and in the English Pale of Ireland.

The second was the Gaelic or Celtic worlds of the Scottish Highlands and most of Ireland, worlds closely linked and partially integrated one with another, and in the largely disconnected but cognate world of the Welsh Celts. The former was post-feudal, rooted in primogeniture and writ-culture; the latter was rooted in a tribal, clan or 'name' culture, and in its own sophisticated processes of arbitration and dispute-settlement. In eighty percent of the land mass of Ireland, and half the land mass of Scotland and Wales, it was Celtic law and rules of property-holding and transmission which prevailed.

The whole archipelago was nominally Christian and all parts nominally part of the Western Catholic Church, but the Anglo-Norman parts had settled dioceses and diocesan financial and judicial structures, under the administrative oversight of Rome. They had settled parochial ministries and pastoral strategies, while the Celtic regions had less fixed and developed patterns, with few bishops and fewer recognised by Rome, with itinerant friars rather than settled parish ministries, and religious orders rather than secular clergy dominant. Wealth and power within the English church lay with an intellectual élite mostly of humble origin; ecclesiastical wealth and power

---

[3] Welsh, Cornish and Breton form one ("Brittonic") group of Celtic languages; Irish and Scottish Gaelic, together with Manx (the language of the Isle of Man) a second ("Gaelic") group. See ed.D.MacAulay, *The Celtic Languages* (Cambridge, 1992).

elsewhere lay with relatives of those who controlled the regions within which they operated. Senior ecclesiastical benefices were a form of outdoor relief for the kin of great lords.

Indeed it is possible to argue that each of the four major historic building blocks of the archipelago - England, Ireland, Scotland and Wales - consisted of an Anglo-Norman core and a Celtic periphery and that the story of the early modern period is the two-fold story of the expansion of each of the cores to incorporate its own periphery and of the English core to assimilate or at any rate to effect control over the other cores. Such a process reached a climax in the 1650s when the English Commonwealth achieved an astonishing military conquest of Ireland and Scotland and incorporated them into an expanded English commonwealth with a single head of state, a single decision-making executive council, and a single Parliament with 374 representatives from England, twenty-six from Wales, and thirty each from Ireland and Scotland. There was a commitment to the introduction of a single legal system throughout the extended commonwealth and a single set of guidelines within which religious pluralism was to flourish. It was even intended that Jersey and Guernsey should be represented. It was a bold experiment, which disintegrated with the death of Oliver Cromwell and the restoration of the Stuarts to rule over three disparate kingdoms.

The following sections will look first at the forces that shaped the development of a British state system in the sixteenth and seventeenth centuries, and then those that transformed the character of the peoples of the archipelago in the same period. We will then seek to establish the links between the two processes.

II

The development of a British state system occurred in a series of lurches followed by times of consolidation, even of reaction. The four crucial stages were the years 1534-47, 1603-10, 1639/49-1660 and 1689-1707. Let us briefly examine each of these spasms of change, and then the cumulative effect on each of the component parts of the 'system'.

Between 1534 and 1547, Henry VIII assumed enormous responsibilities as Supreme Head of the Church in England and as *rex imperator*. These new responsibilities - together with the real and anticipated potential violent resistance to them - led him (or more particularly Thomas Cromwell and his successors) to make sweeping changes to the constitutional and institutional arrangements within much of the Atlantic archipelago.

Within England, this led to the reform of the palatinates and of the liberties and franchises that limited the authority of royal writs and the activities of royal officers in many parts of England; the incorporation of Wales into England - with the shiring of the principality, the extension of English law to the whole of Wales, and the granting of representation in the English Parliament to the twelve Welsh shires and to the principal Welsh boroughs; and the creation of the kingly title for Henry VIII as King of Ireland, with the accompanying claims to title of land and jurisdiction throughout the island and not just within the English Pale. Only with respect to Scotland was this not a significant period, for although the accession of a week-old girl to the Scottish throne in 1542 encouraged Henry to restate emphatically English claims to feudal over-lordship, there was no accompanying constitutional redefinition or institutional innovation.

The second half of the sixteenth century saw much consequential consolidation of the changes wrought by Henry VIII's revolution in government. This was most obviously true of Ireland, where the creation of the Irish kingdom and the subsequent and gradual failure of the Reformation created the circumstances in which violent enforcement of royal power, resistance, widespread confiscation and (colonial) plantation took place. In England and Wales there was a 'thickening' of the textures of government as royal commissioners took on an ever wider range of responsibilities. Meanwhile Anglo-Scottish relations were dominated by dynastic rather than constitutional development as it became ever more possible that the Scottish line would succeed to the English throne.

It was that union of the Crowns in 1603 that set in train the second of the lurches. Most - but not all - of James's attempts to promote a greater union of the kingdoms were defeated by the Scottish hesitancy and English lack of co-operation, but the two kingdoms had to be governed, and a series of ad hoc developments - such as a re-arrangement of the powers and responsibilities of the various royal councils and the creation of a British court at Whitehall - should not be overlooked. The policy of plantation in Ireland and the handing over of much devolved responsibility for government to a colonial elite was greatly enhanced by the Plantation of Ulster in the early years of the reign, a Plantation that brought Scots as well as English settlers to Ireland; and as a result Scots Presbyterianism as well as a sour English Protestantism.

The crisis in the mid-seventeenth century, for too long inaccurately known as the "English Revolution," can in fact be better known either as "the war of the three kingdoms" or as "the wars of the three kingdoms". There are parallels here with the succession of revolts that rocked the Spanish composite monarchy in the period 1640-48. However there were differences too, such as the absence of war-burdens as a cause of the British crisis and the presence of religious conflicts - albeit distinct religious conflicts - at the heart of the wars in England, Scotland and Ireland. In each case, however, as the internal and interlocking wars developed, the future constitutional arrangements as 'between' the component parts (as against 'within' each of them) came to dominate the struggle. The Scots wanted a fully federal or confederal constitution for the British monarchies, and joint Anglo-Scottish control of Ireland; different groups in Ireland wanted different kinds of independence of the English state and parliament; and the victorious English Parliamentarians wanted to turn Ireland into a full-scale colony of the English state, and to have as loose a connection to Scotland as possible. Indeed when the English - without consultation - executed Charles I in 1649, they sought to float off Scotland. In English constitutional eyes, the union of 1603 had failed, and Scotland was free (Portugal-like) to resume its historic course as an independent free-standing monarchy. The English abolished monarchy in England and Ireland but not Scotland. It was an absolute Scottish refusal to accept the abolition of monarchy in England and Ireland, or the severing of the links between the kingdoms, which provoked the English into conquest and into an incorporating union, which was then extended to Ireland. By 1655 there was one executive council of state, one Parliament, and one legal system for the whole archipelago. By then, too, there had been a revolution in Irish land-owning that led to a reduction in the proportion of Irish land held by Catholics from two-thirds to one fifth. What Cromwell sowed would yield bitter harvests for centuries to come.[4]

---

[4] In contrast, less than five percent of English and Scottish land was permanently transferred by confiscation and sale.

That mid-century lurch left fewer marks than the others, Ireland excepted. Its main provisions were rescinded in 1660-1 and the restored Stuarts showed little interest in developing the constitutional and institutional ties between their kingdoms. Under Charles II and James II, there were spasmodic attempts to heighten royal power within each kingdom, but almost an aversion to strengthening links between them.

The final lurch was therefore left until after 1689 when it was the loss of royal control within Scotland and a new dynastic crisis that created the imperatives. In 1689 the Scottish nobility and the Scottish Parliament gained a degree of independence of royal control that rendered insecure the smooth transition from the heir-less Queen Anne, last of the Stuarts, to a remote but Protestant line - that of Hanover. At last the Scots had the leverage to secure from the English binding guarantees for the things that most mattered to them: free trade with England and free access to English overseas markets; the Scottish Kirk; and Scots law. In return for these binding guarantees, the Scots surrendered their legislative and executive independence. It seemed to many at the time a fair swap. Meanwhile, the Crown was allowing the descendants of the Elizabethan and seventeenth-century planters to strengthen their control of Ireland by ever-fiercer controls on the Catholic majority, especially in the years around the turn of the seventeenth and eighteenth centuries. There was now in a real sense a British state, and Ireland was somewhere between an extension of that state and a colony. With its own Parliament, its own peerage, and its own representatives within the royal court, Ireland was more than a colony; but with the English Parliament able to legislate for it, with appeals from its courts running so regularly to Westminster Hall and with its executive appointed directly by Whitehall and working under guidelines so precisely worked out by Whitehall, it was far from an independent unit within a composite monarchy.

Much had thus been transformed between 1500 and 1720. A royal house imported from North Germany and based in south-east England now laid effective claim to govern the whole archipelago with the simple exception of the Isle of Man off the Cumbrian coast (which remained the private possession of the Stanleys earls of Derby until 1753). What had been created, however, was a state system and not a state. Although the English and Scottish royal houses had been united as a delayed consequence of a game of dynastic roulette in 1603, the union of the executive and

141

legislative bodies of the kingdoms was delayed until 1707; and they retained wholly separate legal systems and churches.

There was, it is true, a British Court dominated (at least in the first half of the century) by Scots, and that had profound effects on the development of a British as against an Anglicised high culture, and there was considerable intermingling of the nobilities of the three kingdoms - both by intermarriage and the acquisition by Scots and Irish peers of English titles to hold alongside their existing ones. But the high-water mark of most of these developments lay in the early part of the century, and it failed to pave the way for formal constitutional forms, whether integrative or confederal.

The constitutional relationship of England and Scotland remained fairly strictly segregated down to 1707. The English elite seem to have preferred it that way, and when they did spasmodically consider any development of that relationship - as in 1604-7 or 1647-60, they would look at integrationist schemes, an incorporating Union of the kind that had made Wales governmentally part of England between 1536 and 1543. The Scots became increasingly concerned to achieve a federal or confederal union, with strong co-ordinate powers binding independent Councils and Parliaments in England and Scotland to work in close co-operation with one another (e.g by the presence of delegates of each parliament at sessions of the other, by a *liberum veto* in *conservatores pacis* for both kingdoms in the making of war and peace, approving royal marriages etc.). When union came in 1707, it was a strange hybrid form. But it represented a sublimation of long-term Scottish desires for commercial union and the guaranteed independence of Scottish law and Kirk, and short-term English anxieties about the succession to the heir-less Queen Anne.

The constitutional relationship of Ireland to England remained even more confused and disputed. There was a separate Irish Parliament which could not prevent the English Parliament from time to time legislating directly for Ireland. There was an Irish nobility consisting largely of emigré Englishmen. There was a separate Irish judiciary administering English-made and Irish-made law by English process appealable to England. Government policy for Ireland was made in England but implemented by a Council in Dublin which resembled a colonial council - headed by English administrators sent over for the purpose and consisting largely of second, third or fourth generation settlers from England rooted in their Irish lands. And there was a Church of Ireland, formally replicating the Church of England, technically self-governing and self-determining, but again a church that had the hallmarks of a colonial outreach, and which only ten per cent of the population recognised or supported. As political structures tightened over the 220 years from 1500 to 1720, so ecclesiastical structures became firmer, more antagonistic. And the process by which this state system had developed had produced firmer, more antagonistic peoples throughout the archipelago.

III

In comparison with the French, Scottish and Spanish royal houses, the English royal house in the medieval and early modern period went through constant crises and violent changes. More than half the monarchs crowned between the mid-eleventh and the late-fifteenth century came to the throne despite their being better claimants by strict right of inheritance.

The Tudors came to the throne in 1485 in especially dubious circumstances and their hold on the throne remained precarious for a generation, after which there was constant insecurity caused by the lack of a male heir, by the childlessness of all Henry's children, and by the doubtful legitimacy (in Catholic eyes) of Elizabeth. The accession of the Stewart line from Scotland - in defiance of an Act of Parliament (and Henry VIII's will) which barred the line deriving from Henry's elder sister, Queen to King James IV of Scotland - was less contested than might have been expected, but the deposition of James VII and II and the parliamentary transfer of the title to a Dutch prince and later to a North German Duke, only perpetuated the legacy of dynastic disruption.

At the heart of the creation of the British state system, then, was one of the breaks at the dynastic roulette table that transformed the geopolitical map of Europe in the sixteenth century.[5] Like so many of the dynastic unions of the early modern period, the Anglo-Scottish union was unanticipated and unplanned, a consequence of the childlessness of all Henry VIII's legitimate issue. It is a contingency no-one could

---

[5] Represented above all by the career of Charles V, born to rule the rump of the Duchy of Burgundy and the unruly German provinces to its north, who inherited the Iberian Kingdoms and their dependencies and the Habsburg territories in central and eastern Europe and with them reversionary claim to the Holy Roman Empire; or the dynastic marriage that brought one ruler to both France and Brittany.

have foreseen, less predictable than many alternative dynastic scenarios that would have transformed European history if they had happened.[6] Dynastic chance therefore brought the throne to the great-grandson of James IV of Scotland and Margaret, elder of Henry VIII's two sisters almost one hundred years after the marriage treaty intended to stabilise relations between two hostile neighbours, a peace which had lasted for less than a decade.

Dynastic roulette thus did a great deal to create the new British state system. There was no pressure within English political culture - and certainly no economic or commercial imperative - driving England towards any form of union with Scotland. On the other hand, it was considerations of national security and the requirements of confessionalism that drove the Tudors towards the extension of royal control over Wales and Ireland, and the deployment of English force where co-operation amongst established local éites was not forthcoming. Perhaps the English, denied the option of continued expansion in western and southern regions of what was becoming France (e.g. Normandy and Gascony), were always likely to look to the west and the north as a second best. But the imperatives seem to be more defensive than aggressive, the need to defend their own Reformation from the forces of counter-Reformation.

IV

In 1534 Henry VIII effected his schism from Rome and had himself declared "Supreme Head" of the Church in England. He simultaneously began a propaganda assault aimed at his subjects, at foreign princes and not least at himself, emphasising that "this realm of England is an Empire" - its King knowing no equal, let alone superior, with respect to anything done within the realm. The King was not *primus inter pares*, the manager of a system in which much authority was franchised out, and in which much of the land and the social power that went with land-ownership lay in the hands of monastic orders which were the multinational corporations of Renaissance Europe. The image of the King was displayed in the frontispiece of all

---

[6] What if Charles V and Francis I had built on either of the alternatives provided for in the Treaty of Crépy (permitting the transfer to French royal control by marriage treaty of either Spanish Italy or the Low Countries)? Or what if Henry VIII had persuaded the Scottish to honour the treaty of Greenwich and had been able to marry an Anglicized Mary of Scotland to his son Edward before that unfortunate youth's early death? Or – most dramatically, what if Francis II had fathered a male child by Mary Queen of Scots before he died of an ear infection, a son that would have been the undoubted heir to France and Scotland and (in French and Scottish if not English and Spanish eyes) to England? Then indeed there would have been a War of the English Succession.

seven editions of the Great Bible that appeared in his reign and that he had had chained in every church of the land. He, the King, bestrides the page, delivering Bibles with one hand to Archbishop Cranmer and with the other to Secretary Cromwell. Each receives them humbly, bareheaded, and with expressions of deep piety; Then in a second tableau, dressed in appropriate headgear, Cranmer hands them out to the clergy and Cromwell to the laity. Henry was co-equally the Head of Church and State.[7]

In England, there were striking moves towards the integration of the whole realm under the English Crown. The "Act for recontinuing of certain Liberties and Franchises heretofore taken from the Crown" (1536) revoked all grants of jurisdiction over treasons, felonies and outlawries, all authority to appoint justices of eyre, the peace or gaol delivery, and specified that "all original writs and judicial writs, all manner of indictments of treason, felony or trespass, and all manner of process to be made upon the same in every county palatine or other liberty", that they all be "united and knit to the imperial Crown of this realm"[8] Only the Palatinate of Durham and the Archbishop of York's Liberty were (in a final clause) made exempt from this Act. This represents most graphically what Geoffrey Elton termed "the omnicompetence of Statute" in and after the 1530s. King-in-Parliament simply cancelled immemorial grants both by Henry and by his predecessors, and alienated to the Crown that which had been inalienably granted away. This was the beginning of a sustained campaign to make ubiquitous the royal writ and the presence of those acting in the King's name and on his warrant. Many of the greatest Liberties belonged to the great religious houses, so the coincidence of the Franchises Act with the dissolution of the monasteries quickly promoted the visibility and effectiveness of royal commissioners, royal sheriffs, and (within a generation) royal Lords Lieutenant and their deputies. England became administratively and politically integrated.

As the century progressed, King and M.P.s co-operated in building on the foundations of the 1530s. The new royal privy council, a body that not only deliberated and made policy, but which - again in Elton's evocative phrase - "did

---

[7] I take this description from the discussion by A G Dickens, *Thomas Cromwell and the English Reformation* (1959), p. 141.
[8] *Statutes of the Realm*, III, pp. 555-8.

things"[9] monitored what was happening throughout England, regulated the activities of local governors, assisted them in enforcing policy and in maintaining order, and disciplined them when they failed to carry out their duties. Parliament laid literally hundreds of new responsibilities on local governors, especially in the area of economic and social regulation - employment, housing the maintenance of roads and bridges, poor relief, the marketing of grain and much else. All these regulations were monitored and policed by the Council. It led to the proliferation of questionnaires from centre to locality, from county officers to parish officers and village constables. It made the institutions of the county - the twice yearly assizes, the four-times yearly sessions of the peace, the gathering of the Lord Lieutenant and his deputies - rather than the magnate's hall or solar the fulcrum of local power. It was the county court, not the noble audience, that decided the issues of greatest moment, and in the county court the power of the king and identification with the realm was more unambiguously stated and represented than in the noble household of previous centuries.

The thickening of the texture of "royal" government went along with a thickening of the texture of law. This became a profoundly litigious society, with more actions begun per 1000 of the population than in all modern societies barring that of the USA. And litigiousness demonstrated law-abidingness, a willingness to see personal disputes resolved in the King's court by due process of law. And increasingly there was a centralisation of justice. All legal roads increasingly led to Westminster Hall, as the regional jurisdictions created or strengthened by the reforms of the 1530s weakened or were abolished. In 1547, almost half the English shires had regional courts that acted in place of the national courts such as King's Bench, Common Pleas, Exchequer and Chancery. After 1641, this was no longer the case. It may also be, as Dr Andrew Wood has suggested with reference to the lead-miners of Derbyshire, that local jurisdictions upholding local custom and local practice were set aside as litigants appealed to national courts to uphold national standards and rules imposed (in that case to the benefit of landowners and detriment of free miners).[10]

---

[9] G R Elton, "Tudor Government, the Points of Contact: II – the Council" in G R Elton, *Studies in Tudor and Stuart Politics and Government* (4 vols., Cambridge, 1974-92), III, 23.

[10] A. Wood, "Industrial Development, Social Change and Popular Politics in the mining area of north-west Derbyshire, c.1600-1700" (Univ. of Cambridge Phd thesis, 1993), ch.4

When to all this we add the penetration of a print culture that was essentially London-based we can see the development of a much stronger sense of the English polity growing over the period as a whole. And nothing that happened in the seventeenth century would do anything but consolidate it. The kind of accessible, inexpensive material that was freely distributed by and after the early seventeenth century emphasised a Protestant nationalism and a profound legalism. By the mid-seventeenth century, to be English was to be a particular kind of Protestant, and to be protected by particular laws and a particular structure of law and law-enforcement.

V

Between 1536 and 1543 Wales was incorporated into the English state: the Welshry was divided into shires on the English pattern and all the characteristic commissions introduced; each shire and its county town were granted parliamentary representation; English criminal and land law and inheritance customs were all introduced. In the words of one of the Union statutes, the dominion, principality and country of Wales were incorporated, united, annexed and subject to and under "the imperial crown of this realm". As Peter Roberts puts it: the union was not introduced "as an administrative convenience for its own sake, but because uniformity in patterns of jurisdictions was considered by the makers of policy to be desirable, if not indeed essential, for the successful enforcement of the statutes of the Reformation Parliament" (ie the enactment and enforcement of the schism from Rome and of the royal supremacy).[11]

Just as important, Thomas Cromwell and his successors transformed the authority of the Council of the Marches in Wales with an immediate administrative and judicial oversight of Wales (and, importantly, of five [later four] English shires contiguous with Wales). Within this area, a Council headed by an English courtier together with magnates and lawyers from within the region, possessed all the supervisory and quasi-legal authority of the Privy Council, while its conciliar committees and judges, with experience of Westminster Hall but independent of it, provided civil and criminal justice in Ludlow and on circuit. Yet the policies which the Council enforced and the laws which the judges upheld were those made by King,

---

[11] P Roberts, "The English Crown, the Principality of Wales and the Council of the Marches",in B Bradshaw and J Morrill, (eds.) *The British Problem: State Formation in the Atlantic Archipelago c.1534-1707* (London 1996), p.122.

Council and Parliament in Whitehall and in the Palace of Westminster. Wales was centralised within itself and tied much more closely into the English polity.

Thereafter, although Welsh language, Welsh literary culture, Welshness, survived and adapted (as we will see), there was no such thing as a distinctive Welsh political culture. As Philip Jenkins has put it: "the position of Wales within the early modern British state can be discussed in terms of negatives. Between about 1560 and 1790, there were no distinctively Welsh risings or insurrections, and nationalism and separatism plays no role in what riots or disturbances did occur."[12] Welshmen held more than their fair share of the senior offices of state during the seventeenth century, including three law officers, two secretaries of state, several senior judges and an archbishop of York. None brought anything distinctively Welsh to the jobs they held. More typical was the response of Judge David Jenkins, who told his gaolers in 1648 that rather than acknowledge the authority of the kingless Parliament he would die "with the bible in one hand and magna carta in the other." As Philip Jenkins puts it: "in Welsh political correspondence, magna carta was cited more often than any national concept such as the Celtic church or the Saxon yoke," a remarkable fact when it is considered that the Welsh, as Welsh, got nothing out of it.[13]

This integration owes much to the Anglicisation of social and ecclesiastical élites in the course of the sixteenth century, although (as again we will see) the result was the creation of amphibious Anglo-Welshmen. Here the contrast with the New English in Ireland is especially striking. Part of the reason for the success of the political integration of Wales lies in the promulgation and dissemination of powerful historical myths portraying the Welsh as the ancient Britons and prior occupants of the island, the Tudors as a Welsh dynasty (something that would have been even more powerfully effected if Henry VII's elder son Arthur had succeeded him as King), and the royal supremacy as the restoration of the freedoms of the Celtic church. Part of the success also lay in the geography of Wales, which inhibited contact between North and South Wales and encouraged ever-greater links into the Severn and Dee valleys and across the Bristol Channel and Wirral. Wales was the only Celtic region economically plugged into the lowlands British economy. With no urban centre of

---

[12] P. Jenkins, "Identities in seventeenth-century Wales", unpublished paper given at a Trevelyan Colloquium in Queens' College, Cambridge in July 1993.
[13] Ibid.

more than 3,000 until the mid-eighteenth century, all Welsh upper and middling sorts had to find their consumer goods within English towns.

VI

Scotland remained a decentralised but independent country until 1603. Scottish state formation therefore took two starkly contrasted forms in the early modern period: internally, there were weak but persistent centrifugal tendencies, present since the twelfth century, strengthening from the mid-fifteenth century and strongest at the turn of the sixteenth century; while externally, there were strong centripetal tendencies from the time of the union.

There were two Scotlands in the sixteenth century, and little cultural tension between them: the Anglo-Norman Lowlands and the Celtic Highlands. Language, land-holding and inheritance customs, religious structures all contrasted sharply between the two; but there was a much stronger sense of 'Scottishness' in Scotland than of 'Irishness' in Ireland. As Alexander Grant puts it: "although medieval Scotland had much the same ethnic and linguistic divisions as Wales and Ireland, Scottish Celts did not suffer from the institutionalised racialism found in Wales and Ireland; in Scotland there was no legal gulf between Celt and non-Celt, no exclusion of Celts from the political processes, no treatment of them as second-class citizens or hostile enemies, no sense that the normal state of affairs in the country was one of internal warfare." Throughout the Lowlands and Highlands there was a developing sense of 'Scottishness' by the late fourteenth century: "Alexander III's Scotland, instead of being split between Celt and Norman, or Gael and Gall, was a hybrid country - with hybrid kingship, hybrid institutions, hybrid law, a hybrid church, and an increasingly hybrid landed class."[14]

In part this happened because of the sluggish growth of royal institutions even in the central lowlands where the administration of justice lay still with the lords and not the king, and where the characteristic royal officials of Angevin and Plantagenet England failed to evolve. Scots kings lived of their own, with little resort to taxation, and parliament failed to evolve as it had in England. Laws were passed, but were not generally binding on those Lords not present when they were made. In these

---

[14] Alexander Grant, "Scotland's 'Celtic Fringe' in the late middle ages: the Macdonald Lords of the Isles and the Kingdom of Scotland", in R R Davies, (ed.), *The British Isles 1100-1500* (Edinburgh, 1988), p.119.

circumstances the political consequences of the social, cultural and linguistic blurrings, which increased as one went further into the Highlands, mattered little. The Highlanders were an integral of the Scottish people in an exceptionally loose Scottish state.

From the reign of James III (1460-88) and rather more James IV (1488-1512), there were strenuous efforts to change this. Sadly, Scotland experienced royal minorities for almost exactly half of the sixteenth century (1513-28, 1542-60, 1568-85), so every two steps forward was followed by at least one back. Nonetheless, writ culture did slowly spread in the central lowlands: the development in the fifteenth century of a Court of Session to supervise the nobles' administration of justice, and under James V, of a College of Justice modelled on the Parlement of Paris to systematise it, gradually had some limited impact. More important was the rapid rise in the later sixteenth century of a service nobility of educated lawyers and administrators benefiting from the redistribution of Church lands; and more important still was the creation of uniform structures of Protestant ecclesiastical jurisdiction, first in the towns and their rural hinterlands, and then throughout the Lowlands. We must not exaggerate the growth of 'national' institutions. There was no 'royal' militia in Scotland, and no Scottish equivalent to the English assizes; and attempts to introduce Justices of the Peace in the 1580s, 1610 and 1650s came to nought. But there was more sense of collective responsibility and of the authority of national bodies - Council, General Assembly, even Parliament - in the central Lowlands by 1600 than there had been in 1500. That process maintained a glacial momentum throughout the seventeenth century.

The introduction of much of this to the Western and Northern Highlands is a more disjointed story. It is best illustrated through the story of the gradual assault on the power of the Macdonald Lordship of the Isles - which really was effectively an independent territory. From the 1490s the Crown sought formally to abolish their independence both in theory and through curtailment in practice, a process much assisted by the internal feuds within the clan. Similar action was taken against other over-mighty subjects elsewhere in the north-west and north-east, but the story of the West is the most significant. To cut the clan down to size, successive kings had to build up the power of the (Lowland) Campbells in the region. But it is not without significance that unlike the other new earls of the fifteenth century, the Campbells took the name of the whole region. Indeed the name, Earl of Argyll, was all too reminiscent of the original Macdonald title - *ri airir Goidel* (pronounced Ray AirGile). The crown found itself forced to set a magnate to catch a magnate, and but for the Reformation would probably have found it had a Campbell problem as large as its old Macdonald problem. As it was, the introduction of the Reformation to the west mitigated Campbell independence; and the Campbells remained "Lowlandised" in the process. Even so, the clans in the west could still engage in private wars as late as 1600 - in one pitched battle between the Macdonalds and the Macleans in August 1598 more than 300 were killed. The crown could attempt to bring royal justice and royal writs to the Highlands. Allegiance remained notional and contingent. James VI therefore began a series of draconian measures to compel the Highland clan leaders to have all their children educated in the Lowlands, to learn English (which became a condition of inheritance from 1609) and to spend long periods attending the Court. He also sought to introduce a modified version of the policy of surrender and re-grant, by which Gaelic Lords in Ireland had been required to prove their right to their lands, which were then re-granted to them on the terms that reflected Anglo-Norman and not Gaelic land ownership custom. It was a policy which caused much violence, which the Crown half-welcomed since it was piecemeal, since it led to piecemeal suppression and the transfer of lands to the military undertakers from the Lowlands who had received contracts to put it down. No wonder the Highlanders welcomed Charles I's government and hated the Covenanters. They preferred erratic and ignorant government from London to purposeful disruption from Edinburgh. Thus there was a process of piecemeal centralisation within Scotland alongside the long trials and tribulations involved in the redefinition of the relations of England and Scotland.

Henry VIII and Protector Somerset did try to secure a union of England and Scotland in the 1540s, first by marriage treaty (1543) and then by restating more forcefully than for more than 200 years English feudal suzerainty over Scotland. But even though strong words were accompanied by invasion and "rough wooing" of the Lowlands, English hopes were frustrated. There was no change in the constitutional relationship of the two kingdoms until the union of the Crowns.

And yet, this is not a simple story of two independent but contiguous kingdoms, grating against one another and troubled by dynastic rivalries. For there was a Protestant Reformation in Scotland that owed much to the experience of its clerical leaders (and some of its noble sponsors) in exile in England during the reign of Edward VI, and in exile in Switzerland with English Evangelicals during the reign of Mary Tudor. Scottish liturgy in particular drew on the kind of radical traditions that the English Puritans sought to introduce into Elizabethan England. Those leaders of the Scottish Reformation - headed by John Knox - who had closest links with English Reformers also developed a British apocalyptic rhetoric, arguing that the 'pure' religion of the Scots was to be the cleansing agent by which the half-reformed Church of England was to complete its Reformation, so that together the Churches could be the agent of upholding the Protestant Cause internationally and to secure the overthrow of Antichrist and the establishment of the reign of Christ. English (Foxeian) eschatology remained resolutely English[15]

There was another cross-fertilisation, however, as successive Regents (especially Morton), and then James himself, looked to England for ideas about freeing the Crown from the theocratic bonds forged by the Scottish clergy and their noble sponsors, and particularly looked to introduce the royal supremacy and to restore the episcopate. Contacts of "descending-power" churchmen and "ascending power" churchmen in each country with kindred spirits in the other intensified in the 1580s and represent an important context for the Union of 1603.

This was first and foremost a dynastic union, and it implied no inevitable further institutional or constitutional union. And despite James' strenuous intellectualising and his spasmodic political campaigning, his dreams of a "union of hearts and minds" of the peoples of England and Scotland and of the creation of a new "Kingdom of Great Britain" with its own new institutions and constitutional arrangements and a new 'British' people, he was to die with little apparently achieved. And even this unrealised vision was centred on the island of Britain. At no stage did he envisage the incorporation of the Kingdom of Ireland into his plans for "perfect union" or into the concept of "the Kingdom of Great Britain", nor did he

---

[15] On this theme, see especially R.A. Mason, 'Scotching the Brut' in R. Mason, (ed.)*Scotland and England 1286-1815* (Edinburgh, 1987), pp61-82; A. Williamson, *Scottish National Consciousness in the Age of James VI* (Edinburgh, 1986).

envisage the incorporation of any of the existing peoples of Ireland into his new British nation.

While leading members of the English Council had planned for the dynastic union, they appear to have thought little about the implications for the English state or the English nation. In the months and years that followed, it became clear that the only kind of greater union that a majority of the English political élite were willing to contemplate was an incorporating union on the Welsh model. If that was not practical or feasible, they were content to settle for regnal union without constitutional or cultural frills. The English had no interest acquiring Scottish land, Scottish brides or Scottish jobs. No English clerics lobbied for Scottish bishoprics - as they lobbied for Irish bishoprics - for example. They lobbied instead to keep Scotsmen in Scotland - especially Scottish courtiers and Scottish merchants - and they resented James suggesting that the English had anything to learn from the experience of Scotland - such as a settled preaching ministry in every parish.

James had, however, spent much time over the previous fifteen years thinking through the implications of the regnal union; and he was full of schemes. Whether he hoped for an eventual fusion of the kingdoms to create a "perfect union" based on new institutional structures and legal systems that improved on those pre-existing in each kingdom is disputed. My own view is that he did; but that he recognised it as a distant goal. In the meantime, James wanted to see the peoples come closer together. He wished to facilitate "a union of hearts and minds". He wished to foster a sense of British nationhood as a prelude to the creation of a British state.

Thus James arrived at Robert Cecil's house at Theobalds in May 1603 apparently committed to a plan that would have combined a peripatetic style of government that would take him back to Scotland triennially and to given Scotsmen a share of the top jobs in England and Englishmen a share of the top jobs in Scotland (e.g. English Lord Chancellors in Scotland and Scottish Lord Chancellors in England; Scottish Masters of the Rolls and Chancellors of the Exchequer in England, with comparable placements in Scotland). This scheme ran into such a frozen reception at Theobalds that it was dropped.[16]

---

[16] N. Cuddy, "The revolution in the entourage"in D Starkey et al., (eds.) *The English Court 1450-1640* (London, 1985), 173-225.

But it was replaced by alternatives. James actively promoted joint citizenship, free exchange of goods and of ideas (the Authorised Version of the Bible is a major British endeavour in execution and intent). He sought the repeal of all hostile laws between the kingdoms. He sought to remove from the churches of each kingdom those elements that were offensive in the eyes of the other church (e.g. the lack of an apostolic succession in the Scottish churches, the abuses condemned by James at the end of the Hampton Court Conference in 1604 in the case of the English Church). He encouraged and rewarded intermarriage between English and Scots, the free movement of clergy between the kingdoms. His aim was so to improve the relations between the peoples, and so to mingle aspects of their cultures that a new 'British' identity would develop. Perhaps this is seen with particular force in Ulster where he was determined to create a Plantation rooted both in the Elizabethan experience of Conquest and his own Scottish experience of resettling the Highlands, and to create a British community from the merging of English and Scottish settlers, laymen and clergy.

Most of these ideas withered on the vine. And yet the early Stuart period was not without its institutional developments. Henry VIII had concentrated all his deliberative, policy-making activity in a single council based in Whitehall - his Privy Council - while devolving the enforcement and implementation of policy for twenty-three of the fifty-two English and Welsh counties onto regional councils in Ludlow (Council in the Marches of Wales) and York (Council in the North). In a sense James and Charles I built on this plan by increasingly transferring policy-making responsibility for the whole archipelago to a Whitehall English-dominated council (and its committees) with added Scottish representatives and Irish links, while retaining Councils in Edinburgh and Dublin for the monitoring and enforcement of policy. Furthermore, the dominance of Scotsmen within the Royal Household in general and Bedchamber in particular created a kind of informal *conseil d'en haut*. And although James, and even Charles, were careful not to make any formal claims for the Church of England and its leaders to exercise any jurisdiction over the Scottish or Irish churches, efforts were strenuously made to bring them into closer contact and more congruent patterns of worship and belief. Irish and Scottish bishops were involved in the consecration of English bishops, for example, and Scottish preachers installed in English cathedral chapters.

James yearned to create a new United Kingdom of Britain, and a British presence in the dependent kingdom of Ireland. He achieved a good deal less; but arguably his desire to promote a union of hearts and minds was advanced. Intermarriage of Scottish nobles and lairds to English brides reached a peak in the last years of James's reign, and the awarding of English titles of honour to Scotsmen and Irishmen was matched by the award of Scots and Irish titles to Englishmen. At the élite level, there was emerging a 'British' court nobility. The two senior figures in the Scottish nobility, for example - the Dukes of Lennox and Hamilton - became the Duke of Richmond and Earl of Cambridge in the English peerage. The archipelago was moving towards a new nobility, members of which held office at a British court and lands in two or more of the kingdoms of England, Scotland and Ireland. And the values of this new élite could be expected to permeate down through those who were associated with each of their areas of influence. It is striking that in 1638 the Scots at the English court petitioned Charles I using the form, "we your Majesty's British nobility". Britishness, if not a British state, was advancing in the early seventeenth century.

It was smashed on the anvil of Charles I's authoritarianism. He had no vision of union. He sought to maximise his power in each of his kingdoms with reference to only his distinctive powers and prerogatives within each of his kingdoms. Since he utterly mistook what those powers and prerogatives were in Scotland - especially in relation to religion - he provoked a national revolt against himself in 1638 (expressed in the National Covenant, February 1638). For three years, the Covenanters concentrated on modifying the constitutional arrangements within Scotland. Charles was to be made an absent Doge. As has been frequently pointed out, Covenanting propaganda and political thought drew heavily on the Dutch experience in the 1560s and 1570s (for Charles V and Philip II read James VI and Charles I). But Charles reacted not as king of Scotland but as King of Britain, and he sought to use the resources of all his kingdoms against his northern 'rebels'. With some reluctance, the Scots came to see that there was no long-term security for themselves outside a redefined 'Britain'. Unless "true religion" - Scottish religion - was imposed on England and Ireland, unless the King of England and Ireland was as constrained as he was as King of Scotland, the constitutional constraints imposed in 1639-41 would not hold. And there needed to be a new confederal constitution for the whole of Britain, with representatives of each participating in the councils and assemblies of the other, and joint military and civil control of Ireland. It was for this cause that the Scots sent armies into England on three occasions in the years 1643-51, and it was a determination to uphold Charles II's rights as a covenanted king of a confederated Britain that brought catastrophe on themselves and induced the Cromwellian conquest and incorporation mentioned above.

Many Scots continued to test the water for federal union throughout the later seventeenth century, but when the next major opportunity for a redefinition of constitutional relationships came - in the early 1700s - it took a different form, again, one we have already noticed. The English had no constitutional means to induce the Scots to promote the Hanoverians to the succession to the Crown of Scotland; and the Scots economy was so weakened by the exclusion of Scots from English markets that at last there was overwhelming mutual self-interest in a form of union that safeguarded those institutions that reflected Scottish national identity. The struggle for the succession saw some pulling away of Highlanders into Jacobite activity subversive of everything the Lowland élite stood for. But it must never be forgotten that the Jacobites wanted a Jacobite Britain and not just a Jacobite Scotland, let alone an independent Jacobite Kingdom of the Highlands and Islands.

VII

The two hinges in early modern Irish History lay in the first and the third of the "lurches" discussed in section III; and each of those hinges had two defining moments: the Fitzgerald rebellion of 1534 and the Act for the Kingly Title in Ireland of 1541; the Rebellion of October/November 1641 and the Cromwellian Conquest inaugurated in the autumn of 1649.

At its height, the Angevin Empire in Ireland had spread over the whole of the south, east and central Ireland and more patchily into the north and west. English Lords holding from the Crown under Norman law and inheritance customs were free to run things within their Lordships more or less as they chose. But the Gaelic revival of the fourteenth and fifteenth centuries had seen the reclaiming of much of the land by the great Gaelic families and the "degeneration" of many of the settler families into

Gaelic language, law and manners. By 1500 there were perhaps sixty Lordships, less than one in five of which acknowledged the authority of the King's government in the Pale - i.e. sent representatives to the Dublin Parliament, attended the Council or used the courts. The Pale itself, where full "English" institutions were in force, consisted of an area of barely 1,000 square miles mainly to the north of Dublin; the Lordships responsive to Dublin lay in a much larger area within Leinster and east Munster. Much of this was militarised "borderland" or "march", and the Crown relied completely for the defence and opportunistic expansion of the Lordship upon the most powerful of the "Old English" families of the region and their extensive network of clients, the Fitzgerald Earls of Kildare, semi-permanent Lord Deputies of Ireland under Henry VII and Henry VIII.

As Henry's anxieties about the succession and about "the Great Matter" of the Divorce grew, he became more afraid of the overmighty subjects who policed the peripheries of his *imperium*. In the very years of the schism from Rome and the creation of the Royal Supremacy, Henry broke the power of the Dacres on the Scottish Borders, of ap Gruffyth in the Welsh Principality. The trumped-up charges of treason against Kildare drove him into a rapidly suppressed rebellion and execution. In place of Fitzgerald retainers, Henry determined to rule Ireland through an English Lord Deputy, a remodelled Council and as many English troops as were necessary. But with the opportunities and the insecurities created by the schism from Rome, this could be no more than a palliative. In 1541, Henry accepted a plan from within the Lordship for a radical redefinition of his status in Ireland. An Irish Parliament - at which, surely significantly, many Gaelic lords were present as observers - passed in 1541 the Act for the Kingly Title. Henry VIII became the uncrowned King of Ireland. He laid claim to the allegiance of all the inhabitants of Ireland and guaranteed them all the same rights and protections as his subjects in England and elsewhere. To turn this empty assertion into something of substance, Henry, and more particularly successive Lord Deputies, sought to reach agreements with the Gaelic lords which were equivalent to the deals successfully struck with the Welsh landowners. The policy was threefold: the policy of surrender and regrant; the policy of composition; and the anglicisation of law and legal administration. It would be introduced piecemeal until all sixty or so Lordships were integrated into the new kingdom.

Gaelic lords were encouraged to surrender their lands to the Crown, with the expectation that they would be regranted in forms that guaranteed their titles and which regulated their possession and transmission. Heads of septs and their eldest sons had much to gain; younger sons and other kin who benefited under Gaelic extended-family arrangements had much to lose, and formed an important band of malcontents.

Gaelic lords depended for their revenues on systems of enforced tribute from their tenants known as coyne and livery. This required substantial private armies to collect it, and ensured that Gaelic lordships were rooted in violence and oppression. In its place the Dublin administration offered to supervise the transmission of the enforced payments into fixed sums acceptable to all parties and to provide access to law, with the back-up of state force, to police the "compositions". Part of these agreements would be the surcharges payable to government as brokerage fees. Such a scheme was attractive to many of the lords and even more of the tenants, but it created a second group of malcontents, especially amongst the swordsmen whom the compositions would reduce to unemployment or a return to the plough. It was to be particularly unpopular in Ulster, because of the destabilising arrival of so many Scots mercenaries, driven out by Stewart assault on the Clans of the West such as the Macdonalds.

It was always envisaged that the Crown would need to compel some reluctant lords into going along with the policy, by surrender without regrant. So the policy of Plantation was not an alternative part of the strategy but an intrinsic dimension to it.

The third prong of the policy was the Anglicisation of the regions brought into recognition of the Irish Kingdom. Areas "settled" were to be shired, and the characteristic institutions of English local government introduced. The judges would begin to hold twice-yearly assizes in every shire, and, in recognition of the need to devolve power in these transitional times, regional Councils were - in the 1570s - settled in Munster and Connacht along the lines of the Council in the North and the Council of the Marches across the Irish Sea.

The leading student of this process - Ciaran Brady - has concluded that it had much going for it, and that the outcome was by no means a foregone conclusion. Nor should it be seen as a complete failure. Many lords - mainly "lapsed" Anglo-Norman lords - did surrender and did have their lands and titles regranted, and they did compound; and royal justice did inexorably spread outwards. Only in Ulster was progress seriously impeded. Yet it became an increasingly doomed policy because governments in Whitehall wanted the policy introduced too fast and too completely, and because successive Viceroys failed to manipulate faction and get a critical mass of support within the key areas for the implementation of the policy. The result was a cycle of rush, destabilisation, rebellion, expensive suppression and plantation: Leix and Offaly (1556), Munster (1568-73, 1579-83) and Ulster (in the "Nine Years War" of 1594-1603). There was no rush by English governments to undertake the direct rule of Ireland or to assimilate Ireland into England. But it was English ministers who laid down unrealistic timetables and provided inadequate resources. They hold the main responsibility for the failure to achieve a policy of peaceful piecemeal development. Levels of public violence declined decade by decade in Britain throughout the early modem period to 1640. In Ireland the trajectory was quite the reverse.[17]

Somewhere at the heart of all this lay the English government's determination to make Ireland a Protestant country and the inhabitants a Protestant people. Nothing has proved more contentious in early modem historiography than the question of why the Reformation failed in Ireland - in contradiction to the general rule of sixteenth-century Europe, *cuius regio, eius religio*. There is fairly wide agreement that those drawn to the rest of the Crown's reform package of the 1540s - surrender and regrant, composition, etc. - were persuadable to its religious corollary, the royal supremacy. It is true that there was no great confiscation and redistribution of church lands to secure the secular loyalties of those of uncertain conscience; but it is also true that the more ideologically challenging aspects of the Edwardian Reformation did not have time to cross the Irish Sea before Mary's accession. Ireland lacked a record of plunder and of martyrdom before the succession of Elizabeth. The key to the refusal of so many of the Old English and de-Gaelicized lords, as well of as of the Gaelic majority, to embrace the Reformation lies almost certainly within her reign. It began with a

---

[17] Brady's fullest account is in *The Chief Governors: the Rise and Fall of Reform Government in Tudor Ireland* (Cambridge, 1995). There are excellent short accounts of his ideas in his essays in C. Brady and R. Gillespie, (eds.) *Natives and Newcomers* (Dublin. 1986) and in Bradshaw and Morrill, *The British Problem*.

religious settlement that softened the full effects of the simultaneous English settlement - e.g. liturgies could be in Latin as well as English and there was no attempt to introduce the 39 Articles into Ireland; but there was no effort to provide for worship - or even for a translation of the Bible into Gaelic. In that sense the English behaved differently in Ireland and in Wales. Part of the explanation of the failure of the Reformation outside the Pale and the areas of Plantation lies in the failure to train up a generation of ministers able to teach and administer the new religion through Gaelic; and in the failure to recruit missionaries from England willing to acclimatise themselves to prevailing social and cultural conditions. On the contrary, the only ministers willing to go to Ireland were those (of strongly Calvinist stamp) who found the English *via media* uncomfortable, and who migrated so as to be garrison chaplains proclaiming the truth of the gospel against the wickedness and damnation of the native population. The Irish Protestant Church thus became a more hard-line and 'puritan' version of the English one. It became the religion of the colonial Planter, and Catholicism the religion of all those who rejected the Plantation mode of settling Ireland.

The Plantation of Ulster early in James's reign completed the first phase of the transformation of Ireland within a British context. It was the only one in which not only those who owned the land but also those who worked it were removed and replaced by settlers from both England and Scotland. It created an unstable polity. In Ireland as a whole, Protestants owned one-third of the land, represented one-tenth of the population, but claimed a near-monopoly on political power, gerrymandering representation in the Irish Parliament to secure a built-in Protestant majority in both Houses, dominating the Council and the judiciary and spasmodically launching pogroms against Catholic clergy and threatening further large-scale Plantation.

In other respects the union of the Crowns of England and Scotland had little effect on Ireland. It was left out of James's plans for a union of the Kingdoms of Britain and for an immediate constitutional and gradual institutional fusion of the two. It was a kingdom run by English Viceroys, Old English and New English councillors, a Parliament of and for those who accepted the Tudor Revolution in Irish government and society, and a Protestant Church focused on the souls of the New English. It was a church drifting further away from the English Church, with its own clergy emerging from the newly-founded University of Dublin and its own Articles of Religion.

By 1625 Ireland was a kingdom in which the King's writ was as ubiquitous, his justice as settled, his peace as firm as in the Kingdom of Scotland. The English Pale had expanded to control its periphery; but there was limited control by the English metropolitan centre over this peripheral kingdom. Irish rebels had been tried and executed in London; appeals from the Irish courts were occasionally heard at Westminster; Irish appointments were usually made after lobbying (and Viceroys destroyed by intrigue) at Whitehall; and the English Parliament had made law for Ireland, but very occasionally.

The Lord Deputyship of Thomas Wentworth, Earl of Strafford was a turning point. His master-plan was to make Ireland pay for itself for the first time ever (Charles I, determined not to recall the English Parliament, could not afford to subsidise it), and that meant, in the short term, that he had ruthlessly to mulct the community with most flesh on the bone and the least opportunity to resist: the New English, who had engorged themselves with lands - much fraudulently acquired - in the previous half century. In the long term there would be further ruthless expropriation of Gaelic Irish lands in Connacht and Munster; meanwhile the Catholic population must be placated and allowed to worship openly in return for guarantees from a publicly recognised episcopate of political acquiescence. Meanwhile, Strafford and Bishop Bramhall of Derry set out to strengthen the finances, jurisdiction, teaching authority and unity of the Protestant Church by a rigorous series of reforms aimed against greedy landowners, Calvinist rigourists and Scottish Presbyterian infiltrators in almost equal degrees. In due course a reinvigorated Laudian Church would be unleashed to evangelise the Catholic population as part of stage II of the master-plan. It was a regime intent on transforming the wealth of the Irish monarchy, the Church of Ireland and of the Earl of Strafford, although not necessarily in that order; and on destroying - but not yet - the last vestiges of Irish cultural separatism.

As Charles's power in Scotland vanished and his power in England collapsed in 1640, so his Irish régime faltered; and being based on momentum more than force, it crashed. A day of reckoning arrived not only for the Straffordians, but for the Irish Catholic community. The New English wanted not only to take revenge on all who

161

had oppressed them; they wished to ensure that there could be no repetition, and that meant placing authority in Ireland in the English Parliament and not in the English Crown. They petitioned and lobbied for English parliamentary investigation of past "crimes" in Ireland, parliamentary legislation to reshape the institutions of Ireland and a closer integration of the governments of the kingdoms. They also signalled their intention to launch new pogroms against the Catholic community and new plantations. And they signalled this at a time when they lacked the military muscle to intimidate their intended victims into sullen acquiescence.

The result was the Irish rebellion of 1641 and the great massacres of perhaps 2,000 to 3,000 in Ulster. For the next decade, Ireland was like a modern-day Lebanon or Yugoslavia. The Catholic population fought the Protestant population, although both at times divided against themselves and fought one another; and armies from Scotland and from England fought one another and each of the groups in Ireland - the Catholics, the Protestant royalists, the Protestant Parliamentarians. And every group fought for its own control of a post-war Ireland and for a different vision of the post-war relationship between England and Ireland. A few Catholics wanted a free commonwealth under Spanish (or perhaps French) Protector-ship, (ironically) on the model of the Netherlands in the 1570s; more wanted an Irish Kingdom nominally loyal to Charles but completely self-contained and self-governing, with its own native counsellors and Catholic-dominated Parliament freed from the constraints of Poynings' Law. Some Protestants wanted that same constitutional relationship to underpin a Protestant ascendancy ; others accepted the need for a closer integration into the British state system. And that was increasingly the will of the victorious English Parliamentarians, and their intention by the time they sent an army of vengeance and conquest over in 1649. All those in rebellion against them - all Catholics and many Protestants - were to be expropriated and one in ten executed. Indeed all Catholics were to be killed, exiled or herded into the area between the Shannon and the Sea, and three quarters of Ireland reserved for Protestant settlers, an unprecedented act of ethnic cleansing. In the event this proved beyond the resources of the English state; but well over forty percent of Irish land was newly transferred from Irish to English ownership and ten per cent of the Catholic population fled abroad or was transported. This was the damning legacy of Cromwellian rule. The full integration of Ireland into the English state ended in 1660 and left few marks, however.

The "Glorious Revolution" may have been bloodless in England; it was bloody indeed in Ireland, and ended with victory for William III, his international army and the Protestant interest, and to a further halving of Catholic/Irish land-owning, from twenty to eight per cent. This was followed by draconian new penal laws against the residual population, aimed at dividing and ruling them and harassing all overt witness to their Catholic faith. Ireland remained a hybrid Kingdom: retaining its own Parliament of Protestant landowners, subject to Poynings' Law and to the superior legislative authority of the English Parliament; its own system of courts staffed by English-trained lawyers and subject to appeal to Westminster Hall; its own executive Council, dominated by Lord Deputies appointed by and usually from not only the British Council, but the partisan British cabinet. With its Parliament, its own peerage and its increasing rather than declining ties of kinship and élite property ownership in metropolitan Britain and in Ireland, this was more than a colony and less than a free-standing state. It was an integral part of the British state system.

VIII

There was thus an inexorable growth of a British state system if not a British state between 1500 and 1720. It did not produce a British people. And yet this was also a period in which there were dramatic changes in the way the peoples of the British Isles defined themselves. (We should speak of peoples - the better translation of the Latin gens/gentes - rather than anachronistically of nations.)[18] Everyone defined themselves in a series of ways: in England and the Englishries outside England, by locating themselves within a social framework. Significant if rapidly declining numbers of people still defined themselves by the livery or liveries they on occasion wore and the affinity or affinities to which they were sworn. But they also defined themselves by a succession of geographical descriptors (someone might describe himself separately or in any combination as a man of Hoylake, a man of the Wirral, a man of Cheshire and an Englishman). Each individual would weigh these

---

[18] See on this R.R. Davies, "the Peoples of Britain and Ireland, 1100-1400: I. Identities" *Trans. of the Royal Historical Society* 6th ser. Vol. 4 (1994), 1-20.

differently, and each would give a different weighting to the various descriptors according to where he was and who he was with. Since by no later than 1300 forms of the same word covered the territory of England, the language, and the inhabitants who spoke the language. The English had a strong sense of regnal identity, of being subjects of a king to whom they owed loyalty and from whom they derived justice and protection, and a strong sense of the boundaries of an English kingdom. We can be fairly sure that no one in the English lowlands or the Englishries ever before 1600 called himself 'British' and that the use of 'English' would be much rarer than later.

The situation in Scotland was more complex. There, fluid boundaries and the delayed appearance of regnal solidarity, together with linguistic diversity, allowed chronic conceptual instability to linger - not least over whether the land was to be called *Alba* or *Scotia*. For centuries, the Scotia were the Gaels who dwelt north of the Clyde and the Forth and also the people of Ireland. Indeed Ireland was known as *Scuitt*. The region of Strathclyde and the Borders was known as Alba. Scotland only became the whole in the thirteenth and fourteenth centuries. No foundation myth for Scotland can be traced before that of the (Lowland) Declaration of Arbroath of 1320 and its defences in the writings of Fordun, Wyntoun and Bower. Indeed the Lowlanders viewed the Gaels much as the English Palesmen of Ireland viewed the Irish Gaels. A sense of "Scottish-ness" was thus a fairly recent and fragile plant by 1500. It had, as we have seen, few institutional forms.

The Celtic-speaking people of Wales came over the centuries before 1000 to call themselves *Cymry* (literally "people of the region") instead of the older *Brytanaiad*. Welshness was very territorially located - it was the country between the sea and Offa's Dyke. As with Engl[and]/Engl[lish], the same root covered the territory, the language and those inhabitants who spoke the language (*Cymry, Cymru*).

In Ireland, things were more fragmented still. The categories of 'Irish' and "English-in-Ireland" used by the English and by the English in Ireland were clearer in concept given the de-*gene*ration of so many of the heirs of the Norman settlers in Ireland. The native Gaelic population had a series of overlapping identities: that of the tribe, clan or sept; that of the region (men of Ulster, men of Connacht etc); that of the people of Ireland *fir Erenn*); that of the Gael (*Gaedhill*), an identity which united the Celtic peoples of Scotland and Ireland. These distinct and overlapping identities ebbed and flowed in relation to one another over time and between regions. But, as a broad generalisation, the most important in the two hundred years up to 1500 were the ties of lordship and kin *(tighearnas)* and of Gaelic solidarity; while over the next two hundred it was the intermediate ones (regional and Irish) that strengthened as the others - and especially the sense of pan-Gaelic identity - weakened. In that sense, "Irish identity" is in large part the product of having Irishness thrust upon them by the English - in the creation of the Kingdom of Ireland, in the development of an Irish constitutionalism that excluded them and settled Western Scottish protestantised colonists amongst them. Stripped of much of what had previously defined them as Gaedhil, they became much more self-consciously and determinedly *fir Erenn*.[19]

By 1720, things had been transformed. In lowland England the social descriptors still existed, but the fine gradations mattered less. There was less obsession (except at the very top) with exact location within the peerage or gentry. The crucial thing was to be "noble" - a peer or a member of the gentry - and not ignoble (in Saxon *ceorl*-ish or churlish). Increasingly descriptors outside the nobility were simple descriptions of economic function. There were no longer affinities, and maintenance and livery had come to an end. Our man of Hoylake would still refer to himself as a man of Hoylake, of the Wirral, of Cheshire, and he would now refer to himself as English or British, without recognising there was any difference - that is the crucial point. The more educated people were, the more likely they were to use the term British - and use it inaccurately. And more of them would refer to themselves as one or other than in the sixteenth century. Nation-mindedess would be greater, locality- and region-mindedness would be in retreat. Yet if educated men like Camden could write of the antiquities of England (and Wales) under the title Britannia and Milton could write a pre-Conquest history of England as *The History of Britain*, others were likely to be confused. Englishmen then - and now - simply used the terms England and Britain interchangeably.[20]

The Welsh would refer to themselves freely as Welsh and as British, but they

---

[19] This draws heavily on an unpublished paper by Steven Ellis. I have dwelt on these matters at greater length in "The British Problem 1534-1707" in B. Bradshaw and J.Morrill, (eds.), *The British Problem 1534-1707* (London 1996)

[20] This is explored at length by John Pocock in his writings, as in an infamous exchange with A.J.P. Taylor in *Journal of Modern History*, 47 (1975-6), in which Taylor rejoiced in the fact that he could be shown to have used the two terms slackly and interchangeably in his work. Margaret Thatcher notoriously said that "The history of the English people is our national history and should be at the heart of the curriculum in all British schools".

would know exactly what the difference was and when to use each.[21] They were Welsh when they spoke of their language, culture, region; British when they spoke of their involvement in, rights in the kingdom that comprised England and Wales. They were comfortable with both concepts and had no problem in deploying them precisely. It is important to say this because it is often said that the success of the Anglo-Welsh Union and the political acquiescence of the Welsh rested on the Anglicisation of the Welsh élite. This concept is far too freely trotted out. In fact, there was what could be better described as a 'briticization' of the Welsh élite. There was no triumph of the English language over the Welsh language by 1720; simply a triumph of bi-lingualism.[22] The nobility of Wales commissioned and patronised all kinds of work that celebrated the Welsh contribution to British life and civilisation - from Percy Enderbie's *Cambria Triumphans* (which celebrated the ancient Welsh roots of the royal family and many of the great families of England and which was sponsored by a long list of peers and gentry from Glamorgan and Monmouthshire) to the gentry of the "Englishry" of west Wales who campaigned for the appointment of a royal printer for the Welsh language books. The exposing of the supposed Celtic roots of the 'English' Church were also stressed. One incident sums it up. When Charles, Prince of Wales, was sent to Raglan in 1642 on a highly successful mission to recruit Welsh troops for the Royalist cause in the Civil War, he was presented to the people surrounded by the Marquis of Worcester's tapestries, "full of lively figures and ancient British stones", while bardic poets and prophets performed and the traditional Welsh drink, metheglin, was drunk. As Philip Jenkins put it: "the rhetorical framework appears to assert nationalism, but the conclusion [was] resolutely unionist". The Welsh were Welsh and British. They were not English.

Much the same can be said of the Scots. There was a weakening (but not elimination) of clan and regional identities - except in the far north and especially the far north-west - but the Highland Line remained a cultural Rubicon. Highlanders and Lowlanders knew when to call themselves Highlanders or Lowlanders and when to call themselves Scots. It was still a nation made up of two largely monoglot groups -

---

[21] This paragraph owes much to an unpublished paper by Philip Jenkins given at the Trevelyan Colloquium on "The British Problem 1534-1707" at Queens' College Cambridge in 1993.

[22] Philip Jenkins thinks that in the early -eighteenth century 90% of the population could speak Welsh "with some fluency". It is often overlooked outside Wales that 60% could do so as late as 1914. What had changed was the proportion who could also speak English – perhaps 10% in 1500, 50% by 1720, 90% by 1914.

bi-lingualism was probably less than half the ratio for Wales - but the social, religious and legal cultures of the Lowlands had made steady progress. As Allan Macinnes has put it: "the clan fine remained de facto agents of local government - as they assimilated politically, commercially and socially with the [Lowland] Scottish landed classes".[23] Highland society was therefore very different from how it had been; and it was more isolated. The enforced presence of Protestant missions and parishes and the passive acceptance of Protestantism by most chiefs created a great schism between Irish and Scottish Gaeldom. In Ireland, the bardic schools thrived and a bardic tradition of Catholic patriotism thrived with them; in Scotland, the bardic schools waned, and an impoverished tradition was appropriated from the 1640s by anti-Covenanting and pro-royalist patrons and not by the disorganised and spasmodic Catholic mission to Scotland. Pan-Gaelic identity greatly weakened.

Lowland Scots knew when to be Scottish and when to be British. They, like the Welsh, were never English even when they acquired English titles, wives, offices. The great Scottish gold rush to Whitehall, their Cuzco, peaked in the 1610s and 1620s and had slowed to a dribble by the 1670s and 1680s. There were some complaints about the way those who had dwelt in England brought effete English manners back to Scotland; and while in England some Scots tried to be more English than the English (e.g. in the late 1620s the Duke of Lennox and Richmond commissioned George Herbert to upgrade the church at Leighton Bromswold on his estates near the Great North Road, to the west of Huntingdon, and Herbert responded with fittings that reflected the new piety of the times). But a strong commitment to the Scottish Reformation - whether in its Episcopal or Presbyterian forms, to Scottish education and to Scottish law - preserved the Scots from forgetting their primary identity. Since not one Englishman acquired a Scottish heiress or a Scottish seat in the century between the Union of the Crowns and the Union of the Kingdoms, Scottish identities were less changed than those of the rest of the archipelago.

In Ireland, the situation was very different. From the maelstroms of the sixteenth and seventeenth centuries two substantially new identities emerged: the Irish and the English, or the English in Ireland. The term Anglo-Irish is emerging as a

---

[23] A.I. Macinnes, "Gaelic culture in the seventeenth century: polarisation and assimilation" in S.G. Ellis and S. Barber, (eds.), *Conquest and Union: Fashioning a British State 1584-1725* (1995), p.194.

synonym for the latter, but not yet as a dominant term. Only one group, the Scots of Ulster, ever referred to themselves as British. And no one called themselves Irish and English. The sixty per cent of the population that was Gaelic-speaking and the Catholics of the east who had abandoned Gaelic or who were the residue of the Old English, resolutely saw themselves as Irish rather than as Gaelic. That old *Gaedhill/Gall* distinction had lost much of its force except in relation to the island of Ireland. The Irish were defined by their religion first and foremost, for they had been forced to abandon the distinctive inheritance customs and legal codes of Gaelic society. Ironically, the English of Ireland imposed inheritance laws on them at the turn of the seventeenth century that were distinctive both from their own tradition and the Norman tradition. To break the remaining Catholic families, inheritance was to pass first to any son who embraced the Protestant religion, failing which the land was to be divided between all legitimate male heirs. And the Catholicism of eighteenth-century Ireland owed more to the Council of Trent than to the tradition of St Patrick. The English determination to impose the concept of Ireland on the island, the unique and distinctive sufferings of the Catholic population from 1609, and especially in the mid- century attempts at ethnic cleansing and under the Penal Laws of the 1690s, created a new Irish identity very different from the old Gaelic one.

Meanwhile the Protestant community, secure in its control of ninety per cent of the land, and of the political, administrative and military institutions of Ireland, had no intention of forging the kind of historic identity for itself that the Old English of the sixteenth and seventeenth centuries had sought to manufacture on the model of the Anglo-Welsh. They were fully content to be the English of Ireland, and to maintain the links with metropolitan England that the Scottish élite was abandoning. There were tensions within the community - especially between the almost equal numbers of "Church of Ireland" families and the rainbow coalition of Presbyterians and sectaries - but they had little difficulty in assimilating themselves to a single ethnic identity.

So Ireland was the exception. The Anglo-Scottish Union strengthened the links within Britain; and the peoples of the whole of Britain called themselves British whenever it suited them to do so. Ireland retained its own Parliament, its own executive councils, however susceptible they were to being overruled by their English equivalents. And it was peopled by those who saw themselves either as less than

British or more. There was a British state system if not a state, and there was no British people. There was a series of separate histories, and there was also a single history. In John Pocock's words: British History is the story of "the problematic and uncompleted experiment in the creation and interaction of several nations."[24]

Bibliography

This essay draws heavily on the work of others, but is very much a digest of the thought of others rather than a series of specific derivations. Direct quotations and close renderings of the work of specific scholars are acknowledged in the footnotes, but much is derived in general from the following list of works, all of which make significant contributions to the evolution of a 'British' or 'archipelagic' historiography:

R.Asch (ed.), *Three Nations: A Common History* (Bochum),

B.Bradshaw and J.Morrill (eds.), *The British Problem. State Formation in the Atlantic Archipelago c. 1534-1707* (London, 1996)

C.Brady, *The Chief Governors: The Rise and Fall of Reform Government in Tudor Ireland* (Cambridge, 1995).

C.Brady & R.Gillespie(eds.), *Natives and Newcomers* (Dublin.1986)

K.Brown, *Kingdom or Province? Scotland and the Regnal Union 1603-1707* (London, 1992)

N.P.Canny, *Kingdom or Colony: Ireland in the Atlantic World 1560-1800* (London, 1988)

S.J. Connolly, *Law, Religion and Power: The Making of Protestant Ireland 1660-1760* (1992)

R.R.Davies, *Dominion and Conquest: The Experience of Ireland, Scotland and Wales 1100~1300* (Oxford, 1990)

R.R.Davies & R.Frame (eds.), *The Political Development of the British Isles, 1100-1400* (Oxford, 1991)

[24] J.G.A. Pocock, "The Limits and Divisions of British History", *American Historical Review* 87.2 (1982), p.318.

R.R.Davies,   "The Peoples of Britain and Ireland 1100-1400", Four Presidential Addresses, published in *The Transactions of the Royal Historical Society* 6th ser. Vols.4-7 (1994-7)

S. G.Ellis,   *Tudor Frontiers and Noble Power the Making of the British State* (Oxford, 1995)

S.G. Ellis & S. Barber (eds.), *Conquest and Union: The Fashioning of a British State 1485-1725* (London, 1995)

W.Ferguson,   *Scotland's Relations with England: a Survey to 1707* (Edinburgh, 1977)

A.Grant & K. Stringer (eds.), *Uniting the Kingdom? The enigma of British History* (London, 1996)

P.Hodge,   *Scotland and the Union* (Edinburgh, 1994)

P.Jenkins,   *A History of Modern Wales, 1536-1990* (London, 1992)

B.P.Levack,   *The Formation of the British State: England, Scotland and the Union 1603-1707* (Oxford, 1987)

R.Mason,   *Scots and Britons: Scottish Political Thought and the Union of 1603* (Cambridge, 1994)

J.Morrill,   *The Scottish National Covenant in its British Context* (Edinburgh, 1991)

J.Ohlmeyer (ed.),   *Ireland: from Independence to Occupation 1641-1660* (Cambridge, 1995)

J.G.A.Pocock,   "British History, A Plea for a new subject", Journal of Modern History, 47 (1975), 601-28; "The limits and divisions of British History", *American Historical Review* 87/2 (1982), 311-36

J.Robertson,   *A Union for Empire: Political Thought and the Union of 1707* (Cambridge, 1995)

C.Russell,   *The Causes of the English Civil War* (Oxford, 1990)

C.Russell.   *Unrevolutionary England* (London, 1991)

LAS FORMACIÓN DEL ESTADO EN LAS ISLAD BRITÁNICAS: EL CASO DE IRLANDA BAJO LOS TUDOR

STEVEN G. ELLIS
(National University of Ireland, Galway)

PRESENTACIÓN POR COLIN DAVIS

Steven Ellis es catedrático de historia en la universidad de Galway en Irlanda. Sus importantes publicaciones versan sobre la Irlanda de los Tudor, la formación del estado, y los problemas administrativos y sociales característicos de una zona fronteriza en esa época crítica para la evolución del sistema ge gobierno inglés.

Su communicación empieza con señalar el contraste entre los cambios significativos producidos en la constitución del estado irlandés entre 1485 y 1603, y su marginación en cuanto al pensamiento político y constitucional inglés. Los Tudor lograron consolidar su poder en una Inglaterra que, por primera y única vez en su historia medieval o moderna, no formaba parte de ninguna federación monárquica. Tal situación, más la ausencia relativa de guerras durante este largo periodo, hizo que el estado inglés no tuviera ninguna necesidad apremiante de desarrollar su sistema burocrático, fiscal o militar. Visto esto, hay que pensar que la tentativa de integrar Irlanda en una civilización británica pecaba de ambiciosa y de muy arriesgada. Se iba a intentar en Irlanda lo que no había conseguido su objeto en la frontera norteña de Inglaterrra. Para darle un mínimo de viabilidad a su política, los Tudor tuvieron que crear un ejército permanente además de una fiscalidad innovadora en Irlanda. Sin embargo, el carácter marginal de este país en la conciencia política inglesa hizo que no se sacara partido de esta experiencia para aplicarla luego en otras partes de la monarquía de los Tudor.

STATE FORMATION IN THE BRITISH ISLES: THE CASE OF TUDOR IRELAND

STEVEN G. ELLIS

(National University of Ireland, Galway)

Ireland enjoys a unique position in the context of British state formation.[1] For over eight centuries, from the establishment of a conquest lordship in medieval Ireland in 1169 to the modern province of Northern Ireland, Ireland has been linked politically to the emerging British state. Rule from London was consolidated by two distinct waves of colonization from Britain, during the medieval and early modern periods. At different times, Ireland has been a colony, a lordship or dominion of the medieval English crown, from 1541 a dependent kingdom of the crown of England, and from 1603 a kingdom in a triple monarchy: since 1800 it has been a constituent part of the United Kingdom which, until 1922, included the whole of Ireland and is now confined to the six counties comprising Northern Ireland. Yet Ireland's fluctuating constitutional status obscures a remarkable stability in its practical position within the British state. Other later additions to the original Anglo-Saxon kingdom, such as Wales and the far north of England, were gradually incorporated and assimilated more closely to the centre, and some overseas territories, like Normandy and Gascony, or the American colonies of the first British empire, were later incorporated into independent states. Yet Ireland - neither fully assimilated nor totally independent - has effectively retained its marginal status within an English or British context from 1169 to the present.[2]

The purpose of this paper is to offer a short survey of Ireland's role in the development of what was to become the British state in a formative period of that process, the events leading up to the Tudor conquest of Ireland and the unification of the British Isles in 1603. The Irish role was, in general, both quite considerable and essentially negative. In this context, the Tudor conquest of Ireland marked the point of transition from the medieval English traditions of expansion and settlement to the

---

[1] The historiography of British state formation is a comparatively new phenomenon. Recent surveys focusing on the early modern period are Brendan Bradshaw and John Morrill (ed.),*The British Problem, c.1534-1707: State Formation in the Atlantic Archipelago* (London, 1996); S.G. Ellis and S. Barber (ed.), *Conquest and Union: Fashioning a British State 1485-1725* (London, 1995).

[2] S.G. Ellis, 'The Inveterate Dominion: Ireland in the English State, a survey to 1700' in Hans-Heinrich Nolte (ed)*Internal Peripheries in European History* (Göttingen, 1991), pp 29-43.

early modern pattern of colonial expansion which characterized the first British empire. The conquest of the predominantly Gaelic northern and western parts of Ireland comprised the only considerable addition to the English state throughout the Tudor period. Yet this ill-starred and long-drawn-out process, which resulted in the establishment of a second Tudor kingdom in Ireland, had a fundamental impact on English ideas of state formation. In effect, it encouraged the London government to pursue a strategy of state building which was both quite exceptional in a European context and also ultimately unviable.[3]

In more modern times, the English state and its British successor have usually been viewed as an insular, naval power, which was not part of continental Europe. In the later Middle Ages, however, the English monarchy was inextricably involved in the politics of continental Europe: English armies of 'bills and bows' established it as a major European power which, for much of the period, held the duchies of Gascony and Normandy. When Henry VI was crowned king of France in Paris in 1431, he headed a dual monarchy which ruled vast stretches of territory in northern and western France.[4] Yet with the French conquest of Gascony and Normandy (1449-53), English claims to the crown of France ceased to have any real meaning: English possessions in continental Europe were reduced to the military outpost of Calais (and even that was lost in 1558). Subsequently, the English state was plunged into a disastrous civil war, the Wars of the Roses (1455-87); and in the partial recovery of English royal power which characterized the Tudor period (1485-1603), the accent was on the consolidation of monarchical authority within the British Isles. By the time the English government was again confronted with a problem of a multiple monarchy, following the accession of James VI of Scotland as James I of England, the experience of administering the Lancastrian dual monarchy had long faded from the official memory.[5]

Thus, the years of the Tudor conquest of Ireland and of England's first emergence as an island, naval power coincided with a relatively short period in medieval and early modern times when the English state was not part of a composite

---

[3] Recent studies of the Tudor conquest include Ciaran Brady,*The Chief Governors: the Rise and Fall of Reform Government in Tudor Ireland, 1536-1588* (Cambridge, 1994); S.G. Ellis,*Ireland in the Age of the Tudors, 1447-1603: English Expansion and the end of Gaelic Rule* (London, 1998); Colm Lennon, *Sixteenth-Century Ireland: the Incomplete Conquest* (Dublin, 1994).

[4] For a general survey, see Nigel Saul (ed.), *England in Europe 1066-1453* (London, 1994).

[5] D.M. Loades, *Politics and the Nation*, 1450-1660 (London, 1974).

monarchy. Moreover, the conquest of Ireland was itself only the most prominent aspect of a wider process of Tudor centralization which saw the final assimilation of what were essentially conquest lordships in Wales and the far north of England to create a Tudor state, which was actually multi-national in character but yet not part of a dual monarchy, or dynastic union. At one level, indeed, the Tudor achievement was impressive. The 1530s in particular saw the emergence of the doctrine of state sovereignty based on the king-in-parliament, the establishment of a national church, the associated changes in central administration known to some as 'the Tudor revolution in government', and the extension to outlying Tudor provinces of the uniform and centralized system of English law and government.[6] Inevitably, these Tudor developments had a major long-term influence on the strategies of state-building pursued by the London government. Yet it also needs to be emphasized that, during the Tudor period, the English state lost ground fairly disastrously *vis-à-vis* comparable west European powers - France and Spain. It failed to develop a professional bureaucracy, a standing army, and an effective system of national taxation.

English nationalist historiography has generally put a positive gloss on these failings, which were significant in the context of the rise of parliamentary democracy and individual liberties. Yet the fact remains that the ground lost under the Tudors had to be recovered later on by abandoning the Tudor system and adopting a more typically European strategy of state formation.[7] And if we analyze the reasons for this 'wrong' turning under the Tudors, they seem to relate chiefly to the loss of 'core' territories in France and the problematic experience of acquiring new territory in a 'peripheral', and underdeveloped region like Ireland.

Until their capture by the French c.1450, Gascony and Normandy comprised much the most considerable exception to the late medieval English state system. They were predominantly French in language and culture, not English; English common law and parliamentary statutes did not apply there; nor were they governed

---

[6] G.R. Elton, *Reform and Reformation: England, 1509-1558* (London, 1977), esp. chs. 7-12.

[7] The development of the Tudor state in a comparative European context promises to be much clearer following the publication of the remaining volumes of the European Science Foundation's project on *The Origins of the Modern State in Europe*; but see M.J. Braddick, *The Nerves of State: Taxation and the Financing of the English State, 1558-1714* (Manchester, 1996); John Brewer, *The Sinews of Power: War, Money and the English State, 1688-1783* (London, 1989), ch. 1; and the chapters by John Guy, Richard Hoyle, and David Potter in Diarmaid MacCulloch (ed.), *The Reign of Henry VIII: Politics,Policy and Piety* (London, 1995).

by the normal, highly centralized system of English administration.[8] On the other hand, the Lancastrian regime in the 1430's had come close to developing a standing army to police and defend these valuable but very vulnerable territories.[9] Thus, had the English monarchy held on to these territories in the later fifteenth century, it would in all probability have been forced to modernize along the same lines as continental monarchies, simply in order to defend these remote possessions. Unlike the English conquest lordships in Ireland, Wales, and what is now the far north of England, they could not have been ruled as extensions of England because of the far greater power and resources of the neighbouring French monarchy. In consequence, the Tudor state would have seemed far less uniform and centralized in terms of law and administration, and the dominance of England, the English language, and English culture would have been that much less.[10] Admittedly, the Tudor state still had two long land frontiers with Scotland and Gaelic Ireland, with whom relations were usually poor, but these were not frontiers with powerful neighbours which needed to be closely guarded and defended.[11] Apart from the war with Spain in the period 1585-1604, the English state experienced no extended period of major hostilities between 1453 and 1642. Indeed, for much of the sixteenth century, Tudor monarchs were in the happy position of being able to intervene in continental Europe, or to withdraw, as they chose; but they were not under the same pressure as continental monarchs to centralise or modernise.[12]

In reality, the one significant achievement of the Tudors in terms of state building seemed to be the unification of the British Isles. Yet even this success was less than it seemed. The dynastic union with Scotland was a lucky chance, and the actual manner of the Tudor conquest of Ireland stored up as many problems as it solved (as any study of the origins of the present 'Northern Ireland problem' quickly discloses). If we look at the question of Ireland's traditional ties with England, the

---

[8] C.T. Allmand, *Lancastrian Normandy, 1415-1450: the History of a Medieval Occupation* (Oxford, 1983); G.L. Thompson, *Paris and its People Under English Rule: the Anglo-Burgundian Regime, 1420-1436* (Oxford, 1991); M.G.A. Vale,*English Gascony, 1399-1453* (Oxford, 1970).

[9] Anne Curry, 'The first English standing army? Military organization in Lancastrian Normandy, 1420-1450' in Charles Ross (ed.), *Patronage, Pedigree and Power in Later Medieval England* (Gloucester, 1979), pp 193-214.

[10] S.G. Ellis, 'Tudor state formation and the shaping of the British Isles' in Ellis and Barber (ed.),*Conquest and Union*, pp 40-63.

[11] S.G. Ellis, *Tudor Frontiers and Noble Power: the Making of the British State* (Oxford, 1995).

[12] I owe these points to discussions with Professor Wallace MacCaffrey. See especially his*Elizabeth I: War and Politics 1588-1603* (Princeton, 1992).

position was that until the 1530s the English lordship of Ireland (that part of Ireland which was ruled by English kings through Dublin and comprising about a third of the island c.1500) was actually comparatively well integrated into the English state. Alone of the English territories, it was governed by English common law, was subject to legislation by the English parliament, and the work of the king's court and council there was subject to review at Westminster.[13] Wales was only made subject to this kind of supervision from 1536 onwards. In other ways, however, this English frontier with the independent chieftaincies of Gaelic Ireland was in Tudor times without parallel in western Europe. It was fragmented and fluid, and more like the contemporary Russian frontier with the nomadic population of the southern steppes: it was a genuine frontier, not an international border between sovereign states. The 'wild Irish' were not nomads of course, and English kings had long claimed overlordship throughout Ireland, but the very fact that the English did not regard the Gaelic peoples as a civilized nation meant that, in the reduction of Ireland to peace and civility, Gaelic law and culture were of no account.[14]

Medieval men expected to be governed in accordance with their own law, and medieval English kings had generally abided by this principle, most recently in the English occupation of Normandy (1415-49). Yet this principle did not apply to primitive peoples like the Welsh or the Irish. They had to be trained to 'civility', and what better way to do so than to impose on them central aspects of English forms of law and administration (but not all aspects!), as King Edward I attempted to do in the late thirteenth century. From the conquest of Wales in 1283 to the conquest of Ireland in 1603, the assumption underpinning this strategy seems to have been that the imposition of English law and administration would automatically promote 'English civility' among the natives.[15] Conversely, the failure to uphold English law and administrative structures in those parts would lead to English settlers and 'true subjects' degenerating and growing wild like the natives. Thus, the English strategy for the reduction of Gaelic Ireland to peace and 'civility' - once English expansion in

---

[13] S.G. Ellis, 'Crown, community and government in the English territories, 1450-1575' in *History*, lxxi (1986), pp 187-204.

[14] See especially the essays by Rees Davies, Robin Frame, and Katharine Simms, in Robert Bartlett and Angus MacKay (ed.), *Medieval Frontier Societies* (Oxford, 1989); Ellis, *Tudor Frontiers*, pt. 1. Cf. Michael Khodarkovsky, 'From frontier to empire: the concept of the frontier in Russia, sixteenth-eighteenth centuries' in *Russian History*, xix (1992), pp 115-28.

[15] R.R. Davies, *The Age of Conquest: Wales 1063-1415* (Oxford, 1987); Art Cosgrove (ed.),*A New History of Ireland. II, Medieval Ireland, 1169-1534* (Oxford, 1987); Ellis,*Tudor Frontiers*, pt. 1; Joep Leerssen, 'Wildness, Wilderness, and Ireland: Medieval and early-modern patterns in the demarcation of civility' in *Journal of the History of Ideas*, (1995), pp 25-39.

Ireland resumed in the late fifteenth century - was radical in the extreme: the whole island was to be thoroughly anglicized, in terms of law, language, government, and society. The 'wild Irish' were to be turned into 'civil Englishmen' wearing cloaks and leggings and shoes, instead of going barefoot in Gaelic mantles; they were to build stone houses in place of mud huts, and live in towns and nucleated villages instead of wandering in the mountains; and Gaelic lordships and the clan-system were to be replaced by English social and administrative structures based on shires.[16]

Given the great differences between English and Gaelic society, this was a highly ambitious strategy, requiring considerable administrative resources to have even a measurable impact on Gaelic Ireland. The 1530s witnessed the extension of the uniform and highly centralized system of government as it operated in lowland England throughout the Tudor territories. Yet, even where regional councils were established to supervise the administration of justice in outlying parts, the standard English system of shire government proved less than effective in remote upland regions like the far north of England because society there (although fully English!) was quite different. The far north was a region of compact lordships, where power was more fragmented, with a turbulent lineage-based society and few gentry, and where the policing and defence of an exposed march demanded greater administrative devolution. What was involved in Tudor policy was a decisive shift of power in the region, away from marcher lords and feudal franchises to shire government through county gentry. Concurrently, a great expansion occurred in the duties of Tudor justices of the peace. These changes placed great strains on northern society, where peace commissions were much smaller and where military service was more important than law and order. Lacking a professional bureaucracy and a standing army, English monarchs had no effective means of governing and defending the borders once the traditional structures of border rule were dismantled in the early Tudor period; hence the string of revolts in the region from 1487 to 1569-70.[17]

In Ireland, however, royal government faced all these problems and more, since Gaelic lordship, law and culture were quite unlike anything encountered in England. Sooner or later, therefore, the Tudor regime was forced into sanctioning

---

[16] Ellis, *Ireland in the age of the Tudors*, passim.

[17] Ellis, *Tudor Frontiers*, passim.

significant departures from its basic strategy of anglicization, simply in order to reduce Gaelic Ireland to English rule. It is interesting to note what these departures were. Most significantly, it was obliged after 1534 to build up a standing army to quell mounting resistance from Gaelic chiefs and, later, to override opposition from the local Englishry. Large parts of the country had to be placed under martial law, and a series of quasi-military offices (seneschals and provost-marshals) was developed to strengthen local government. The Irish parliament was seldom called after 1543, but instead a system of military taxation was built up to finance an administration which was less and less responsive to the local English community there. In short, Tudor absolutism was imposed.[18]

The main question this raises, however, is how much of this Tudor experience in Ireland was perceived as relevant to the wider problems of British state formation and so was transferable elsewhere. In principle, since the conquest of Gaelic Ireland represented the only considerable addition of new territory by the Tudor state, the Irish experience should have been very relevant to the wider problem of state formation. There is indeed some evidence that conquest and colonization in Ireland were seen as relevant to the problems of English exploration and settlement in British North America, but significantly, this was in connection with the founding of colonies among another group of savages.[19] It was not seen as offering lessons for the government of a settled territory inhabited by a civilized people. Thus, after 1603, the broad thrust of crown policy towards Ireland was to normalize its administration on English lines. In particular, the size of the army was rapidly reduced to save money. It was only gradually (in the late 1630s, and more especially under Charles II) that the stationing of a larger army in Ireland began to be seen by the crown as a means of circumventing opposition to a standing army in England. Military taxation was likewise cut back, with the reduction in the army's size, and an English-style system of parliamentary taxation was introduced in the Irish parliament of 1613-15. Finally, in the long period of peace after 1603, military officials and martial law virtually

---

[18] Ellis, *Ireland in the age of the Tudors*, chs. 6,8-9; idem. 'Parliament and community in Yorkist and Tudor Ireland' in Art Cosgrove and J.I. McGuire (ed.), *Parliament and Community: Historical Studies XIV* (Belfast, 1983), pp 43-68; Brady*The Chief Governors*, passim; Nicholas Canny, *The Elizabethan Conquest of Ireland: a Pattern Established, 1565-76* (Hassocks, 1976).
[19] Nicholas Canny, *Kingdom and Colony; Ireland in the Atlantic World*, 1560-1800 (Baltimore, 1988).

disappeared.[20] It is hard to believe that if a civilized and settled country like Normandy or the Netherlands had been conquered, instead of 'the wild Irish', the experience of a standing army, military taxation, and martial law would not have been seen as holding lessons for English government elsewhere.

On the other hand, those aspects of Irish administration which accorded more closely with English traditions of government exercised a continuing influence on English officials. Just as Wales and the far north had been assimilated and incorporated into the English realm by extending standard English administrative structures and common law to these parts, so now too had Ireland (even if the desired results had taken longer to achieve in Ireland where the natives were only now, after 1603, learning English manners and growing civil!). In this context too, it should be noted that Tudor strategy was to anglicise Ireland and to incorporate it as far as possible into the kingdom of England - as 'a member appending and rightfully belonging to the imperial crown of the said realm of England and united to the same'.[21] The crown's aim was not to establish a sovereign kingdom of Ireland as part of a dual monarchy, even though things occasionally looked otherwise, notably in 1541. In 1541, Ireland was erected into a kingdom, whereas hitherto it had been a lordship; but this made absolutely no difference in terms of the constitutional relationship between England and Ireland.[22]

The Union of the Crowns in 1603 prompted King James to advance the concept of Britain - closer congruity between three kingdoms in a multiple monarchy - as a means of uniting his English and Scottish kingdoms in a common allegiance to a new British monarchy. Potentially at least, this marked a significant departure from the rigidly anglicizing strategy of state formation which had characterized Tudor policy to one which was a little more flexible and pluralist. Yet in terms of Ireland's status within this new British polity, what is so striking is that there was so little

---

[20] The essays by Aidan Clarke in T W Moody, F .X. Martin, and F.J. Byrne (ed.),*A New History of Ireland. III Early Modern Ireland, 1534-1691* (Oxford, 1976), chs. 7-9. On the army, see esp. the comments in the essays by John Morrill and Toby Barnard in Ellis and Barber, (eds.), *Conquest and Union*, pp. 28-31, 270-73.

[21] *The Statutes at Large Passed in the Parliaments Held in Ireland* (20 vols., Dublin, 1786-1801), I, 156.

[22] Ciaran Brady, 'Court, castle and country: the framework of government in Tudor Ireland' in C. Brady and R. Gillespie (ed), *Natives and Newcomers: Essays on the Making of Irish Colonial Society 1534-1641* (Dublin, 1986), pp 27-9; Ellis, 'Tudor state formation', pp 56-7; Ciaran Brady, 'The decline of the Irish kingdom' in Mark Greengrass (ed.)*Conquest and Coalescence: the Shaping of the State in Early Modern Europe* (London, 1991), ch.6. For a different view, see Brendan Bradhsaw*The Irish Constitutional Revolution of the Sixteenth Century* (Cambridge, 1979).

attempt to subsume the third Stuart kingdom within Britain after 1603.[23] In the longer term, this was to prove a significant omission: well before 1603, 'the British Isles' was current as a geographic term for the group of islands of which Britain and Ireland were the largest, but despite attempts in the nineteenth century to coin the term 'West Britain' for Ireland, Ireland never became part of Britain. (In recent years too, some Irish historians have begun to take exception to the use of the term 'the British Isles', with reference to Ireland, preferring instead to describe the islands collectively as the Atlantic archipelago, although this overlooks other groups of islands in the Atlantic, such as the Azores or the Canaries.)[24] Yet in the short term, the Stuart monarchy saw no need to stress Ireland's British identity, since Ireland was not a sovereign kingdom but annexed to the crown of the realm of England. Indeed, to do so was politically inadvisable in an English context, since it might appear to open Ireland to the attention of King James's Scottish subjects. In the event, however, the London government found it increasingly difficult to maintain this legal fiction in the changed circumstances after 1603.

In general, therefore, the importance of Ireland in the development of the British state system is that it supplied a flexible and adaptable, but ultimately quite misleading model of state formation which could be cited or ignored, as appropriate, in support of English prejudices. Thus for instance, Ireland's peculiar status as a dependent kingdom was held up by English officials after 1603 as a perfect model for Scotland's incorporation into the English state.[25] In fact, however, in the circumstances of the early seventeenth century, King James's concept of Britain was actually a much more realistic strategy. Any attempt to impose the inflexible and overcentralised English administrative system on Scotland was certain to be just as disastrous as it proved in Ireland. Where further research may well be needed, however, is concerning the precise reasons underpinning the English preference for an incorporating union with Scotland: was it simply that incorporation was a good deal less disruptive for England and was now also, as the case of Ireland and Wales showed, a tried and tested method of state formation? (In this respect, the Scottish

---

[23] John Morrill, 'State formation and nationhood', pp. 177-186; Jenny Wormald, 'James VI, James I and the identity of Britain' in Bradshaw and Morrill (ed.), *The British Problem*, ch.6.
[24] S.G. Ellis, 'Writing Irish history: revisionism, colonialism, and the British Isles' in *The Irish Review*, xix (1996), pp 1-21; Carl Moreland and David Bannister, *Antique Maps* (London, 1993), chs. 17-18.
[25] Wormald, 'Identity of Britain', pp 150-52.

experience too was of incorporating unions, as with the Western and Northern Isles acquired from Norway in 1266 and 1468/9.)[26] Or was it that the Scots too, particularly the 'wild Irish', of the Highlands and Western Isles, were perceived by the English as a savage people in need of 'English civility'?[27] However this may be, one reason why King James's British strategy was not taken up more enthusiastically was because, with the exception of Scotland for which alternative methods had to be devised, central control over dependencies of the English crown could always be consolidated by traditional Tudor methods of incorporation and anglicization. By contrast, what from a European perspective ought to have been the more valuable lesson which the Irish experience held for state formation - a standing army and a more effective system of taxation - was discounted and had to be learned afresh at great cost during the Wars of the Three Kingdoms (1638-52) and after.

---

[26] Ranald Nicholson, *Scotland, the Later Middle Ages* (Edinburgh, 1974), pp 46 413-18.

[27] The remarks in Derek Hirst, 'The English Republic and the meaning of Britain' in Bradshaw and Morrill (ed.), *The British Problem*, ch. 8 (esp. pp 201, 208) suggest that this too was an influence on English perceptions of Scotland.

THE PROBLEM OF THE 'COMPOSITE MONARCHY' IN SPAIN

PABLO FERNANDEZ ALBALADEJO
(*Autonomous University of Madrid*)

From a comparative point of view Professor Morrill's paper posits some interesting parallels between the Spanish and the British situation. Under pressure from internal nationalist movements and current moves towards European self-definition, both countries have begun parallel processes of state reorganisation and the redefinition of 'national'. Quite independently of the differences which exist between the origins of both processes and the individual collective attitude towards potential European goals, both situations share the need for a re-examination of a past history which appears to have been written to exalt an image of a nation, that nowadays turns out to be no longer generally shared. The very terms 'Spain' and 'Britain', with their respective implications of *Hispanidad* and *Britishness*, count in this sense as the first victims. In the face of the imminent disintegration of what has been considered up to now as the history of a relatively united past, the claim put forward for a 'British' history along the lines formulated by Morrill, constitutes an enriching methodological advance, which can equally be applied to the Spanish situation. This is especially so if we bear in mind that, unlike *Britannia*, *Hispania* had been a much more consistent political and cultural reality right from the late Middle Ages.

This paper tries to show to what extent, during the sixteenth and seventeenth centuries, we can really talk about a single idea and history of Spain which would integrate the histories of each of the kingdoms which composed the Spanish monarchy. These kingdoms had both a traditional identity of their own, and also a common factor of service to the Spanish crown. To a large degree, the present Spanish crisis of identity is tied up with the failure during the eighteenth and nineteenth centuries to define an alternative national identity to the one which was forged during the early modern period.

EL PROBLEMA DE LA "COMPOSITE MONARCHY" EN ESPAÑA

PABLO FERNÁNDEZ ALBALADEJO

(*Universidad Autónoma de Madrid*)

La primera consideración que me sugiere la excelente ponencia de John Morrill es de orden historiográfico. Aunque sin duda resulte algo más que obvio para los colegas del archipiélago que nos hospedan en estas jornadas, permítaseme que amparándome justamente en mi condición de huesped comience mi comentario refiriendo algunas cosas sabidas - sobre todo por los isleños - que pueden ayudar a encuadrar debidamente mi propio comentario. Así pues, y desde ese punto de vista estrictamente historiográfico, creo que la aportación de Morrill no viene sino a poner de manifesto la extraordinaria importancia que ha llegado a adquirir el toque de atencion a favor de una 'British History' que hace ya más de veinte años (1975) efectuara John Pocock desde las páginas del *Journal of Modern History*. Y cuya proyección con toda probabilidad habría sido menor de no haber mediado la presencia de un grupo de historiadores dispuestos a hacerse cargo, desarrollar y contrastar debidamente las sugerencias que acababan de ser formuladas. Dentro de esta estela hay que situar la serie de trabajos con los que desde hace algún tiempo nos viene obsequiando John Morrill, cuyos últimos planteamientos pueden verse ahora en el reciente libro editado conjuntamente con Brendan Bradshaw.[1] El trabajo de Morrill refleja así un quehacer historiográfico compartido que, según se nos indica en el primer ensayo de ese *reading*, aparece especialmente interesado en abordar de otra forma la historia de un espacio territorial y marítimo cuya identificación, hasta hace relativamente poco, no parecía plantear mayores problemas.

El hecho de que últimamente hayan podido suscitarse algunas dudas a este respecto, e incluso el que en estos momentos se debata intensamente sobre esa identificación, no es algo que por lo demás deba imputarse mecánica ni exclusivamente a la aparición del artículo de Pocock. La discusión, como es sabido, tiene que ver con transformaciones de auténtico calado, con procesos que eran ya más que evidentes por las fechas en las que Pocock lanzaba su manifesto. Tom Nairn los

---

[1] *The British Problem c. 1534-1707* (Londres, MacMillan, 1996), y asimismo, "The fashioning of Britain", en S. Ellis y S. Barber (eds.) *Conquest & Union*, (Londres, Longman, 1995), pp. 8-39.

analizaría en 1977 en un libro que gozó de cierta audiencia en España, y cuyo título ya denota de por sí bastante: *The Break-Up of Britain*.[2] Supongo que, de alguna manera, el título de la ponencia que nos acaba de exponer John Morrill tampoco es ajeno a esa *quiebra* en cuestión. Que su trabajo se identifique como una indagación sobre el proceso de *state formation* en Gran Bretaña así parece apuntarlo, poniendo de manifesto hasta qué punto la mencionada quiebra parece afectar a los supuestos mismos con los que ese concreto presente estatal se ha venido imaginando el propio pasado. Hasta el extremo de que se haya llegado a producir la desaparición - dentro del mismo título de la ponencia - de quien hasta la fecha había venido siendo el protagonista indiscutible en esa secuencia de *staatsbildung*. Y ante cuya llamativa ausencia Morrill se ve obligado a dar explicaciones: ya se nos advierte desde la primera nota a pie de página que el análisis de la *state formation* que va abordarse sucede dentro del escenario de un *atlantic archipelago*. No es por tanto historia de Inglaterra ni aún de Gran Bretaña de lo que va a tratarse; no al menos de lo que tradicionalmente ha venido entendiéndose como historia de «Gran Bretaña».

Así pues *State Formation and Nationhood in the Atlantic Archipelago* constituye algo más que un pacífico ejercicio de revisión historiográfica. Siendo eso, es también y sobretodo la constatación de que tal vez los historiadores tengan algo que decir ante lo que ya ellos mismos identifican como *The British Problem*. Por de pronto la propia hipótesis de partida que - en mayor o menor medida- comparte ese conjunto de investigaciones encierra en sí misma un claro mensaje: si la *break-up of Britain* acaba por consumarse ello no deberá significar - cualquiera que sea el escenario político que acabe asentándose- que por extensión deba quebrar asimismo la *British History*. Salvo que deliberadamente quiera utilizarse el *big-bang* político que eventualmente pudiera desencadenarse para borrar la memoria de un pasado, si no idílico y común, por lo menos compartido. Entiéndase bien: el sentido de la operación no es el de reclamar como algo metafísicamente irrenunclable una historia de Gran Bretaña - tácitamente hegemonizada por Inglaterra - sino el de señalar que tanto la historia de Inglaterra como la de Gales, Escocia e Irlanda sólo pueden llegar a entenderse plenamente si se ubican dentro de una "British dimension". Lo contrario

---

[2] La traducción española, por razones de mercado, adornó el sentido del libro titulándolo en portada como*Los Nuevos Nacionalismos en Europa* (Barcelona, 1979); una consideración no muy complaciente con el planteamiento marxista de Nairn, en B. ANDERSON, *Imagined Communities* (Londres, Verso, 1991).

equivaldría a una auténtica automutilación. Reivindicar una *British History* no implica en cualquier caso el abandono de los "national frameworks", sustituir la historia de cuatro naciones por la de una sola, sino el reconocer que por encima de cada una de esas historias ha ido tejiéndose un espacio de interacciones mutuas que solicita asimismo su propio lugar al sol. Tal sería en puridad la apuesta que subyace tras la *British History*, algo que consecuentemente debe percibirse dentro de un cierto *esprit*, como una suerte de experimento historiográfico cuyos logros deberán ser oportunamente contrastados.[3]

Si existe un *British problem* la historiografía de las Islas no ha permanecido muda ante él. Si me he entretenido en glosar su respuesta ha sido porque me parece que puede resultar de interés a la hora de establecer alguna comparación con el caso español. Al igual que Gran Bretaña, España se enfrenta asimismo a la decisiva reorientación política que supone el actual momento de definición europea. Pero la respuesta que en líneas generales se está produciendo ante esa presión no es desde luego la misma. La «reticencia inglesa» se transforma en nuestro caso en aceptación prácticamente generalizada, un relativo «eurooptimismo» se contrapone al «euroescepticismo». Hay sus razones como es sabido, pero no me corresponde ni procede el analizarlas aquí y ahora en detalle. Tan sólo quisiera señalar que en la misma medida que tras el euroescepticismo británico se arrastra un problema de desaparición de *empire* y de subsiguiente pérdida de soberanía,[4] tras el eurooptimismo español subyace - paradójicamente - un problema de continuidad misma de «España», entiéndase, de la idea de España como *una* comunidad nacional. No es, como cabe imaginar, una cuestión que se haya susitado en estos últimos tiempos. Es una historia que tiene su espesor y sus alternativas.[5] El franquismo encarnó, como se sabe, una de ellas, imponiendo violenta y autoritariamente una idea unidimensional de comunidad nacional. El llamado «Estado de las autonomías», la discutida expresión que se ha acuñado para designar nuestra actual forma de Estado, fue diseñado como una respuesta democrática frente a esa imposición. Es por tanto una apuesta política que

---

[3] "A problematic and uncompleted experiment in the creation and interaction of several nations", en palabras del propio Pocock retomadas por Morrill; todas las referencias proceden de los trabajos citados en la nota primera.
[4] El argumento, condensando su extensa investigación al respecto, en J.G. POCOCK,*La recostruzione di un impero. Sovranitá britannica e federalismo americano* (Roma, 1996).
[5] Un resumen en P. FERNANDEZ ALBALADEJO, "Les traditions nationales d'historiographie de l'État: L'Espagne", en *Visions sur le développement des États européens* (Roma, 1993), pp. 219-233.

ALBALADEJO

explícitamente quiere incorporar además un distinto entendimiento de España.
Francisco Tomás y Valiente, el ex-presidente de nuestro Tribunal Constitucional y
formidable historiador asesinado por los terroristas de ETA, gustaba hablar en este
sentido de la posibilidad de España como una "nación de naciones", rememorando así
la idea unamuniana de España como «sobrenación».[6]

No está nada claro sin embargo que esa propuesta cuente con demasiada
audiencia. Se diria incluso que las cosas apuntan en sentido contrario. En el
momento actual «España» resulta un término que, en el lenguaje cotidiano, tiende más
bien a eludirse, sustituído por la referencia a un abstracto y genérico «Estado». Como
si se sobreentendiese que la actual forma política estatal fuera asimismo la sede
precaria y sustitoria de una comunidad nacional puramente provisional. De hecho su
existencia no deja de ser puesta un dia y otro en cuestión. El «Estado» al que nos
venimos refiriendo - no se olvide - lo es «de las autonomías» y, en el equilibrio
interno de esa particular composición política, el segundo de los dos elementos
frecuentemente cuenta más que el primero. En la práctica ello significa que,
obviamente, ese estado concreto no se corresponde con una sola comunidad nacional;
y que incluso algunas de las comunidades autónomas que lo constituyen
(especialmente las llamadas «históricas», aquellas cuya evolución presenta rasgos
supuestamente diferenciales, como sucede en los casos de Cataluña y Euskadi)
puedan llegar a proclamar sin mayores problemas su desentendimiento explícito en
relación con el proyecto de una sola nación. Se diría que tales comunidades
autónomas aceptan *estar* en España, pero aparentemente no parecen dispuestas a *ser*
España.[7] Ni siquiera en los términos de «sobrenación» antes referidos: a estos efectos
es «Europa» quien aparece para ellas como la tierra prometida, como una opción
política y estratégicamente preferible a la de «España». En esa opción,
paradójicamente, las aspiraciones del nacionalismo radical periférico vienen a
coincidir con las de buena parte de la derecha española, no exenta tampoco en sus
planteamientos de un componente nacionalista propio, pero en líneas generales
consciente de las dificultades que el reciente pasado impondría al éxito de una apuesta

---

[6] F. TOMAS Y VALIENTE, *A orillas del Estado* (Madrid, Taurus, 1996), pp. 87-92, esp. 92; la referencia y oportuna contextualización de la expresión de Miguel de Unamuno en, P. CEREZO GALÁN,*Las máscaras de lo trágico* (Madrid, 1996), p.771.
[7] Generalizo aqui una idea expuesta por M.S. BASTENIER a propósito de la relación Cataluña-España ("España tieneun precio", *El País*, 17 de diciembre de 1996).

política pura y exclusivamente «españolista».   El eurooptimismo encubre aquí también intereses muy diversos.

De esta forma la posibilidad de que en el horizonte inmediato pueda llegar a producirse alguna nueva versión de la España-comunidad nacional es algo que, cuando menos, parece incierto. De hecho la propia historiografía así lo viene entendiendo ya desde hace algún tiempo. La instauración de la España autonómica ha generado una eclosión tal de historias nacionales/regionales que, en la reciente reforma de los planes de estudio de las universidades estatales, el Ministerio de Educación ha tenido que defender en más de un caso la presencia de una «Historia de España» con el mismo rango cuando menos que la de la respectiva comunidad autónoma. A la vista de lo que venimos refiriendo se comprenderá que se trata de una batalla perdida.   La europeización de España parece implicar - al menos historiográficamente - la «pérdida de España». Como si la profecía que ha venido pesando sobre ella desde la época de los visigodos - pacifica y silenciosamente - estuviera a punto de cumplirse.[8] Con menos énfasis profético pero con mayor amplitud y precisión ya lo había vaticinado Pocock: la construcción de Europa pasa por la *deconstrucción* de otras realidades.[9] *Britishness* e *hispanidad* pueden contarse entre sus víctimas.

Ya se ha visto no obstante que en el edificio por derribar algunas paredes podían y debían permanecer en pie.   Cuanto en este sentido ha venido argumentándose a favor de una *British History,* puede utilizarse aquí en relación con la necesidad de una «Historia de España». Con las mismas salvedades ciertamente que se han mencionado para el primer caso: si esta historia en cuestión no debe diluirse fragmentada en otras historias más o menos nacionales, tampoco cabe admitir su habitual reducción a la historia de Castilla o, más frecuentemente aún, a la de una dinastía. Sobre todo si tenemos en cuenta que, a diferencia de *Britannia, Hispania* presenta una posición de partida relativamente más nítida. Tanto como para que aquí fuese inimaginable que, como se vio obligado a hacer Jacobo I al principio de su reinado, ningún monarca tuviese que proponer su reconocimiento ante el Parlamento. Aún sin constituir una unidad política e incluso antes de configurarse como una unión

---

[8] A. MILHOU, "De la destruction de l'Espagne a la destruction des Indes", *Études sur l'impact du Nouveau Monde* (Paris, 1981), I, pp. 25-47.
[9] "Deconstructing Europe", *History of European Ideas*, vol. 18,3, 1994, pp.329-345.

dinástica Hispania existía, con unas señas que desde luego iban más allá de la simple expresión geográfica. Había la memoria - tan viva como imaginada - de un momento visigodo que, desde el observatorio del siglo XV, permitía fundar debidamente esa existencia[10] y mantenerla luego incluso en las circunstancias más adversas. La propia diversidad de reinos que había caracterizado el período medieval tampoco se consideraba en este sentido como un argumento que pudiese jugar en su contra; se sobrentendía que el desenvolvimiento de cada una de las identidades regnícolas no excluía su simultánea coexistencia, su encaje, dentro de esa forma primera. Naturalmente las disputas por establecer a cuál de esos *regna* correspondía ocupar la posición preeminente dentro de Hispania no escasearon, pero su propia presencia no venía sino a demostrar la aceptación de esas reglas de juego. El lenguaje lo reconocía: Hispania existía también en plural; «España» podía entenderse también como «las Españas», *Hispaniae*.

Los Reyes Católicos, como es sabido, explotarían exitosamente esa memoria, llegando a presentar su propia labor como la culminación de un proceso plurisecular encaminado desde el principio a conseguir la «restauración» de Hispania.[11] Debe advertirse por lo demás que esta úlitima no se entendía desde una perspective unidimensional, no ajustándose fácilmente a los excluyentes marcos estatales en los que hoy estamos habituados a desenvolvernos. Otra era la cultura entonces operante y, dentro de ella, unas identidades podían solaparse con otras sin mayor problema.[12] Podian darse así identidades eminentes e identidades subordinadas.[13] La nación no se consideraba en este sentido entre las segundas, pero los elementos que la componían nada tenían que ver con los forjados por el discurso nacionalista contemporáneo que los historiadores tienden a proyectar alegremente sobre ese período. La *nascion de España*, a la que en el siglo XV se refieren autores como Alonso de Cartagena, remitía en sus supuestos de fondo a un entendimiento de Hispania como sede de la *gens et patria Gothorum,* firmemente establecida en el

---

[10] S. TEILLET, *Des Goths à la Nation Gothique. Les origines de l'idée de nation en Occident du V au VII siècle* (Paris, 1984); J.A. MARAVALL, *El concepto de España en la Edad Media* (Madrid, IEP, 1964).

[11] R.B. TATE, *Ensayos sobre la historiografía peninsular del siglo XV* (Madrid, 1970).

[12] Lo ha recordado Linda COLLEY a propósito del XVIII británico: "Identities are not like hats. Human beings can and do put on several at a time" (*Britons: Forging the Nation 1707-1837* Londres, 1992, p.6); asimismo, A.D. SMITH*National Identity* (Londres, 1991).

[13] A..M HESPANHA, "A identidade portuguesa", *História de Portugal*, José Mattoso, (ed.) (Lisboa, 1993), vol. IV, pp. 19-37.

imaginario cultural desde la época de San Isidoro. Y dentro de la cual el núcleo verdaderamente identitario venía a componerlo la religión. *Hispania*, la *Hiberiae patria* de algunos textos de ese período visigodo, se entendía en todo caso como la *patria Christiana*. Era el reflejo de la patria auténtica, la *patria superna*, que obviamente estaba en los cielos. La religión devenía así puro lenguaje patriótico. A lo largo de la edad media fue esta una matriz que no perdió operatividad en sus supuestos.[14]

Los textos que a modo de ejemplo se recogen en el apéndice de estas páginas ilustran parte de esa compleja realidad, dejando constancia de las repercusiones que de ello pudieron derivarse a partir del momento en el que se produjo una primera formulación y entendimiento de España. Los textos 1 y 2 informan sobre algunos de los pormenores que acompañaron ese momento en cuestión. El Consejo Real (que sólo lo era de Castilla) podía tener dudas más que fundadas a la hora de aconsejar a Fernando e Isabel su intitulación como *Reyes de España*, unas dudas que probablemente no eran ajenas al hecho de que, desde otros círculos aúlicos (texto 2), se recomendase una solución que como la *monarchia de todas las Españas* cumplía el mismo objetivo de poder y al propio tiempo guardaba las formas. Se admitía así que ese orden político no tenía porqué entenderse en singular. En términos políticos podía admitirse más de una España, cabían en ella varios *territorios* con un monarca que agregadamente los representaba.[15] Esta noción de pluralidad era algo que no podía admitirse en términos de religión. Aquí no cabía pluralidad. No es casual que la unión dinástica de las coronas de Castilla y Aragón fuese en cierto sentido reforzada con la concesión (1496) a Fernando e Isabel -por parte de Alejandro VI- del título de *Católicos*, o más exactamente de «Rey y Reina Católicos de las Españas»[16]

El título en cuestión condensaba, en su sentido más profundo, cuál era la identidad de la nueva monarquía. En él los monarcas hispanos eran reconocidos - ya

---

[14] Ver los trabajos recogidos por J. FONTAINE Y C. PELLISTRANDI (ed.), *L'Europe Héritière de l'Espagne Wisigothique* (Madrid, 1992).
[15] Sobre ese proceso de consitución ver especialmente, B. CLAVERO, "Anatomía de España",*Quaderni Fiorentini*, 34-35, I, pp. 47-86; sobre la idea de monarquá de España, J.A. MARAVALL, "El concepto de monarquía en la edad media española", *Estudios de Historia del pensamiento español* (Madrid, 1973) pp. 69-89. El término territorio se utiliza aquí en la acepción de O. BRUNNER, *Terra e potere*, (Milan, 1983), pp. 229-330.
[16] Ver nuestro trabajo, "«Rey Católico». Gestación y metamorfosis de un título", *El Tratado de Tordesillas y su época* (Valladolid, 1995), I, pp. 209-216.

ALBALADEJO

antes de la llegada de Carlos V - como el nuevo poder imperial *de hecho* dentro de la Cristiandad, y esa sería justamente la forma en la que *España* comenzaría a ser percibida desde el exterior.[17] Visto desde el interior el título no tenía menos sentido. Como escribía Gonzalo de Ayora a Fernando el Católico (texto 4), España, a comienzos del XVI, podía equipararse sin mucha exageración a un monasterio de *observantes*. Pero, para llegar a ese desenlace, de por medio había habido que ingeniar alguna que otra novedosa solución a fin de clausurar un complejo conflicto religioso que desde el siglo anterior venía enfrentando a viejos y nuevos cristianos, a *cristianos viejos* y conversos, y entre cuyas consecuencias no planeadas habría de contarse el establecimiento de la Inquisición. A partir de ella - aunque no sólo por ella - pudo ponerse en marcha un precoz proceso de confesionalización que colocaría a España en una situación de *first comer* dentro de la dinámica de soluciones confesionales que inmediatamente iban a ensayarse en Europa.

Lejos de contradecir esa dinámica, el advenimiento de Carlos V vendría a reforzarla. El tortuoso aunque finalmente efectivo alineamiento de Carlos V con el papado, y por tanto con la confesión católica, acentuaría el papel de la religión -desde esa perspectiva confesional - como referente identitario de España. Así, en 1548, Pedro de Medina colocaba al "celo de la santa fe católica" y al "Santo Oficio de la Santa Inquisición" entre los *bienes* que era preciso consignar dentro del *Libro de grandezas y cosas memorables de España*. La progresiva identificación que llegaría a producirse con la idea imperial no supondría, de otra parte, la difuminación de España dentro del entramado imperial carolino, tal y como dejan entrever las prevenciones que se solicitan en el texto 5. La tradición de *imperio propio* supuso en este sentido un papel fundamental; gracias a ella justamente pudo comenzar a plantearse la presencia de un orden católico que, sustentado sobre la noción de *hispanitas*, superaba ya en grandeza al propio momento imperial romano.[18] Para Juan Ginés de Sepúlveda, el principal ideólogo de esa propuesta, Carlos V aparecía por encima de todo como "Rey de España y de los españoles", y era la historia de estos últimos la que intentaba incorporar en sus trabajos. A efectos de fundar una historia propia, don Pelayo comenzaba a interesar tanto o más que el propio Recaredo, los *españoles* más

---

[17] P. FERNÁNDEZ ALBALADEJO, *Fragmentos de Monarquía* (Madrid, 1993), pp. 168-

[18] J. L. PHELAN, "El imperio cristiano de Las Casas, el imperio espanol de Sepúlveda y el imperio milenario de Mendieta", *Revista de Occidente*, 1974, pp. 293-310; FERNÁNDEZ ALBALADEJO, *Fragmentos*, pp. 60-72.

que los *visigodos*. Haciendo suyo ese planteamiento, Esteban de Garibay llegará a afirmar en 1571 que don Pelayo "no era de nación godo, sino natural español".

La afirmación de Garibay, no por casualidad, procede de *Los XL Libros de las Chronicas y Universal Hisioria de todos los Reinos de España* (1571), una de las realizaciones más imponentes del XVI historiográfico hispano, y un título que con esa pretensión de *universal historia* denota ya bastante. La obra venía a mostrar cómo era possible organizer una «historia de España», exponer ordenadamente una relación de las "muchas cosas notables de la nacion española", acreditar en fin su "mucha santidad y religion" sin desatender, al mismo tiempo, a "los prosperos sucesos de los españoles" en Italia o Indias. Existía por tanto «España» como protagonista de una historia. Pero continuaba siendo una España que, internamente y desde sus primeros momentos, se declinaba en plural. La dominación romana, por ejemplo, sólo había podido asentarse después de una serie de guerras mantenidas "con diversas naciones de España", entre las cuales ocupaban un lugar preferente las llevadas a cabo por "los Españoles Lusitanos y su Capitán Viriato". Dentro de esa pluralidad corporativa Garibay reconocía, sin embargo, que Castilla ocupaba la posición de "cabeza de España". La afirmación pretendía mostrarse como un dato nada conflictivo pero encubría de hecho una importante tensión interna. Los textos 6 a 8 permiten entrever hasta qué punto todos y cada uno de los territorios se percibían como parte integrante de España, aunque no por ello dejaba de haber sus diferencias. Frente a la pretensión de hegemonía castellana reivindicada por López Madera en 1597 se alzará, por ejemplo, la perspectiva aragonesa, sugiriendo que su territorialidad tenía mayor consistencia que la de la propia España; o bien, como se hará desde Portugal en un momento posterior, podía proponerse sin más una pacífica composición.

El espectacular incremento de los costes de la guerra, la enormidad de los objetivos planteados y al propio tiempo la convicción de que -con la religión en juego- se trataba de objetivos irrenuncibles, dió como resultado un agotamiento de energías y recursos más que perceptible ya a finales del siglo XVI. La política de pacificación con la que obligadamente se abrió el siglo XVII fue acompañada de un replanteamiento de los supuestos sobre los que había venido desarrollándose la política universal de la monarquía, e inevitablemente del propio entendimiento de España. A estos efectos, el Gran Memorial (texto 9) constituye sin duda uno de los documentos más representativos. Pero la conversión de Felipe IV en efectivo *rey de España* que allí se sugiere poco tiene que ver con la pretensión de imponer ya desde esa fecha una España centralista y aún castellanizante tal y como tendió a interpretarse desde el siglo XIX. De hecho el memorial no puede entenderse sin considerar otra serie de proyectos simultáneos que venían a completar el diseño de Olivares y que, en su conjunto, ponen de manifiesto que la estrategia principal apuntaba hacia el afianzamiento de un imperio austríaco integral (que reunificase la política de las dos ramas) y monoconfesional.[19] No se pierda de vista que el objetivo primordial, el "fin tan justo y tan glorioso" de la empresa, no era otro que el de la "dilatación de la religión católica". La necesidad de los cambios se explica a partir de este supuesto primero y principal. Desde el punto de vista de la *monarquía de España* la realización de ese diseño aparecía por otra parte como la única forma de acallar la reputación de que esta última no era sino "un cuerpo fantástico" acosado por "la debilidad de sus fuerzas en su raíz" (texto 11). Pero los cambios que eventualmente llegaran a introducirse en ningún caso podrían trascender la esfera de lo que estrictamente fuese *gubernaculum, gobernación*, sin posibilidad de afectar a lo que fuese *justicia, jurisdictio*. Los *fueros* y las *prerrogativas particulares* sólo podrían alterarse dentro de los límites de ese entendimiento.

Apelando a la *necesidad*, pero convencido al mismo tiempo de que con ello no se alteraban los supuestos de fondo por los que se regía la monarquía, Olivares intentaba implementa tácticamente un principio de actuación puramente *político* que permitiese sacar adelante los asuntos de esa misma monarquía. Su planteamiento, como se sabe, no llegaría a conseguir una aquiescencia general. Como en 1631 venía a hacer patente Juan de Palafox, cada reino debía de mantener su particular constitución natural. La integración de la monarquía se fundaba - y se bastaba - en la obediencia y lealtad a un rey común; con ello tenían conseguido "la más principal parte de felicidad en lo político" (texto 10). En España por encima y antes de lo político se situaba siempre la religión, "una y verdadera". Y ello hasta el extremo de que allí donde existía la verdadera religión no se reconocían consecuentemente diferencias nacionales: no cabía "a los ojos de cristianos hacer diferencia de naciones,

[19] E. STRAUB, *Pax et Imperium* (Munich, F. Schonning ed., 1980), pp. 79-129; H. ERNST,*Madrid und Wien 1632-1637* (Munster, 1991), pp. 19-44.

sino de obras"; de hecho, y en este sentido, no había más que "una nación, y esa es Cristianos".[20] Esa era la identidad que componía la nación, y tal era el lenguaje nacional con el que podía operarse. No puede sorprendernos entonces que Francesc Martí Viladamor -uno de los ideólogos de la revuelta catalana que acabaría luego afiliado a posiciones profrancesas- denunciase en 1640 la política de Olivares como una política que tendía a "la ruina y perdición de España" (texto 12). Independientemente de que -contra lo argumentado por López Madera- ninguno de los reinos de España podía abrogarse la sobrelegitimidad histórica pretendida por Castilla (todos descendían de los godos y todos habían surgido como reacción frente al Islam), lo que preocupaba especialmente al autor era poner de manifiesto hasta qué punto Olivares, con su actuación, no venía sino a subvertir lo que habían sido los propios supuestos fundacionales de España en el momento visigótico. La revuelta podía justificarse en este sentido como una defensa de España. No otra cosa era lo que habían hecho los campesinos de una provincia que, tenida por "columna constante de la fe católica", se habían opuesto al herético saqueo de las iglesias realizado por las tropas de la monarquía acantonadas en el Principado. Con el alzamiento no sólo se redimía Cataluña, "sino toda España". La resistencia frente al *privado* era algo que, finalmente, comprometía a todos, ya que "perdida Cataluña lo sería toda España".

No le faltaba razón en este sentido a Matías de Novoa, el cronista de Felipe IV, al considerar que los acontecimientos de 1640 supusieron el inicio de las "guerras de España."[21] Quienes participaron en ellas podían ser de *nación* catalana o castellana, pero ya se ha visto que no por ello dejaban de considerarse al mismo tiempo como *españoles*. *Prima facie* el conflicto se presentaba como una guerra *social*, como un conflicto entre aliados (en el sentido de *socii* que Pocock y el propio Morrill sugieren) dentro de la misma monarquía, pero más sustantivamente quizás el conflicto ejemplificaba también una guerra *civil* entre *españoles*. La finalización de esas guerras no supondría, ya en la segunda mitad del XVII, una alteración de ese entendimiento tradicional de España. Aupándose sobre una victoria militar, Felipe V

---

[20] A. BAUTISTA, *Discurso breve sobre las miserias de la vida*, cit. Por J.Mª JOVER, 1635: *Historia de una polémica y semblanza de una generación* (Madrid, 1949), p.418. (Munster, 1991), pp. 19-44. (Munster, 1991), pp. 19-44.

[21] VARII, *Historia de la cultura espanola: El siglo del Quijote* (*Historia de España de R. Menéndes Pidal*), (Madrid, 1996), I, p.623.

introduciría a comienzos del XVIII unas nuevas reglas de juego. De acuerdo con lo aprendido de la experiencia de su propio abuelo, el nuevo monarca procedería a aplicar en España el modelo absolutista de disposición y tratamiento patrimonial del reino tal y como se había intentado en Francia.[22] Una solución bien distinta por cierto de la que en 1707 había dado lugar al *Treaty of Union*. Si este último sentó las bases para el *forging the nation* dentro del archipiélago, la evolución del reino de España tardaría algún tiempo en vislumbrar ese horizonte. Antes que sobre un planteamiento de eventual afirmación de nación, las lineas de fuerza del XVIII español se articularán sobre una logica de *grandeur dynastique* impuesta a través de una tecnología de poder estrictamente administrativista. De ahí la aparición de un lábil partido *castizo* o *español* opuesto desde el primer momento a la aplicación de un proyecto dinástico que se consideraba desnacionalizador, como asimismo la irrupción a partir del último tercio de siglo de una corriente de crítica ilustrada firmemente decidida a denunciar el despotismo de la monarquía.

Arrancando desde el mismo momento revolucionario gaditano, los dos primeros tercios del siglo XIX conocerán por ello un sostenido esfuerzo a fin de recuperar la memoria histórica de una nación española cuyas señas se consideraban deliberadamente desfiguradas por el absolutismo. Y que, más sustantivamente, irá acompañado por la conformación e imposición de la propia *España* como sujeto político, por su "institución constitucional."[23] Es la gran apuesta que se ventila. De sus vicisitudes no podemos aquí ocuparnos, pero su fracaso resultará determinante en la irrupción a fines de siglo de la radical y angustiosa crisis de identidad que marcará los hombres de 1898. Su estela no se ha perdido todavía de vista. El esfuerzo de los historiadores contemporaneistas por minimizar su presencia e incluso por darla por clausurada de una vez por todas[24] es probablemente la demostración más concluyente de que el problema identitario español esta lejos todavía de haberse clausurado.

[22] Sobre este punto, y lo que sigue, FERNÁNDEZ ALBALADEJO, *Fragmentos*, pp. 353-454.

[23] B. CLAVERO, "Tejido de sueños. La historiografía jurídica española y el problema del Estado",*Historia Contemporánea*, 12, 1995, pp. 25-47.

[24] S. JULIA, "Anatomía, dolor y fracaso de España", *Claves*, 66, 1996, pp. 10-21.

APENDICE. TEXTOS

[1]. "Platicose ansimesmo en el Consejo del Rey e de la Reyna como se devian yntitular, e como quiera que algunos del su consejo eran en voto que se yntitulasen Reyes de España, pues subçediendo en aquellos Reynos e señorios eran señores de toda la mayor parte de ella, pero determinaron de lo no fazer" (Femando del Pulgar, *Crónica*, 1479)

[2] "... nuestra señora doña Ysabel Reyna de España, de Cecilia y Cerdeña, duquesa de Athenas, condesa de Barçalona. Y como quiera, muy esclarescida princesa, que Nuestro Señor vos haya dado no sin gran merescimiento poco menos que la monarchia de todas las Españas" (Diego de Valera, Crónica, circa 1487)

[3] "Creo que actualmente España es el único país feliz, a quien cupo en suerte (cosa que hasta ahora le fue negada) tener unos principes amantes de la religion, defensores acérrimos de la justicia, y de una prudencia consumada: marido y esposa que como divinidades bajadas del cielo, con tanta compenetración y en tal modo la guardan, ilustran y hacen prosperar, que verdaderamente parecen inspirados por algún espiritu divino o guiados por la diestra misma del omnipotente." (Pedro Martir de Angleria, *Epistolario*, 1487)

[4] "E ya muy poco faltava para que todos los pecados del mundo corriesen libremente por españa syn contradiçion alguna. Y vuestra alteza, juntamente con la Reyna nuestra señora, los arrancaron y desterraron, y en lugar de ellos plantaron tantas virtudes que españa, en conparacion de todo el Resto del mundo es casi un monesterio de Relisyon oservante." (Gonzalo de Ayora a Fernando el Católico, 1507)

[5]. "Don Carlos, por la Gracia de Dios, Rey de Romanos, futuro Emperador semper Augusto, y Rey de Castilla y de León, & ... Por quanto despues que plugo a la Divina Clemencia (...) que fuessemos elegido Rey de Romanos, futuro Emperador, y que de Rey Catolico de España (con que eramos bien contentos) fuessemos promovido al Imperio, convino que nuestros titulos se ordenasen ... Fue necesario (conformandonos con razon, segun la qual, el Imperio precede a las otras dignidades seglares ...) de preferir la Dignidad Imperial a la Real ... Y porque de la dicha prelacion no se pueda seguir, ni causar perjuicio, ni confusion adelante a los nuestros Reynos de España, ni

a los Reyes nuestros sucesores, ni a los naturales sus subditos que por tiempo fueren. Por ende... nuestra intencion e voluntad es que la libertad, y exempcion que los dichos Reynos de España, y Reyes de ellos han tenido, y tienen... de no reconocer superior, les sea ahora y de aqui adelante observada" (Carlos V, 5 de septiembre de 1519)

[6] "Con lo qual se entendera la grande razon y causa que ban tenido nuestros Reyes aviendo juntado estos Reynos tan poderosos y grandes para usar de las armas y insignias particulares de cada uno componiendo de ellas el escudo Real ... //... Y no he querido en esta consideracion hazer division alguna de España, porque es para mi cosa certissima y indubitable, que el derecho y verdadero señorio de toda ella siempre estuvo, y se continuo en los Reyes de Leon y Castilla, successores legitimos del Rey Don Pelayo, como esta fundado en toda buena razón y derecho ... //... De manera que el Reyno de España es verdaderamente uno, aunque en señal de las victorias de sus Reyes este dividido en muchos titulos". (Gregorio López Madera, *Excelencias de la Monarchia y Reyno de España*, Madrid, 1597)

[7]. "Maxima autem regio plures ac diversas, magnas regiones comprehendit intra suos fines, & territorium, ut Hispania, intra quam sunt magnae regiones, supra numeratae [Castella, Navarra, Cathalonia Valentia, Lusitania, Aragonia] quae pyrineis montibus circunscribitur... ac sub uno catholico, ac domino nostro Rege Philippo gubernatur, & regitur: que tamen, sub maioribus regionibus comprehendetur, ut sunt Europa, Asia, vel Africa. Ex quibus omnibus, licet parva, & magna regio semper ab uno capite regantur, indeque proprie regiones apellatae, tamen maxime & maiores non semper, nec necessario, sed ex accidenti, uni capiti subsunt, ac in unum regem pervenerunt..." (Pedro Calixto Ramírez, *Analyticus Tractatus de Lege Regia*, Zaragoza, 1616)

[8] "Podran dezirme, que siendo el titulo deste libro *Flores de España, Excelencias de Portugal*, no trato en el de otro algun Reyno de España sino en orden a Portugal, y assi parece que no concuerda el titulo con la materia, y que pudiera quitarse el nombre de *Flores de España*, a lo qual digo, que como Portugal es parte tan principal de España, escriviendo yo las Excelencias deste Reyno, escrivo Flores de España ... // ... Portugal es Reyna de todas las otras tierras, pues la naturaleza, o mas propiamente hablando, Dios le puzo en tal parte que queda no solo con corona, sino cabeça coronada de todo el mundo, y assi Europa es la mejor parte del orbe, España como

cabeça es la principal de Europa, Portugal como corona honra de España..." (Antonio de Sousa Macedo, *Flores de España, Excelencias de Portugal*, Lisboa, 1631)

[9]. "Tenga V. Majd. por el negocio más importante de su Monarquía el hacerse rey de España; quiero decir, señor, que no se contente V. Majd. con ser rey de Portugal, de Aragón, de Valencia, conde de Barcelona, sino que trabaje y piense con consejo maduro y secreto por reducir estos reinos de que se compone España al estilo y leyes de Castilla, sin ninguna diferencia en todo aquello que mira a dividir límites, puertos secos, el poder celebrar cortes de Castilla, Aragón y Portugal en la parte que quisiere, a poder introducir V. Majd. acá y allá ministros de las naciones promiscuamente ... //... deseando este poder para el mayor bien y dilatación de la religión católica, conociendo que la división presente de leyes y fueros enflaquece su poder y le estorba el conseguir fin tan justo y tan glorioso y tan del servicio de nuestro Señor, y conociendo que los fueros y prerrogativas particulares que no tocan en el punto de justicia, que esa en todas partes es una y se ha de guardar..." (Olivares, *Gran Memorial*, 1624)

[10] "Porque así como no vendrá bien el sombrero a la mano, ni el guante a la cabeza, y sería extraño y disforme si se trocasen, así cada reino, conforme a sus naturales, sus inclinaciones, su situación, sus circunstancias, ha de tener diferentes leyes, y con ese cuidado se ha de gobernar, porque sería peligroso alterarles el gobierno que aman, porque con el nacieron y crecieron. Pero como en lo universal, que es el reconocimiento, la lealtad, la obediencia y jurisdicción estén sujetos a un rey, tienen conseguida la más principal parte de felicidad en lo político. En esto, pues, concededme que España se aventaja a todas las naciones, no sólo con una y verdadera. Religión, sino debajo de un Príncipe cristiano, católico, santo, celador de lo bueno, enemigo de lo malo.." (Juan de Palafox y Mendoza, *Diálogo Político del Estado de Alemania*, 1631)

[11] "Todas las grandes monarquías se fundan en gente, dineros y abundancia de lo importante para conducir grandes ejércitos que develen los enemigos; assí los políticos extraños que celosos han atendido con profundidad a nuestros defectos han resuelto que pesa poco la monarquía de España con todas sus provincias por la debilidad de sus fuerzas en su raíz; dicen que es un cuerpo fantástico defendido de la opinión no de la sustancia. Porque, señor, de qué utilidad le pueden ser a V. Majd.

algunos reinos si cuando a V. Majd. le invaden los enemigos, aunque fuese en su corte, ellos no tienen obligación de ampararle" (*El Nicandro*, Madrid, 1643)

[12]. "No teme mi afligido coraçon última ruina a Barcelona y fatal ocasso a Cataluña, porque las ya referidas circunstancias y las preeminencias que luego escriviré, declaran a tan feliz provincia por columna constante de la fe católica y reparo firme de la Iglesia Santa ... //... Y si los de Castilla tuvieron esta pretensión de poder elegir rey según las góticas costumbres... ¿es mucho que los catalanes tengan la misma pretensión... Y es mucho que por la misma razón tengan autoridad para mudar de govierno?... Por la qual mutación de govierno (quando sucediese) nunca se mudaría en los catalanes su innato amor... porque con ella quedaría Cataluña, no sólo con más fuerças para defender a sus naturales, sino también para oponerse con efecto a qualquier designio del Privado, en el qual para lograr sus desseos dispusiese la ruina y perdición de España, siendo mas cierto que perdida Cataluña, lo sería toda España" (Francesc Martí Viladamor, *Noticia Universal de Cataluña*, Barcelona, 1640)

[13]. "Habiendome representado mi Consejo de Estado las grandes conveniencias y utilidades que resultarian a favor de la causa publica y bien universal de mis Reinos y vasallos, de formar un nuevo reglamento para la sucesion de esta Monarquia... a fin de conserver en ella la agnacion rigurosa, [y aunque] para aclarar la regla mas conveniente a lo interior de mi propia familia y descendencia podria pasar como primero y principal interesado y dueño a disponer su establecimiento, quise oir el dictamen del Consejo [de Castilla] ... //Y quiero y mando, que la sucesion de esta Corona proceda de aqui adelante en la forma expresada, estableciendo por Ley fundamental de la sucesion de estos Reinos, sus agregados y que a ella se agregaren, sin embargo de la ley de Partida y de otras qualesquiera leyes..." (Felipe V, 10 de mayo de 1713).

[14]. "Considerando aver perdido los Reinos de Aragon i Valencia, y todos sus habitadores,por el rebelion que cometieron... todos los fueros, privilegios, essenciones i libertades que gozaban... i tocandome el dominio absoluto de los referidos Reinos de Aragon i Valencia... he juzgado por conveniente (assi por esto, como por mi deseo de reducir todos mis Reinos de España a la uniformidad de unas mismas leyes, usos, costumbres y Tribunales, governandose igualmente todos por las Leyes de Castilla, tan loables y plausibles en todo el universo) abolir i derogar enteramente... todos los

referidos fueros, privilegios, practica i costumbre hasta aqui observadas en los referidos Reinos de Aragon i Valencia, siendo mi voluntad que estos se reduzcan a las Leyes de Castilla, i al uso, practica y forma de govierno que se tiene i ha tenido en ella i en sus Tribunales sin diferencia alguna en nada, pudiendo obtener por la razon mis fidelissimos Vasallos los Castellanos, oficios i empleos en Aragon, i Valencia de la misma manera que los Aragoneses i Valenclanos han de poder en adelante gozarlos en Castilla" (Felipe V, 29 de junio de 1707).

IDENTITIES : NATIONS, PROVINCES AND REGIONS 1550-1900
SOME CONCLUDING REMARKS

JAMES CASEY
(University of East Anglia)

Three main themes would seem to emerge from the papers presented at the Anglo-Spanish colloquium in the University of East Anglia in October 1996, of which the present volume is the outcome. In the first place, there is the question of what one might call 'palaeo-nationalism', or the latent or potential identities available to social groups, based on shared territory or customs or environment. Secondly - and this was perhaps one of the most suggestive ideas to emerge from the conference - there is the task of distinguishing (if we can) between historicism and history, between the teleogical view of a national identity developing over time, whose significance in the present distorts the lens through which we regard the past, and the patient reconstruction of the solidarities which had significance for our ancestors. Thirdly and finally, there is the full-blown nationalist movement of the nineteenth and twentieth centuries, which clearly draws on both of the above legacies - on solidarities real and presumed, on a sense of place and on a reinvention of tradition. Some political trigger was clearly required to convert potential nations into nation states, great or small. It will be the aim of my concluding remarks to try and draw out some of the implications of these three points - more than anything, as an invitation to reflection and debate.

The countries on which the participants in this colloquium have focused - the Atlantic Archipelago, the Iberian Peninsula, Scandinavia - have clearly immense reservoirs of customs and languages and cultures which do not always coincide neatly, either today or in the past, with political frontiers. The 'natio' is an old concept, as the great Spanish historian Menéndez Pidal once pointed out, referring to the ninth-century chronicle of Asturias-León, which had no difficulty in distinguishing between the various peoples of Europe with their individual characteristics. The Song of Roland not long afterwards surveyed the well-defined 'national' groups which made up Charlemagne's army - Franks, Bavarians, Normans - whose language, dress and perhaps some lingering myth of tribal ancestry would

203

have marked them out as in some way different from their fellows. Just as Charlemagne relied on national solidarities to give cohesion to his fighting forces, the great thirteenth-century Castilian law book, the Siete Partidas, spelled out the basic solidarities on which a medieval society was constructed: the family, *crianza* (loyalty to the man in whose household one had been reared), vassalage, *amistad* (friendship), and *naturaleza*, whereby two men from the same region "take pleasure in one another's company and help each other in time of need."

In this sense, the 'nation' does not depend on a territory. The great novel of Pío Baroja, *The Restlessness of Shanti Andia* (1911), reminds us of the network of human solidarity created across America and Asia by the Basque diaspora of sailors and traders. A sense of identity for the Irish and the Jews has many parallels with this kind of memory, which depends on a shared culture rather than a defined space. Territory was certainly important as one of the factors in building up the solidarities of pre-modern communities; but the attention that pre-modern writers paid to it depended on the belief that the character of the inhabitants could be explained by the astrological and climatic influences prevailing in particular latitudes. Before the seventeenth century, geographers were concerned to map what one might call the 'sacred landscape' of shrines and historic towns, which, along with the sign of the Zodiac, gave a particular 'nation' its identity. The concern with the physical landscape - with mountains, rivers and roads - grows from that time onwards, as the state (and above all its military men) began to exert greater control of the frontiers, planning for defence and in the process paying careful attention to statistics of population and production. The birth of economics as a science separate from theology and ethics began to change the perceived link between man and his physical environment, as we approach modern times. The whole process might be summarised as the growth of an organised polity, more dependent now on the exercise of fiscal and military power than on ancient clannish or personal loyalties.

Trying to separate out the two different but allied concepts of the state and the nation may help us to acquire a clearer image of each. Menéndez Pidal saw fit to point out that none of the historic peoples of the Iberian peninsula is clearly set off from its neighbours by what one might call 'natural frontiers'. Rather the cultures and languages straddle mountain barriers. Nor did the hand of man play much direct role in the shaping of a people - at least not initially - for the political frontiers drawn at an early date were complex. Thus the kingdom of Asturias-León already in the eighth century included both Romance dialects of Castilian and Galician, while the kingdom of Navarre from the tenth century comprised both Basque and Castilian speakers. From a different perspective, one is impressed by how weakly these political units correspond to what might be termed social groupings. Looking at family systems, for example, one notes the survival down to the twentieth century of a Pyrenean 'community', running from Catalonia through northern Aragon into the Basque Country. Here, the traditions of the single heir have created a stable medium peasantry - and a strong family piety centred on the parish church - which has given these areas a collective identity as strongly Catholic, even Carlist (that is, hostile to the liberal governments of nineteenth-century Madrid). But that collective identity was not translated into a common language or culture, or any sense - except marginally in the Carlist Wars of the nineteenth century - of political solidarity. In the British Isles, as we have been reminded, there was a strong difference within the kingdom of Scotland in language and customs between the Highlands and the Lowlands. For some purposes - as is evident in the correspondence of the Spanish ambassador to the court of James I, the count of Gondomar - the Highlands seem to blend with Ulster as a redoubt of tribal independence, rebelliousness and hostility to the official Protestant culture. Even at the present day, the traveller from London to Belfast or Dublin via Liverpool may find himself wondering whether the significant frontier within the Atlantic Archipelago is not the human one between the 'Celtic' uplands of the north and west, with their distinctive landscapes, climate and architecture, rather than the political and religious divisions between England and Ireland.

It is at this stage that one may reflect on the enormous significance of the 'accidents of history', in cutting through the solidarities of geography and creating identities of a more explicit kind. Medieval and early modern historians are less likely than their modernist colleagues to be immediately interested in the question of national identity. Nationalism is not something which acquires significance until we get towards more modern times - at least, not as a major political force in its own right. But clearly one of the major features of the earlier period is the phenomenon of state-building, and the events associated with this process - however we interpret them - enter into the stream of historical consciousness and become factors in the later growth of the nationalist movements. Thus we have the fact of Portugal's independence of the Spanish crown, established after at least one bitter war (1640-68), and the failure of the contemporaneous revolt of the Catalans (1640-52). The memory of 11 September 1714 when the troops of Philip V stormed into Barcelona lives on in the Catalan national consciousness, even though the event itself and its causes are susceptible of a diversity of interpretations.

Further comparisons between a strong British and a rather weakly integrated Spanish state would no doubt be fruitful. The fiscal strength of the British state after the civil wars of the seventeenth century which established parliamentary sovereignty has been a subject of interest to Marxist historians for some time. It has implications for the growth of the modern world economy - for the dominant position occupied by Britain and a few other states in the Age of Mercantilism, during which military power was critical for the development of capitalism. That Spain did not manage the transition towards a 'bourgeois' state, where an entrepreneurial elite held the reins of power, was one of the spurs to Catalan nationalism after the disastrous loss of the last Spanish colonies in the war of 1898 with the United States. The Catalan cotton manufacturers began to redouble their criticism of a weakly integrated state, in which a kind of informal 'feudalism' (*caciquismo*) characterised government. Lawyers and landlords in Madrid presided over a loose federation of local communities, run by corrupt oligarchies. As Pérez Galdós pointed out in his great novel *Miau* (1886), 'the long battle between the taxpayer and the state' prevented Spain from achieving the political and social reforms on which so much else depended. In that sense it is difficult to separate out the question of national identity from a much wider analysis of the structure of power and the controversies over the relationship between the political centre and its peripheries. Students of Spanish America in the late colonial period are, of course, particularly aware of this problem, as it affects the complex growth of a Creole, 'American' identity around 1800. At some stage the Spanish elites living in Venezuela or Mexico, though barely a fifth of the population, were prepared to take the enormous risk of separating themselves from their metropolitan centre and to construct new homelands, in alliance with the majority Indian, Black and half-breed populations. The countries of Ecuador or Bolivia or Guatemala which emerged from the bitter wars of 1808-25 were interestingly based on the old administrative divisions of the Spanish empire.

The construction of states is a question which has a much wider resonance than the theme of the present conference on national identity. One may wonder how much attention should be paid by early modern historians to the great strength of competing claims by the church to sovereignty in Catholic countries. At the time of the Reformation the universalism of Christendom was broken in Protestant countries, and the state assumed an increasing role as the embodiment of emotional loyalty and spiritual guidance for its citizens. One thinks, for example, of Henry VIII abandoning the title of lord of Ireland, granted to his ancestors by the popes, and calling himself king of Ireland after 1541; one thinks of the enormous significance of the 'Protestant' calendar in seventeenth-century England - the growth of patriotic holidays centred on 5 November (the safeguarding of king and parliament from conspiracy) and 17 November (the providential accession of Elizabeth I in 1558, after the Marian persecution). There is little that is equivalent to this in Spain, where festivities continued to be centred more on the traditional saints identified with localities. Even Saint James was a Castilian rather than a Spanish phenomenon.

If the Spanish state entered modern times, therefore, with a looser structure, both fiscal and spiritual, than its British counterpart, the development of nationalist movements in the nineteenth and twentieth centuries would inevitably take rather different forms. The modern phenomenon of nationalism has generated such a prolific literature in recent years that one may feel a certain trepidation about embarking on this terrain, not least given the constraints of the present concluding summary. Perhaps one could suggest that nationalism was one part of a broader democratic and modernising process. Certainly for Rousseau and Mazzini, two of the leading early theorists, and for Simón Bolívar, the 'Liberator' of South America, nationalism was a form of patriotism - an education in citizenship, which emphasises duties to neighbours and which becomes the more necessary the less one can rely on older hierarchies of kingship, nobility or religion to provide an inspiration for man. Rousseau and Mazzini sought to recreate communities, as a necessary counterpoise to the democratic process of freeing the individual from old hierarchies and subservience, of proclaiming the equality of all men. They believed, in harmony with the dominant Romantic mood of the time, that the individual personality was shaped anyway, for good or ill, by the physical and moral environment in which a man was raised.

This Romantic school of thought, so wedded to the concept of the organic community, still left it rather uncertain how one was to define the real frontiers of the latter. As an intellectual force, Romanticism proved particularly influential in the nineteenth century, and took new forms as it was subjected to the battery of positivism and realism. The arts and crafts movement of the later nineteenth century continued to contribute a certain vitality to the nationalist ideal. But, again, it was not immediately clear what the link between respect for the formative influences on man and the forces of political nationalism would be. The love for local traditions, so evident in the work of Antoni Gaudí (1852-1926), could coexist happily with an attachment to a Catholic universalism and, through his patrons, the great bourgeois families of Barcelona, with a certain Spanish awareness. Reviving the language and literature of Catalonia did not imply separatism. Indeed, in the case of Valencia, the contemporaneous interest in studying the culture and political history of the Middle Ages was allied with a 'conservative' approach to the politics of the present. Defence of Catholicism and of guilds and of local customs gave the late nineteenth-century Valencian bourgeoisie a strong provincial rather than national identity.

If one recalls the atmosphere of those times - evoked in the memoirs of Francesc Cambó (1876-1947), founder of the Catalan home-rule party, the *Lliga*, in 1901 - one realises how difficult a step it was from national awareness to nationalism. Education was, after all, essentially in the classics. One learned good citizenship from the Greeks and Romans - and one's moral responsibility from a universalist church. One's attitudes were formed within the confines of communities separated from one another by great distances in the age of the horse and cart. Cambó recalls the evening discussions round the table lit by the oil lamp, where inevitably the press and mass ideologies made less impact than the solidarity of the local community, with its known families. Politics was, in a sense, the art of avoiding open confrontation, while of course advancing the interests of one's own small group; but the lines of ideological cleavage could not be so neatly drawn as in the comfortable anonymity of the city.

That the Catalan bourgeoisie went on to develop a nationalist movement is a phenomenon that can be explained in terms of certain political triggers activated after 1898. But clearly the phenomenon requires investigation on the social as well as the political level. Historical memory has been invoked in several of the papers given to the present colloquium as a factor which has to be taken into account in explaining the uneven development of national assertiveness. The interesting thing is indeed the way in which events from the past were understood and reinterpreted, and the way they meshed with the attitudes of a later generation. The Catalan bourgeoisie, for example, were able, in a way in which their Valencian counterparts were not, to draw on the 'myth' of a community - on an idea of equality with the tillers of the soil and the workers in the city. Lawyers like Cambó and political leaders like Enric Prat de la Riba, President of the first Catalan home-rule government (1914-16), were proud to trace their descent from the 'peasantry'. The *masia*, the medium farm, passed on over generations in the same family, gave the Catalan elite a self-image of hard work, community spirit and self-reliance - only gradually dispelled in the early twentieth century as labour problems on the land and in Barcelona began to suggest that the Catalonia of the employers and landowners would not be universally acceptable to its inhabitants.

By way of conclusion, one may return to a basic theme of the present volume: is the very concept of 'national identity' an invention? Does it raise a false question and lead the historian to ask the wrong questions of the past? Should we, as Peter Aronsson suggests, be more aware of the alternative solidarities which have long interested the social anthropologist - of regions and folk cultures, of family structures and pilgrimage centres and traditional routes to markets? The concept of the nation invites us perhaps too easily down the path of historicism, towards explaining how what is now came to be, rather than seeking patiently to reconstruct the past on its own terms. The historian can no doubt keep alive the flame of humanism more successfully by recreating 'other cultures' - the ideas and values which have not entered the mainstream of the world in which we live. It was the achievement of the Romantic and Marxist historians to make us aware of the need to situate ideas in relation to the societies which gave them birth. The 'accidents' of history, as the present conference has suggested, have a logic of their own. That they then enter the historical memory and become part of a new alignment of forces becomes particularly evident as we explore the formation of collective identities. But the study of the past on its own terms is not a retreat into mere antiquarianism, but a way of making us all aware of the complexity of the forces shaping the society in which we live.

Bibliography

Benedict Anderson	*Imagined Communities* (London 1983)
Jeremy Black	*Maps and History: Constructing Images of the Past* (London 1997)
David Brading	*The First America: The Spanish Monarchy, Creole Patriots and the Liberal State 1492-1867* (Cambridge 1991)
Francesc Cambó	*Memorias: 1876-1936* (Madrid 1987)
Américo Castro	*The Spaniards: An Introduction to their History* (London 1971)
Agustí Colomines	*El Catalanisme i l'Estat* (Barcelona 1993)
David Cressy	*Bonfires and Bells: National Memory and the Protestant Calendar in Elizabethan and Stuart England* (London 1989)
Ramón Menéndez Pidal	*España en la Historia* (Madrid 1947)
Claudio Sánchez-Albornoz	*Spain: A Historical Enigma* (2 vols., Madrid 1975)